INCLUSIVE GROWTH AND SUSTAINABLE DEVELOPMENT
Ideal for Indian Economy

INCLUSIVE GROWTH AND SUSTAINABLE DEVELOPMENT

Ideal for Indian Economy

Edited by

B.B. TANDON
Senior Advisor, IBS Chandigarh

and

P.K. VASUDEVA
Visiting Fellow, Guru Jambheshwar University, Hisar

DEEP & DEEP PUBLICATIONS PVT. LTD.
F-159, Rajouri Garden, New Delhi-110027

INCLUSIVE GROWTH AND SUSTAINABLE DEVELOPMENT
Ideal for Indian Economy

ISBN 978-81-8450-262-6

Typeset by S.S. COMPOSERS
3190, Mohindra Park, Shakur Basti, Delhi-110034.

Printed in India at MAYUR ENTERPRISES
WZ Plot No. 3, Gujjar Market, Tihar Village, New Delhi-110018.

Published by DEEP & DEEP PUBLICATIONS PVT. LTD.
F-159, Rajouri Garden, New Delhi-110027.
Phones: 25435369, 25440916
E-mail: ddpbooks@yahoo.co.in • ddpubs@gmail.com
Showroom:
2/13, Ansari Road, Daryaganj, New Delhi-110002 • Telefax: 23245122

Contents

Preface

"Earth provides enough to satisfy every man's need, but not every man's greed."

—Mahatma Gandhi

"Generations to come will scarcely believe that such a one as this, ever in flesh and blood walked upon this earth."

—Albert Einstein on Mahatma Gandhi

Growth is not an end in itself. However, it makes it possible to achieve other objectives, by creating resources, such as education, health care, employment and other Millennium Development Goals. In other words growth is necessary but not sufficient condition for human development unless measures are taken to remove poverty and drudgery. Some of these measures are efficient delivering of public goods and services, infrastructure development and appropriate government procedures and regulations. Without rapid growth, potential entrants to the work force will not find a satisfactory job. Maintaining a reasonable growth rate is also essential for social stability and peace.

Growth requires a transformation of economy from agriculture to industry and services. This structural change results in mass displacement of people. To make this economically natural creative destruction acceptable to the society the state must educate, train, retrain and create sufficient jobs. Government should also establish social safety nets for unemployed to get public support for its growth-oriented economic policy.

Sustained growth can lift people below poverty line continuously. However, this virtue of sustained growth is many times missed, as people confuse inequality with failure to make progress against poverty. Growth almost always eliminates extreme poverty. But accelerating growth leads the divergence in incomes for a long time. Economists believe that finally there is narrowing of income differentials. But when it starts, it cannot be correctly predicted.

The type of growth pursued by the developed nations since industrialization and blindly copied by the developing nations has proved to be unsustainable, i.e., it has put pressure on planet's ecology and climate. This global trend, like many others, is beyond the control of few countries. Global Warming can be stopped or reduced by collective action of all developed and developing countries. Just as growth is not the ultimate objective, inclusivity is not either. Both may be admirable but incomplete without sustainability. The humanity will survive only if inclusive growth goes with sustainable development. Unfortunately, human economy is at present growing itself to death.

In 1972, the first major international meeting, under the auspices of the United Nations was held at Stockhom, to discuss the harmful effects of human activity. But there is little to show for nearly 35 years of the efforts to present environmental degradation. Let us hope that there will be international agreement reached in Copenhagen in December, 2009 which will bring paradigm shift in government policies, actions by corporate sector and society in general. Environmental protection requires effective action. Climatic change is the defining human developed challenge of the Millennium. Failure to respond to climate change will stall international efforts to reduce poverty. Unfortunately the poorest countries will suffer the earliest and most damaging setbacks. According to the World Economic and Social Survey, 2009, the world needs to set aside at least one per cent of the world GDP per year as additional investments in instigation and adaption to climate change.

This book brings the views of five environment experts, six academicians and a highly respected national leader. They have examined in depth the complexity of growth, inclusivity, sustainability and their relationship. We have been in touch with the contributors for more than one year. Indeed it has been a pleasure and honor to interact with distinguished scholars from different areas but having a common interest, i.e. to see a happy, peaceful and prosperous India. It is pleasing to note that ecological balance is no longer concern of environmentalists but also of governments, corporate sector and even common man.

Chandigarh

B.B. TANDON
P.K. VASUDEVA

Brief Profile of Authors

Aggarwal, M.R.
M.A. Ph.D. L.L.B. (Pb.)
E mail: mr_aggarwal01@yahoo.com

He is Professor of Economics, Department of Economics, Panjab University, Chandigarh, India for the last more than 30 years. He has done a number of Projects of the University Grant Commission (UGC) and published more than 20 research papers in National and International Journals. Presently he is doing a project on "Economic Growth of South-East Asian Countries" allocated by UGC.

Bhavanishankar, B.S.
E-mail-bhavanishankar@hotmail.com

He is President, 'SAHAYOGA' and former Advisor, Government of Karnataka and former Chief Engineer, Government of India and Government of Madhya Pradesh. He has been Staff Consultant with World Bank and Asian Development Bank.

Somnath Chatterjee

He is Former Speaker, Lok Sabha and a seasoned Statesman of Communist Party of India (CPI). He has been Member of Parliament of the Lok Sabha since 1952 onwards. He is one of the most respected Parliamentarian of his time.

Kewal Raj Dawar

He is Professor in Economics ICFAI Business School, Chandigarh. He has written a number of research papers in the National Journals and Business papers.

Arunesh Garg

He is associated with IBS, Chandigarh as Assistant Professor in Marketing. Having completed his doctorate from GNDU, Amritsar, Dr. Garg is an engineer from Thapar University, Patiala. He has done his MBA from PAU, Ludhiana. He has spent almost 10 years in academics and contributed a number of research papers and articles in various journals and articless.

Neha Kapoor
Email: neha.kapoor@yesbank.in, Tel: +91 022 66209098)

She is Senior Manager, Development and Knowledge Banking, YES BANK Ltd, India.

Sheenu Jain
M: 9766369336
Email: sheenujain@ibsindia.org

She is Assistant Professor, IBS, Goa and now posted at IBS, Noida.

Shyam Saran

He is a well known retired Bureaucrat who has served in a large number of important appointments in India and abroad. Presently he is Advisor PMO on climate change. He has participated in a number of negotiations and acted as an Ambassador of India to a large number of Conferences/Negotiations with Developed and Developing Countries.

Somak Ghosh
Email: somak.ghosh@yesbank.in,

He is Group President, Corporate Finance and Development Banking, YES BANK Ltd, India.

Tandon, B.B.
M.A. (London School of Economics), Ph.D Queen's University, Canada.
Email:bbtandon_sradvisor@ibsindia.org

He is a well-known Economist who has written a large number of research papers in National and International Journals. He has been Dean and Chairman of University Business School, Panjab University, Chandigarh. He has also been Chairman of Ludhiana Stock Exchange. Presently he is Advisor, IBS Chandigarh.

Vasudeva, P.K.
M.A., MBA, Ph.D (WTO)
Email: vasu022@gmail.com

He is a Soldier turned Economist. He is former Senior Executive TATA Exports, Principal, College of Communication and Management, Bharatiya Vidya Bhavan, Member of Consumer Disputes Redressal Commission, U.T., Chandigarh, Senior Professor, ICFA University and President, Chandigarh Management Association (CMA). Presently he is Consultant, Rajiv Gandhi Foundation, Advisor, Institute of Development Studies and Training, Senior Vice-President, National Adventure Club (India) and Expert Panelist, National Institute of Science Communication and Information Resources (NISCARE), Government of India. He has written 8 books, more than 158 research papers and more than 1000 articles in National and International Journals/Newspapers.

Vasudeva, S.P.
M.Sc. (Hons.), M.Phil, Ph.D

B.Sc. (Hons.), M.Sc. (Hons.) Botany, M.Phil (Botany) with Forest Genetics as specialisation and Ph.D in Reproductive biology from Panjab University, Chandigarh. Certificate Course on People's Participation in Rural Development from University of Reading U.K. and MBA on Project Management from University of Hull UK. Indian forest Service of 1962 batch Himachal Pradesh cadre. Worked as Director (External Assistance) in the Ministry of Water Resources, Government of India, Member Secretary of H.P. Environmental Protection and Pollution Control Board. Presently Chief Conservator of Forests, Himachal Pradesh. Awarded the Order of Merit with Samajshri Award in 2006 for Pollution Management by Indian Council of Management Executives, Mumbai.

Acknowledgement

Have you ever seen anyone walking alone? Perhaps not! However, no one walks alone especially when one is walking on the journey of life just from where you start to thank those who joined you, walked beside you, supported you when you are going to fall and finally helped you in the long journey of writing a book

Editors of this book sincerely thank Shri Somnath Chatterjee, former Speaker of Lok Sabha, who initially put forth the idea of writing this book when we met him. This book is result of his initiative and constant motivation when we met him during inauguration at a Seminar on "Sustainable Development" organised by CII at New Delhi in 2008.

We received great inspiration and constant encouragement from Mr. S. K. Sharma, Director IBS HO Hyderabad, Dr. P. D. Kaushik, Director, Rajiv Gandhi Foundation, New Delhi and Professor Bhagat Ram, Dean IBS Chandigarh for their guidance, providing literature from time to time and consultation on the subject as and when required.

Special mention is made of Ms. Seema Arora, Principal Counsellor and Head, CII ITC Centre of Excellence for Sustainable Development of CII and Mr. P.K. Verma, Director HR Alchemist, who gave us valuable inputs.

The publication of this book could not have been possible but for the ungrudging efforts put in by a large number of individuals working for the "Sustainable Development and Inclusive Growth". It is, therefore, only fair that their contributions do not get unacknowledged.

Thanks go to Professor Dinesh K. Gupta, Chairman and Dean, University Business School, Panjab University, Professor H. L. Verma, Department of Business Management, Haryana Business School, Guru Jambheshwar University, Hissar and Professor Arundeep Ahluwalia, Head of the Department, Geology, Panjab University, for their sustained help in guiding and researching on the subject.

We thank Professor S.M. Sharma, Principal, College of Communication and Management, Bharatiya Vidya Bhavan and Wing Commander Harbhajan Singh of IBS for compiling and correcting notes besides providing administrative assistance for the completion of this book. Thanks are also due to Ms. Swati Sabharwal of Bharatiya Vidya Bhavan, Ms. Meenakshi Arora, Research Associate and Ms. Nidhi Batra of IBS Chandigarh, who looked after computer storage and typing and to Mr. Navneet and Professor Vinay Aggarwal who prepared tracings and sketches. We also thank all staff members of IBS, Chandigarh and Bharatiya Vidya Bhavan for secretarial assistance.

We sincerely thank all our contributors who had to burn mid-night oil for writing Research Papers for the preparation of this book. We shall be failing in our duty if we do not thank Mr. G. S. Bhatia of Deep & Deep Publications Pvt. Ltd. who produced such a picturesque and finely printed book in a record time of two months because the Copenhagen Conference due in December 2009.

PROFESSOR B.B. TANDON
P.K. VASUDEVA

EXCELLENCE FOR SUSTAINABILITY DEVELOPMENT

Somnath Chatterjee

ABSTRACT

I greatly appreciate the vision and the concerted efforts of all those spearheading the CII-ITC Centre of Excellence for Sustainability Development (CESD) to develop the requisite capability among Indian Industry by taking several pro-active measures to promote the process of sustainable development while retaining its competitiveness.

We are already becoming the world's third largest source of greenhouse gases. We can turn these challenges into remarkable opportunities, if the country as a whole work together, discarding the ways of negative and confrontational politics, to achieve sustainable development, ensuring ecological efficiency and broadly inclusive growth.

Friends, today we have an opportunity to be the world leader in the movement for ensuring competitive and sustainable development, drawing the rest of the world—including the developed part—into this process of transition in the developmental path, helping to create a mutually profitable relationship between countries in this endeavour. India's vast resources and potential for the sustainability market can be utilized to achieve this objective.

The corporate world should use this opportunity to comprehend and deliberate how you, as part of the world's largest and most vibrant democracy, could play a leadership role in the radical transformation to sustainability.

It gives me immense pleasure to be amidst you all at the "3rd Sustainability Summit: Asia 2008". I am grateful to Shri Y.C. Deveshwar, Chairman, CII-ITC Centre of Excellence for Sustainable Development

Advisory Council, for his initiative and leadership in organizing this Summit and for giving me the opportunity to associate myself with this event. I greatly appreciate the vision and the concerted efforts of all those spearheading the CII-ITC Centre of Excellence for Sustainability Development (CESD) to develop the requisite capability among Indian Industry by taking several pro-active measures to promote the process of sustainable development while retaining its competitiveness.

The goal of sustainability is of special significance to us in view of the prevalence of large-scale deprivation and inequality in access to developmental benefits, more likely to intensify in the context of the current financial crisis which has, in fact, brought in sharper focus the question of sustainability *vis-a-vis* our developmental priorities and strategies. I sincerely hope that the Summit will provide solution for maintaining compatibility between material progress and the sustainability of development—social, economic and environmental. The specter of climate change is looming large over the world and its effects have also started impacting on our social, economic and environmental spheres. Shrinking of glaciers and melting of ice-sheets have posed a serious threat to human settlement. Seasonal and terrestrial ecosystem changes have resulted in inequitable water distribution and affected rainfall patterns, hampering agricultural productivity. Besides, many new water-borne and vector-borne infections have started emerging, posing new challenges to our health-care preparedness. Above all, it has made a dent on our bio-diversity, the essence of the sustenance of our ecosystem.

If we have perpetual poverty and a life of inhuman existence; industrialization and urbanization will have to be seen from the perspective of human concerns. The challenge is to find development strategies that improve the living standards, create employment, and promote opportunities and which, at the same time, are environment friendly. Regrettably, the developed world has failed in its commitment to transfer green technology and additional finance to the developing countries. In such a scenario, we have to find the most appropriate technology that can make development possible while promoting and preserving the environment.

India has proven competence for business model innovation in health, telecom and small-scale products and services. Moving this to the global marketplace could gain enormous competitive advantage to Indian companies. The transition will require radical transformation of the strategies of the corporate world with lot more farsightedness and unraveling the untapped markets existing in different challenges. There are many companies which have generated business from 'waste to wealth' concept. Then there are some who have found a market by providing rechargeable solar LED lamps, an affordable and durable solution to a long-standing issue and replace traditional kerosene-based lamps that are polluting and hugely inefficient. Around two billion people around the world are using kerosene. That is 20% of the global lighting costs, delivering 0.2% of the output. In Kerala, they have packaged Ayurveda and Tourism and created an industry which is providing employment to many people.

According to the Task Force Report of the Ministry of Non-Conventional Energy Resources, India produces, in its talukas, 400 million tons/year of agricultural residue which can produce 53000 mW of power. Even if half of this is possible, coupled with the large scale wind energy production, which holds a potential of 45000 mW, India can develop into an energy secure nation. Less than 40% of the households in India have tap water connections which again is a chance for the business to reach 600 million people. Investment potential for decentralized water purifications systems, itself, exceeds US$ 10 billion. There are enormous opportunities for contributing towards building a dependable health-care infrastructure for our people. All this have to be accomplished with innovations in strategy, in planning, in processes, in designing, and in delivery, without ignoring the environmental sensibilities and, above all, with sincere commitment to the people's causes.

Mahatma Gandhi, had once observed, "Earth provides enough to satisfy every man's need, but not every man's greed."The motto of meeting the needs of the present without compromising the ability of future generations to meet their own needs should guide us in our developmental activities. The traditional business management theory that 'there is one responsibility of business: to use its resources and engage in activities designed to increase its profits' needs to be given an urgent rethink and an overhaul. The paradigm of development and economic growth needs to be transformed, keeping in mind the ecological concerns and value-laden business practices.

Despite all the encouraging talks about economic growth that averaged about 6 per cent annually, across the Asia-Pacific region in recent years, it is indeed an unpalatable fact that millions of people still live in absolute poverty, surviving on less than one dollar a day. A study conducted by the Asian Development Bank has pointed out that the rich are getting richer and faster, than the poor in developing Asia as disparities in standards of living continue to widen in this one of the most dynamic regions in the world. The ADB report has expressed fear that in societies where wealth is concentrated in the hands of a few, there is danger of policy levers being captured by the rich for their own benefit and a wakening of the institutional foundations of the growth process. These findings may further aggravate due to the forecast of recession in advanced economies and the slow growth rate in the Asian nations due to global meltdown.

Friends, India, with a billion-plus population, is endowed with a vast reservoir of resources—natural and human—and is steadily moving into the world domain as a major economic and political force. Nonetheless, we have many challenges to reckon with, both on the domestic and the international fronts. Amidst all the talks of high economic growth, rapid industrialization and phenomenal scientific progress, including the Mission to Moon, we are besieged with the problems of poverty, poverty-induced social hazards, food insecurity, water-conflicts, energy shortages, unemployment, lack of healthcare facilities, inadequate infrastructure, unbalanced social, economic and political growth, environmental degradation, etc. Notwithstanding all the plans and programmes initiated in the aftermath of Independence with a view to ameliorating the lot of our people, we still have 26 per cent of our population living below the poverty line and rank 127th in the World Human Development Index. We are already becoming the world's third largest source of greenhouse gases. Some of the Indian cities are among the most polluted in the world today. While these are some of the domestic challenges, issues such as climate change, the menace of global terrorism and financial crisis are adding to the trouble with varying but significant impact on the country's development. The imbalance in the economy has to be corrected if India has to truly become an important player in the world affairs. We can turn these challenges into remarkable opportunities, if the country as a whole work together, discarding the ways of negative and confrontational politics, to achieve sustainable development, ensuring ecological efficiency and broadly inclusive growth.

As a vital component of the society, the corporate world, whch is immensely benefited by the former, is under obligation to give back to the society its due. Our entrepreneurs in both the corporate organizations and in their individual capacities should turn these challenges into opportunities by meticulously making use of their vision, innovation, state-of-the-art technology and perseverance. They should imbibe the principle of corporate social responsibility (CSR) and fulfil their obligation towards the people.Besides, there is an urgent need to have a re-look at business competitiveness which, even while enhancing its profitability and share-holders' values, creating wealth and pursuing opportunities for growth, can also ensure the sustainability of business itself from all other angles as has been proved by the ITC Limited. As an Indian, I am proud to know that the ITC is a 'carbon positive' and 'water positive' company, besides being able to achieve 100 per cent recycling of solid waste in many of its operations and I sincerely compliment both the management and the employees of the ITC for their splendid achievements and contribution to sustainable development.

I hope and trust all the stakeholders in our national life-the government, corporate houses, individual entrepreneurs, members of the civil society, and the people in general, will come forward in promoting sustainable development. This calls for a new perception of competitiveness that can create the possibility for sustainable development and long-lasting competitiveness. The corporate houses should associate themselves with programmes like 'social forestry', eco-tourism, and promote the use of bio-diesel among our common people and entrepreneurs. They should commit themselves to green technology by complying with the norms of 'water positive', 'carbon positive' and almost absolute recycling of solid waste contents. They can bank upon the unconventional sources of energy like solar energy, wind energy, ocean energy, bio-gas energy, etc. in undertaking their industrial activities.

The Parliament and the government will have to continue to make every possible endeavor to promote economic growth while sustaining the ecology. Today we have in place a National Action Plan on Climate Change, focusing attention on eight priority National Missions namely solar energy, enhanced energy efficiency, sustainable habitat, conserving water, sustaining the Himalayan eco-system, a "Green India", sustainable agriculture and strategic knowledge platform for climate change. Environmental considerations are increasingly being integrated into the planning, designing and implementation of our developmental programmes.

I would like to share with this distinguished gathering some of the developments in this regard at the parliamentary level. Our Parliament, as the highest deliberative and legislative body, has been giving serious attention to this problem and only last year the Lok sabha had about four-and-a-half-hour long debate on global warming. Our Parliament's Departmentally Related Standing Committee on Science and Technology and Environment and Forests has been constantly evaluating the functioning of the Ministries concerned. I have also taken several initiatives to make our elected representatives more aware of the imperative of ecological conversation and sustainable development. I have constituted a Parliamentary Forum on Global Warming and Climate Change and another one on Water conservation and Management, besides the Forum on youth, Forum on Children and the Forum on Population and Public Health with a view to equipping the Members of Parliament with adequate information and knowledge about issues and developments in these vital areas. We have been organizing Lectures by subject experts on topical interest for the benefit of the Members since 2005. The Lectures by global environmental activists like the former US Vice-President and nobel Laureate Mr. Al Gore, Dr. R.K. Pachauri and Dr. Sunita Narayan, among others, were indeed, eye-openers to the gravity of the challenges that the world community is facing on the environmental front today. I am happy to say that water harvesting and water conservation systems have been put in place in Parliament Complex as well as at my official residence. These measures have, no doubt, gone a long way in sensitizing the members of Parliament on the imperative of sustainable development.

Friends, today we have an opportunity to be the world leader in the movement for ensuring competitive and sustainable development, drawing the rest of the world-including the developed part-into this process of transition in the developmental path, helping to create a mutually profitable relationship between countries in this endeavour. India's vast resources and potential for the sustainability market can be utilized to achieve this objective.

As we struggle to provide a better standard of living to our people, our commitment to protect environment remains as strong as before. The 21st Century is being hailed as an Asian Century and India is poised to be one of the robust engines of growth and a leading player. It speaks of our sincerity and commitment that despite our developmental imperatives, we have pledged that our per capita Green House Gas emissions will not exceed the per capita GHG emissions of the developed countries. We must work together to make growth inclusive and both the public and private sectors must build a partnership to find out new economic activities and industrial enterprises to generate employment opportunities that do not overlook or bypass the poor. I am sure, the CESD, in concert with India incorporated, civil society groups and individual entrepreneurs will continue its efforts ceaselessly in maintaining a fine balance between material progress and sustainability of natural resources, a challenging but rewarding responsibility. *I am glad you have chosen to spend two days at this thought-provoking Summit. The corporate world should use this opportunity too comprehend and deliberate how you, as part of* the world's largest and most vibrant democracy, could play a leadership role in the radical transformation to sustainability.

I would like to once again express my thanks to Shri Y.C. Deveshwar for giving the opportunity to share some of my views on such a vital issue having bearing on our people and our environment. I also compliment the organizers of this Summit who have taken so much care to make this event a great success.

CHAPTER

2

SUSTAINABLE DEVELOPMENT AND EXCLUSIVITY IS THE MANTRA FOR INDIA'S ECONOMIC GROWTH

(Extracts of Speeches of Shyam Saran at various Seminars/Conferences/Negotiations at National/International Levels)

INTRODUCTION

The onus to adopt environmentally friendly technologies should not completely lie on the developing world. Science suggests the current climate change is due to accumulated emissions of over 200 years of industrialization. The world, therefore, should work together to achieve sustainability, said Mr. Shyam Saran, Prime Minister of India's Special Envoy on Climate Change. He was speaking at a Seminar on 'Business Response to Climate Change' organized today by the Confederation of Indian Industry (CII)-ITC Centre of Excellence for Sustainable Development.[1]

According to him collaborations become irrelevant when competitive tendencies prevail. He outlined practices like IPR and trade competitiveness as major obstacles for environmentally friendly technology adoption. Positioning India's National Action Plan on Climate Change as a new strategy for sustainable development, Mr. Saran highlighted that the issue of climate change, particularly for India, is closely linked to development. He was of the view that India's development denominator is associated with huge population; ongoing industrialization; extensive urbanization and need for greater agricultural output.

CLIMATE CHANGE AND DEVELOPMENT IMPERATIVES

Seeking to achieve energy security, he further stated, 'if India has to continuously grow at 8-9%, then it should reduce dependence on fossil fuel. According to India's Integrated Energy Policy, by 2030 India will be importing more than 90% of oil and about two-third to three-fourth of coal, and the energy cost will increase.' To this regard he reflected upon the National Solar Energy Mission, which is an ambitious project by the government of India for reducing India's dependence on non-renewable energy sources. The mission is based on the fact that India receives high insolation and is a leading option to innovate and scale up.

Mr. Saran further appraised about the Energy Efficiency National Mission, which builds on India's decoupling of its economic growth and energy intensity. He stated, 'The clearance of Civil Nuclear Energy Agreement will help India to have better energy security. The current economic downturn has turned to India's advantage as the cost of equipment and fuel have come down considerably.

Speaking about the National Mission on Water by the Government of India, which aims to ensure better water management. Mr. Saran stated that the Mission envisages micro and macro-level initiatives. River Basin Management projects are place at Indus, Ganga and Brahmaputra. At the micro level the aim is to ensure involvement by the community. Such projects lend themselves to greater participation from business and industry bodies like CII leading to water-positive practices and water-neutral industrial processes.

Green India Mission has been formulated as an adaptive and mitigating practice for climate change. Mr. Saran highlighted that the mission aims to scale up India's forest cover from the current 22% to 33%. He advocated participation of the in this mission which also links with the Water Mission.

Earlier, giving the welcome address, Mr. Harpal Singh, Chiarman, CII Northern Region and Chairman Emeritus, Fortis Healthcare Ltd. stated, Climate change features in regular discussions as it is closely linked with growth, poverty, equity and the future of the human race. It is optimistic to find Indian companies voluntarily disclosing their carbon footprints and trying to keep emissions under control. CII is now into the 3rd carbon disclosure project for India's top 200 companies. Such voluntary initiatives should be augmented with policies and initiatives, which can help India achieve leadership in climate change mitigation.

In her concluding remarks, Ms. Seema Arora, Principal Counsellor and Head, CII-ITC Centre of Excellence for Sustainable Development, said, as development and climate control are interlinked, industry has to come together. A shift from a mere response to a strategic intervention is imperative for achieving sustainable development.

INDIA AND FOSSIL FUELS

If India has to continuously grow at eight to nine per cent, then it should reduce dependence on fossil fuels. At the same time, the onus to adopt green technologies should not completely lie on the developing world.[2]

Science suggests the current climate change is due to accumulated emissions of over 200 years of industrialisation. The world, therefore, should work together to achieve sustainability.

It is feared that industrialised countries would use intellectual property rights and trade competitiveness in the race to develop and use greener technologies. These would be "major obstacles for environmentally friendly technology adoption".

Positioning India's National Action Plan on Climate Change as a new strategy for sustainable development, it is suggested that if India has to continuously grow at eight to nine per cent, then it should reduce dependence on fossil fuels. According to India's Integrated Energy Policy, by 2030 India will be importing more than 90 per cent of oil and about two-thirds to three-fourths of coal, and the energy cost will increase.

In this regard it is worth reflecting upon the National Solar Energy Mission, which is a project by the government to reduce India's dependence on non-renewable energy sources.

It is also informed about the National Energy Efficiency Mission, which builds on India's decoupling of its economic growth and energy intensity. The clearance of civil nuclear energy agreement (with the US) will help India to have better energy security. The current economic downturn has turned to India's advantage as the cost of equipment and fuel have come down considerably.

The Green India Mission aims to increase India's forest cover from the current 22 per cent to 33 per cent and called upon industrialists to participate in this and in the national water mission.

INDIA AND GLOBAL CLIMATE CHANGE NEGOTIATIONS

"India's stand in international negotiations is based on the simple principle—"The polluter pays", said Shyam Saran, Special Envoy to the Prime Minister on Climate Change, at a seminar on "Climate Change and India" organised by the Confederation of Indian Industry (CII) in Mumbai.[3]

Showing the historical emission of carbon from the period 1850-2000, Saran pointed out that while US leads with 30 per cent, the EU-25 with 27.2 per cent, China with 7.3 per cent, India accounts for only two per cent. Thus in the multilateral negotiations on climate change, India strongly advocates equity, stressed Saran.

Comparing Indian emissions with global emissions, Saran said that they are only four per cent compared to 20 per cent for US and 16 per cent for China.

"India emits about 1.1 tonnes of carbon per capita while the corresponding figure for US is more than 20 tonnes", informed Saran. He went on to explain that India was thus not a major emitter as often argued by the developed countries.

"Though few developed countries have attempted to avoid their legal obligations under UNFCCC and the Kyoto Protocol by arguing that till India and China remains outside emission regime, their own efforts will make little difference. India does not consider itself a major emitter by way of total volume of Carbon emissions or per capita emissions," he pointed out.

Saran also dwelled on the Kyoto Protocol and its implications on India. He clarified that there is no legal obligation on part of India under existing international climate change framework, to take on binding emissions reduction obligations, now or in the post 2012 period. He explained India's negotiating position on climate change thus:

Kyoto Protocol does not expire in 2012, nor are developing countries expected to take on reduction commitments in post-2012 period.

The responsibility to support sustainable development strategies in developing countries, through the transfer of financial resources and technology from developed countries should not be linked to any conditionality on developing countries. While developed countries are free to adopt sectoral approaches as a means to achieve their national emission reduction targets, there can not be an imposition of industry-wide norms on a global basis, nor recourse to arguments about maintaining trade competitiveness or a level playing field. UNFCC framework does not feature trade competitiveness in climate change negotiation.

Post Kyoto framework should have an expanded commitment from developed countries for carbon emission and the global carbon market should also increase. While holding the above position, India has made number of positive and forward looking proposals, Saran said.

He specified:

1. In the G8+G5 Summit in Germany, last year, Prime Minister, Dr. Manmohan Singh gave a public assurance that while India's carbon emissions may rise in the short and medium term, but per capita carbon emissions in India will not, at any time, exceed the average of the developed countries per capita emissions.
2. An active role in Clean Development Mechanism where India has largest portfolio of CDM projects to date.

"We are in the process of formulating India's National Plan on climate change to be released in June this year. It constitutes a strategy for sustainable development and will include major national level missions, such as Solar Mission, a National Solid Waste Management Plan, a nation wide effort to create a huge carbon sink of afforested land, Water

Conservation Mission and adoption of international best practices and efficiency norms for a range of key industries. All these are seen as public private partnerships," he stressed.

Jamshed N. Godrej, Chairman and Managing Director, Godrej and Boyce Mfg. Co. Ltd., said that the issue of climate change poses both challenges and opportunities. He called upon the industry captains to back the government in their efforts to tackle the issue of climate change heads on. (ANI)

SPECIAL ENVOY OF THE PRIME MINISTER FOR CLIMATE CHANGE AT THE CARNEGIE ENDOWMENT FOR INTERNATIONAL PEACE, WASHINGTON DC ON INDIA'S CLIMATE CHANGE INITIATIVES: STRATEGIES FOR A GREENER FUTURE

I wish to thank the Carnegie Endowment for the opportunity to acquaint informed public opinion in the United States of how India is tackling the challenge of Climate Change4.

This is also an area of substantial Indo-US collaboration already and many more opportunities are likely to open up, thanks to President Obama's decision to put Climate Change at the top of his Administration's agenda, including his 10-year, US $ 150 billion Renewable Energy initiative.

At the outset, let me put India's responsibilities as well as constraints, in respect to the challenge of Climate Change in its proper perspective.

It is often stated that India belongs to the category of large emitters which must take on carbon reduction commitments in order to mitigate global climate change. India is described as the third largest emitter after the US and China. The latest data shows that while US and China are each responsible for about 20% of global CO2 emissions, India, with its billion plus population, generates only 4% of such emissions. Furthermore, as against a per capita CO_2 emission of 20 tonnes for the US, India's is a low 1.8 tonnes per capita. Therefore, to club India together with so-called major emitters is misleading and unfair.

I would also like to draw your attention to the fact that despite our low per capita emissions currently, our Prime Minister has declared that even as we pursue our goals of economic and social development, we will not allow our per capita emissions to exceed the average per capita emissions of developed countries. The significance of this commitment is not fully appreciated. India is after all still a developing country. Our per capita energy consumption is about 500 Kg against the world average of 1800 and there are an estimated 400 million Indians who do not have access to commercial energy. The developmental imperatives are huge and yet we are determined to meet them with a sense of ecological responsibility.

Despite the growth of population and the need to ensure food security, India is increasing its forest cover and intends to raise it from the current 22% of total land area to 33%. This amounts to creating a huge carbon sink for absorbing CO2 in the atmosphere something quite unprecedented in any developing country. The developmental challenges which India faces and is attempting to address within a democratic polity should not be ignored when applying the principle of equal burden sharing in addressing climate change.

India draws upon its civilizational legacy in raising public awareness and promote community activism and initiative on Climate Change. Safeguarding the environment looking upon Nature, not as a dark force to be conquered and subdued, but as a Mother, and a source of nurture, to be respected and preserved, is a concept deeply ingrained in Indian tradition. Let me quote from an ancient prayer in the sacred Hindu scriptures, the Vedas:

Let there be peace in the Universe and in infinite space, Peace upon this earth and in the oceans,

Let peace reign over plants and over trees, May the Gods enjoy peace; may the Creator, Brahma dwell in tranquility. Let there be peace everywhere, but most of all Let Peace reside within our hearts.

Traditionally, the Indian world view has looked upon human existence as an integral part of Nature and in harmony with Nature's cycle of birth, growth, decay and regeneration. Modern industrial development and concepts of progress are linear in nature, not cyclical but today most of humanity is beginning to realize the wisdom of sustainability as the depletion of the planet's resources near their finite limits and the very sources of nurture, i.e. earth, water and air are ravaged beyond Nature's power to regenerate. As a country most significantly impacted by Climate Change, India has already embarked on a strategic shift from a pattern of development that relies on an ever more generous consumption of resources to one based on sustainability. There is now a clear and compelling recognition in government as well as in civil society, that India's growth story will soon hit a dead-end if we do not embrace sustainable growth. It is for this reason, that Climate Change has now been fully integrated into the national development process.

At the heart of this strategic shift to a strategy of sustainable development is accelerated change, from production and consumption processes that are based on carbon fuels to those based on renewable sources of energy. For India, the climate change argument and the energy security argument have come together in compelling fashion. If a growth rate of 8% to 10% per annum in our GDP is essential to eradicate poverty in our lifetime, then India must overcome the energy constraint on its growth and must do so in a global environment of increasingly finite and depleting sources of energy. Today, over 70% of our oil requirements are met through imports. It is likely to exceed 90% by 2030. This is no energy security.

India announced its National Action Plan on Climate Change on June 30, 2008. In launching the Plan, Prime Minister, Dr. Manmohan Singh said:

> "Our people have a right to economic and social development and to discard the ignominy of widespread poverty. For this we need rapid economic growth. But I also believe that ecologically sustainable development need not be in contradiction to achieving our growth objectives. In fact, we must have a broader perspective on development. It must include the quality of life, not merely the quantitative accretion of goods and services. Our people want higher standards of living, but they also want clean water to drink, fresh air to breathe and a green earth to walk on."

This Prime Ministerial directive is what the National Action Plan seeks to translate into concrete policy interventions.

The Plan has identified Eight broad areas for focussed action, encompassing both mitigation and adaptation. These National Missions are:

1. National Solar Mission,
2. National Mission for Enhanced Energy Efficiency,
3. National Mission on Sustainable Habitat,
4. National Water Mission,
5. National Mission for Sustaining the Himalayan Ecosystem,
6. National Mission for a "Green India",
7. National Mission for Sustainable Agriculture, and
8. National Mission on Strategic Knowledge for Climate Change.

Each of these Missions has a technology development and R&D component, while the Mission on Strategic knowledge seeks to fill the many gaps that continue to exist in our understanding of climate change phenomenon and its impact specifically on India and our region. India is already using its Space capabilities for this purpose and future plans include using indigenously developed Automatic Weather Station (AWS), Agromet Towers, Doppler Weather Radars and GPS applications for more detailed climate studies and developing simulation models.

Currently, each of these Missions is being elaborated through a very wide-ranging consultative process involving all stakeholders, including Central Ministries and agencies, State Governments, business and industry, civil society and community level organisations and representatives. We want each of the Missions to proceed with what may be called PPP or public/private and people partnerships. The elaboration of these Missions is taking somewhat longer than we had envisaged, but the results, we hope, will be to deliver an ambitious but effective, visionary but realistic strategy for India's sustainable development.

REDUCTION OF DEPENDENCE ON FOSSIL FUELS

If India has to continuously grow at eight to nine per cent, then it should reduce dependence on fossil fuels, the Prime Minister's Special Envoy on Climate Change Shyam Saran said here on Monday. At the same time, the onus to adopt green technologies should not completely lie on the developing world, he pointed out. "Science suggests the current climate change is due to accumulated emissions of over 200 years of industrialisation. The world, therefore, should work together to achieve sustainability," Saran said while speaking at a seminar on Business Response to Climate Change organised by the Confederation of Indian Industry (CII)-ITC Centre of Excellence for Sustainable Development.

Saran referred to the fear that industrialised countries would use intellectual property rights and trade competitiveness in the race to develop and use greener technologies. He said these would be "major obstacles for environmentally friendly technology adoption".

Positioning India's National Action Plan on Climate Change as a new strategy for sustainable development, Saran said, "If India has to continuously grow at eight to nine per cent, then it should reduce dependence on fossil fuels. According to India's Integrated Energy Policy, by 2030 India will be importing more than 90 per cent of oil and about two-thirds to three-fourths of coal, and the energy cost will increase."

In this regard he reflected upon the National Solar Energy Mission, which is a project by the government to reduce India's dependence on non-renewable energy sources.

Saran also informed about the National Energy Efficiency Mission, which builds on India's decoupling of its economic growth and energy intensity. He said, "The clearance of civil nuclear energy agreement (with the US) will help India to have better energy security. The current economic downturn has turned to India's advantage as the cost of equipment and fuel have come down considerably."

He also said the Green India Mission aims to increase India's forest cover from the current 22 per cent to 33 per cent and called upon industrialists to participate in this and in the national water mission. (IANS)[4]

FINALISATION OF MISSION ON CLIMATE CHANGE

(Discussions held with scientists, academics, NGOs)

The eight missions identified in the National Action Plan on Climate Change are being elaborated and the exercise is drawing to a close.

The missions are: National Solar Mission, National Mission for Enhanced Energy Efficiency, National Mission on Sustainable Habitat, National Water Mission, National Mission for Sustaining the Himalayan Ecosystem, National Mission for a Green India, National Mission for

Sustainable Agriculture, and National Mission on Strategic Knowledge for Climate Change.

Talking to journalists here on Friday, Prime Minister's Special Envoy for Climate Change, Shyam Saran said comprehensive discussions were held with scientists, technologists, academia and the community representatives, including the non-governmental organisations, to consider their opinions also.

"The exercise is close to finalisation with the last meeting scheduled shortly following which the final draft would be prepared and placed before the Prime Minister's Council on Climate Change," Mr. Saran said.

Dismissing criticism that India was resisting calls by the developed countries to take on specific targets for the reduction of its greenhouse gas emissions, and thereby stalling any agreement at the international level, Mr. Saran said India had consistently favoured a fair and equitable outcome in accordance with the principle of common but differentiated responsibilities and respective capabilities.

Expecting an ambitious outcome at the 15th Conference of Parties at Copenhagen in December, Mr. Saran said as a developing nation, India would continue to be severely impacted by the climate change at a time when it is confronted with huge development imperatives. "We would expect the Copenhagen outcome to provide us with the space we require for accelerated social and economic development in order to eradicate widespread poverty."

Further, Mr. Saran accused the developed nations of deviating from the United Nations Framework Convention on Climate Change on various pretexts, and said India had already declared that even as it pursued its social and economic development objectives, it would not allow its per capita emissions to exceed the average of the developed countries.

Appreciating the new recognition given to climate change by the U.S. President Barack Obama, who has announced a 10-year $150 billion Renewable Energy Initiative, Mr. Saran said the renewed focus on this sector fits very well into India's strategy.

Investment in addressing climate change especially in renewable energy could create new industries, new jobs and spur technological innovation.

"Action on climate change must become part of the solution to the financial and economic crisis," he added.

SPEECH BY SHYAM SARAN, SPECIAL ENVOY OF THE PRIME MINISTER FOR CLIMATE CHANGE "FROM BALI TO COPENHAGEN—TACKLING CLIMATE CHANGE WITH RENEWABLE SOLUTIONS"

India welcomes the opportunity to share with this prestigious Forum, its vision for tackling Climate Change as a collaborative Global Mission.[5]

Such a Global Mission requires us to recognize that what we face, as humanity, is an extraordinary challenge and this requires an extraordinary response. While there is talk of Climate Change being an extraordinary challenge, what we have seen so far in multilateral negotiations, is best described as "under-ordinary".

An extraordinary response cannot be delivered by a traditional negotiating process, which is by its nature, adversarial, in which each negotiating partner or a group of negotiating partners, seeks to safeguard and advance its own perceived self-interest and the result is usually a least common denominator outcome. This may be appropriate for less challenging areas such as trade or even security-related issues. A least common denominator outcome to the Bali Process will not be appropriate to the elemental challenge that Climate Change poses to collective humanity.

What we need is a collaborative approach based on a common and shared vision, but one which can only succeed if it incorporates the principle of equity and fairness.

As India sees it, the Copenhagen Outcome must be based on the principle that each citizen of the globe has an equal entitlement to the global atmospheric space. This is similar to the principle recognized, for example, in the Outer Space Treaty, that Outer Space "shall be the province of all mankind". Therefore, our objective should be to aim eventually for a per capita convergence of greenhouse gas emissions.

The Prime Minister of India has solemnly declared that even while India pursues its economic and social development goals, it will not permit its per capita GHG emissions to exceed, at any point of time, the average per capita emissions of developed countries.

A successful outcome, which is equitable, must take into account historical responsibility. It is not current levels of emissions alone which are responsible for climate change. Climate change is taking place as a consequence of accumulated GHGs in the atmosphere, as a result of several decades of carbon-based industrialization in the developed world. Therefore, as the UNFCCC itself acknowledges, it is the developed countries who occupy the limited carbon capacity of the earth's atmosphere, who must achieve urgent and significant reductions in their emissions.

Developing countries have the responsibility to engage in sustainable development but their emission reductions will be the result of sustainable development, not the other way around. This is an important distinction. To enable enhancement of sustainable development in developing countries, there has to be support in terms of technology transfer and financial resources.

What developed and developing countries together need to achieve is an accelerated and substantial shift from fossil fuels to non-fossil fuels and from non-renewable sources to renewable sources of energy. There must be a global plan to change the very nature of growth, from one based on carbon that has remained virtually unchanged since the dawn of the industrial revolution to one based on clean and renewable sources of energy. This radical and in a sense revolutionary shift is the extraordinary response required to an extraordinary challenge. We are prepared to be a part of this global effort, but I repeat, this must be on the basis of equitable burden-sharing.

India has announced its own National Action Plan on Climate Change on June 30, 2008. It is, in essence, our own strategy for sustainable development. It is based on the recognition that both in terms of energy security and tackling climate change, India must achieve a graduated shift from reliance on carbon-based fossil fuels to non-fossil fuels and from non-renewable to renewable sources of energy. Therefore, the pride of place has been given to a National Solar Mission to promote the use of the sun's energy, which is available plentifully in tropical India. There is also a focus on other renewables such as bio-mass and bio-fuels as also nuclear energy. We would welcome international collaboration to accelerate the implementation of this strategy.

The extraordinary nature of the global challenge of climate change also leads us to recommend other collaborative agreements on technology transfer, technology collaboration and financing instruments. If there are current patented technologies, whether from the developed or developing countries, whose widespread diffusion would make a significant impact on climate change, then let us acquire these patents through a global fund and make them available widely as public goods. We as a developing country, are prepared to contribute to such a fund in accordance with our economic capacity.

Similarly, we must put in an unprecedented effort in collaborative R&D to generate technological innovations that are cost-effective and convenient. This too, can be financed through a Global Venture Fund to which we are also prepared to contribute, and whose results similarly could widely be diffused as public goods.

There is no doubt that the financing required to achieve a substantial shift from a carbon-based economy to a renewables-based economy, will be of an unprecedented scale. Given the current economic gloom world-wide, this may seem unrealistic. I would, however, argue that deploying resources to tackle the global challenge of climate change, is itself a means of "energizing" the world economy. It will unleash a veritable surge of innovation, enterprise and development unmatched in history.

The capital required must be deployed nationally as well as on a multilateral basis to support sustainable development in developing countries. The location and disbursement of these funds are best achieved through the UNFCCC framework itself rather than in a traditional donor-driven approach, where the priorities of developing countries tend to be ignored. This will require a mind-set change both among developed and developing countries. Financing for climate change should not be seen as another form of ODA but rather payments for 'entitlements' of developing countries under an equitable global regime.

India is prepared to work actively and constructively for an ambitious, equitable and effective outcome from Copenhagen.

INDIA HITS OUT AT DEVELOPED NATIONS ON CLIMATE CHANGE

India strongly hit out at developed nations for putting "conditions" and "adding dimensions" such as carbon tariff and trade competitiveness for action on climate change.

"Action on climate change cannot be based on conditions. Once we start going in that directions than it means we start going for protectionism under green label and it is harmful to India's interest seeking sustainable development," said Shyam Saran, India's special envoy on climate change.

He was speaking at a seminar on 'Business response to climate change' organised by the CII-ITC Centre of Excellence for Sustainable Development.

"So in that context we see issues coming up, sometimes in the form of carbon tariff or greater tariff change or opening up of market which the developed countries want to impose on us on the pretext of tackling climate change," Saran added.

Sharing the concern of corporates that imposition of carbon tariff would go against the interest of business and industry in India, he said, "This is what we have been resisting. Collaborations become irrelevant when competitive tendencies prevail."

"In international negotiations we have taken the position that climate change is a challenge which must be dealt on its own and through supportive global regime," he said while indicating India's stand to be taken at Copenhagen at the end of the year when countries will meet to discuss a global policy on climate change.

CLIMATE CHANGE PLAN TO FOCUS ON SUSTAINABLE DEVELOPMENT

The country's strategy for sustainable development known as the National Action Plan on climate change, would be in place by June this year, a top Prime Ministerial aide said.[6]

"The National Action Plan on climate change is essentially a kind of strategy for sustainable development and aims to bring about shift from fossil fuels to non-fossil fuels," former Foreign Secretary and Special Envoy of Prime Minister, Shyam Saran, said at a conference on climate change in India, organised by the Confederation of Indian Industry (CII).

Saran said that the strategy was also about how to bring about a shift from non-renewable to renewable source of energy as well as conventional to non-conventional source of energy.

He said that such a shift was requird so that energy does not become a constraint to growth.

Responding to a question on India's position in the on-going multilateral dialogues over the carbon emission reduction issue, Saran said that developed countries have undertaken certain committments to reduce their carbon missions by a certain amount up to 2012.

"Now we are discussing amongst ourselves as to what could be the post 2012-committment which could be made again by the industrialised countries," Saran said.

Saran said the formulation of the action plan, as agreed at Bali last November, was to make more effective the implementation of the objectives of the original framework of the Convention on Climate Change.

"There are a number of objectives which have not been effectively implemented. The Bali Action Plan is about how to implement these objectives effectively. It also talks about the trasnfer of resources and technology from the developed to developing countries to enable the developing countries to engage in sustainble development," he said.

THE GREENHOUSE GAS PROTOCOL INITIATIVE

The Foundation for Sound and Sustainable Climate Strategies

The Greenhouse Gas Protocol (GHG Protocol) is the most widely used international accounting tool for government and business leaders to understand, quantify, and manage greenhouse gas emissions. The GHG Protocol, a decade-long partnership between the World Resources Institute and the World Business Council for Sustainable Development, is working with businesses, governments, and environmental groups around the world to build a new generation of credible and effective programs for tackling climate change.

It provides the accounting framework for nearly every GHG standard and program in the world—from the International Standards Organization to The Climate Registry—as well as hundreds of GHG inventories prepared by individual companies.

The GHG Protocol also offers developing countries an internationally accepted management tool to help their businesses to compete in the global marketplace and their governments to make informed decisions about climate change.

INDIA'S CLIMATE CHANGE INITIATIVES: STRATEGIES FOR A GREENER FUTURE

India's National Action Plan on Climate Change reflects the recognition that its economic growth will hit a dead-end if it does not embrace sustainable growth as a goal, asserted Shyam Saran, the Prime Minister's Special Envoy for Climate Change. In an engaging presentation moderated by William Chandler, Saran outlined India's strategies for tackling the challenge of climate change while simultaneously promoting economic growth and poverty reduction.[7]

Sustainable Growth and Energy Security

For India, climate change and security concerns have come together in a way that draws increasing attention to energy policy. If India is to achieve an 8-10% growth rate, which is necessary to eradicate poverty rapidly, the country has to overcome its rising energy constraints. Imports currently meet 70% of India's oil requirements and this figure is likely to increase to 90% by 2030. Such dependence on foreign oil is neither secure nor sustainable.

Because India is still in the process of building its energy, transport and industrial infrastructure, it has the opportunity to invest in energy efficient technologies that can help the country "leapfrog" over the carbon-intensive phase of development and move toward an advanced low-carbon economy.

With regards to the current state of energy infrastructure and emissions, Saran objected to India being labeled as a "large emitter." He argued that even though India is often cited as the third largest emitter in the world, its 4 per cent contribution to global carbon dioxide (CO_2) emissions is dwarfed by United States and China, each of which account for about 20 per cent. India's current emissions amount to just 1.8 tons of CO_2 per capita while the United States emits 20 tons per capita.

India's low per-capita emissions are, in part, a result of the fact that there are 400 million Indians who do not have access to commercial electricity today. Despite India's growing energy needs as more of those citizens gain access to electricity, the prime minister has committed to remaining below the per capita emissions rate of developed countries, reiterating the country's commitment to sustainable growth.

National Action Plan

The need to address both climate change and energy security has given rise to a Prime Ministerial directive called the National Action Plan (NAP) which identifies eight areas or "missions" for focused energy and climate policy interventions: solar energy, energy efficiency, sustainable habitat, water, Himalayan ecosystems, sustainable agriculture, strategic knowledge for climate change and a "Green India". Each of the missions will proceed in what are known as Public, Private and People (PPP) partnerships, which bring together central and state governments, businesses, civil society and community organizations to create an effective and realistic strategy for the implementation of the eight missions.

- *Solar Energy*: India enjoys intense sunlight across the country during most of the year, making it a prime location for solar power. The potential for rapid expansion means that there is still room for significant cost reductions in solar energy. The government's strategy is to scale up existing solar applications through supportive regulations and incentives. If the cost of solar power falls to the level of coal-fired power, market forces could help solar energy expand to reach the same scale as nuclear power—which is currently at 10,000 megawatts of capacity but could reach as high as 60,000 megawatts by 2030.

- *Enhanced energy efficiency*: Part of the impetus to conserve energy comes from the fact that Indians face some of the highest energy prices in the world—relative to median income, energy prices in India are a staggering 100 times greater than prices in the United States. India has therefore tried to decrease the energy requirements of its economic growth. Since 2004, the economy has grown by 9 per cent but energy use has grown by just 4 per cent and the ratio between the two is better than in the past. In one major initiative, the Indian government identified nine energy intensive sectors and set efficiency benchmarks for each sector, with an overall target of 20% greater efficiency by 2012. This target is enforced through mandatory energy audits, and the NAP plans to introduce trading of Energy Efficiency certificates to encourage higher standards.

India also launched an Energy Conservation Building Code (ECBC) in 2007 which encourages the design of 30% more energy efficient buildings. In an example of effective Indo-U.S. cooperation, USAID provided strong technical support in training Indian architects to use ECBC.

The Indian government has also undertaken efforts to increase energy efficiency at the level of individual consumers, including a major drive to popularize highly efficient compact fluorescent lamps (CFLs). The government hopes to increase sales of these bulbs by making them available for less than the market price, using the sale of carbon credits to fund this subsidy.

- *Himalayan ecosystem*: The NAP seeks to fill in gaps in knowledge about the ecology of the Himalayas by using India's space capabilities for climate studies. This research is crucial for understanding and adapting to the retreat of Himalayan glaciers, which are the primary source of fresh water for much of the country.
- *Sustainable agriculture*: Several villages in South India have switched from high-input intensive agriculture—which uses large amounts of water, fertilizers and seeds—to a more diversified cropping pattern. If scaled up, this sustainable strategy could significantly lower greenhouse gas emissions from agriculture.

Successful India-U.S. Cooperation

As the world prepares to negotiate a successor to the Kyoto Protocol in Copenhagen this December, India's main hope is that the new global regime will provide sufficient financial and technical support for mitigation and adaptation efforts in developing countries. India believes United States must be a key driver of this process not only because of its emissions-reduction responsibility but also because it is the chief source of technological innovation and creative entrepreneurship.

On the bilateral front, India and the U.S. have collaborated on many specific climate-related projects including the 'Methane to Market' partnership for the commercial utilization of coal-bed methane. India was also a partner in the U.S.-led Future Gen project to develop a zero-emission coal based thermal power plant. The U.S. was a leader in development of methane technology until low oil prices led to its neglect. India believes methanol can be used as a low-emission transportation fuel and is therefore ready to support the resumption of aggressive R&D on methane technology.

The positive experience of working together on energy and climate issues, including the Indo-U.S. Civil Nuclear Agreement, has enabled these two countries to plan a much more ambitious agenda for collaboration under President Obama's Renewable Energy Initiative. While the Indian government is already taking significant domestic action, India needs the United States to lead the initiative to build a multilateral framework that is fair and equitable and helps India make the transition to a low-carbon economy.

Questions and Answers

In the question and answer session, Saran addressed a number of international and multilateral issues, reiterating India's willingness to engage in productive negotiations in Copenhagen as long as the U.S. takes a leadership role. He expressed hope that the negotiations might find a way to streamline and reform the Clean Development Mechanism (established under the Kyoto Protocol), which could be more effective if it were based on large-scale programs rather than specific projects.

Saran also stated his view that trade and competitiveness issues should be addressed in a separate sphere from climate issues, saying it would be "most unfortunate" if countries like the U.S. decided to place border adjustment taxes on goods produced under less stringent emissions regulations. Finally, Saran left the door open to future collaboration with China, Nepal, and Bhutan—particularly on climate issues affecting the Himalayan region—but he added that India must resolve many domestic challenges before focusing too heavily on reaching out to its neighbors.

Saran answered a range of audience questions relating to domestic energy issues as well, including practical questions relating to the implementation and monitoring of the National Action Plan. He said he was confident that the ambitious solar power initiative could be implemented effectively, beginning with property owned by the public sector, where as much as 50% of available roof space may someday be used for solar panels. Yet many details of the NAP missions are still in the works; at present, the Prime Minister's office is holding a series of brainstorming sessions to seek input on the NAP from businesses, industry leaders, NGOs, academics, and science and technology experts.

A trading scheme for Energy Efficiency Certificates is also in the development stage. The government is looking for a way to incentivize efficiency without ignoring the fact that some plants and factories already have much greater energy efficiency than others. After ironing out these details, monitoring the progress of all these initiatives will pose the next big hurtle. For help with this, the Indian government plans to draw on local and regional networks, which has been a successful strategy in past monitoring efforts.

Finally, several questions addressed India's future energy prospects, ranging from conventional fossil fuels to nuclear energy and renewables. Saran explained that India does not believe carbon capture and sequestration is an economically viable solution; instead, India hopes to continue collaborating with the U.S. on other technology to reduce coal emissions, such super-critical power plants. Cleaner coal is especially important, he said, because at least 50% of the country's electricity needs will still be met by coal in the coming decades. Similarly, India will continue to rely heavily on petroleum in the next few decades, particularly because biofuels are an unlikely and unpopular substitute in a country with many people on the brink of starvation.

But even as fossil fuels continue to play an important role, nuclear power will provide an increasing share of India's energy. Saran, as a key negotiator in the U.S.-India civil nuclear deal, expressed his hope for a rapid expansion of nuclear power. With the door opened for nuclear energy commerce, India hopes to reach 60,000 megawatts by 2030 and perhaps as much as 250,000 megawatts by 2050. On nuclear energy as well as on other low-carbon energy sources, Saran concluded, India looks forward to working with the U.S. to find solutions that benefit both countries.

STRATEGIES FOR A GREENER FUTURE

India's National Action Plan on Climate Change reflects the recognition that its economic growth will hit a dead-end if it does not embrace sustainable growth as a goal, asserted Shyam Saran, the Prime Minister's Special Envoy for Climate Change. In an engaging presentation moderated by William Chandler, Saran outlined India's strategies for tackling the challenge of climate change while simultaneously promoting economic growth and poverty reduction8.

Sustainable Growth and Energy Security

For India, climate change and security concerns have come together in a way that draws increasing attention to energy policy. If India is to achieve an 8-10% growth rate, which is necessary to eradicate poverty rapidly, the country has to overcome its rising energy constraints. Imports currently meet 70% of India's oil requirements and this figure is likely to increase to 90% by 2030. Such dependence on foreign oil is neither secure nor sustainable.

Because India is still in the process of building its energy, transport and industrial infrastructure, it has the opportunity to invest in energy efficient technologies that can help the country "leapfrog" over the carbon-intensive phase of development and move toward an advanced low-carbon economy.

With regards to the current state of energy infrastructure and emissions, Saran objected to India being labeled as a "large emitter." He argued that even though India is often cited as the third largest emitter in the world, its 4 per cent contribution to global carbon dioxide (CO_2) emissions is dwarfed by United States and China, each of which account for about 20 per cent. India's current emissions amount to just 1.8 tons of CO_2 per capita while the United States emits 20 tons per capita.

India's low per-capita emissions are, in part, a result of the fact that there are 400 million Indians who do not have access to commercial electricity today. Despite India's growing energy needs as more of those citizens gain access to electricity, the prime minister has committed to remaining below the per capita emissions rate of developed countries, reiterating the country's commitment to sustainable growth.

National Action Plan

The need to address both climate change and energy security has given rise to a Prime Ministerial directive called the National Action Plan (NAP) which identifies eight areas or "missions" for focused energy and climate policy interventions: solar energy, energy efficiency, sustainable habitat, water, Himalayan ecosystems, sustainable agriculture, strategic knowledge for climate change and a "Green India". Each of the missions will proceed in what are known as Public, Private and People (PPP) partnerships, which bring together central and state governments, businesses, civil society and community organizations to create an effective and realistic strategy for the implementation of the eight missions.

- *Solar Energy*: India enjoys intense sunlight across the country during most of the year, making it a prime location for solar power. The potential for rapid expansion means that there is still room for significant cost reductions in solar energy. The government's strategy is to scale up existing solar applications through supportive regulations and incentives. If the cost of solar power falls to the level of coal-fired power, market forces could help solar energy expand to reach the same scale as nuclear power—which is currently at 10,000 megawatts of capacity but could reach as high as 60,000 megawatts by 2030.
- *Enhanced energy efficiency*: Part of the impetus to conserve energy comes from the fact that Indians face some of the highest energy prices in the world—relative to median income, energy prices in India are a staggering 100 times greater than prices in the United States. India has therefore tried to decrease the energy requirements of its economic growth. Since 2004, the economy has grown by 9 per cent but energy use has grown by just 4 per cent and the ratio between the two is better than in the past. In

one major initiative, the Indian government identified nine energy intensive sectors and set efficiency benchmarks for each sector, with an overall target of 20% greater efficiency by 2012. This target is enforced through mandatory energy audits, and the NAP plans to introduce trading of Energy Efficiency certificates to encourage higher standards.

India also launched an Energy Conservation Building Code (ECBC) in 2007 which encourages the design of 30% more energy efficient buildings. In an example of effective Indo-U.S. cooperation, USAID provided strong technical support in training Indian architects to use ECBC.

The Indian government has also undertaken efforts to increase energy efficiency at the level of individual consumers, including a major drive to popularize highly efficient compact fluorescent lamps (CFLs). The government hopes to increase sales of these bulbs by making them available for less than the market price, using the sale of carbon credits to fund this subsidy.

- *Himalayan ecosystem*: The NAP seeks to fill in gaps in knowledge about the ecology of the Himalayas by using India's space capabilities for climate studies. This research is crucial for understanding and adapting to the retreat of Himalayan glaciers, which are the primary source of fresh water for much of the country.
- *Sustainable agriculture*: Several villages in South India have switched from high-input intensive agriculture—which uses large amounts of water, fertilizers and seeds—to a more diversified cropping pattern. If scaled up, this sustainable strategy could significantly lower greenhouse gas emissions from agriculture.

Successful India-U.S. Cooperation

As the world prepares to negotiate a successor to the Kyoto Protocol in Copenhagen this December, India's main hope is that the new global regime will provide sufficient financial and technical support for mitigation and adaptation efforts in developing countries. India believes United States must be a key driver of this process not only because of its emissions-reduction responsibility but also because it is the chief source of technological innovation and creative entrepreneurship.

On the bilateral front, India and the U.S. have collaborated on many specific climate-related projects including the 'Methane to Market' partnership for the commercial utilization of coal-bed methane. India was also a partner in the U.S.-led Future Gen project to develop a zero-emission coal based thermal power plant. The U.S. was a leader in development of methane technology until low oil prices led to its neglect. India believes methanol can be used as a low-emission transportation fuel and is therefore ready to support the resumption of aggressive R&D on methane technology.

The positive experience of working together on energy and climate issues, including the Indo-U.S. Civil Nuclear Agreement, has enabled these two countries to plan a much more ambitious agenda for collaboration under President Obama's Renewable Energy Initiative. While the Indian government is already taking significant domestic action, India needs the United States to lead the initiative to build a multilateral framework that is fair and equitable and helps India make the transition to a low-carbon economy.

Questions and Answers

In the question and answer session, Saran addressed a number of international and multilateral issues, reiterating India's willingness to engage in productive negotiations in Copenhagen as long as the U.S. takes a leadership role. He expressed hope that the negotiations might find a way to streamline and reform the Clean Development Mechanism (established under the Kyoto Protocol), which could be more effective if it were based on large-scale programs rather than specific projects.

Saran also stated his view that trade and competitiveness issues should be addressed in a separate sphere from climate issues, saying it would be "most unfortunate" if countries like the U.S. decided to place border adjustment taxes on goods produced under less stringent emissions regulations. Finally, Saran left the door open to future collaboration with China, Nepal, and Bhutan—particularly on climate issues affecting the Himalayan region—but he added that India must resolve many domestic challenges before focusing too heavily on reaching out to its neighbors.

Saran answered a range of audience questions relating to domestic energy issues as well, including practical questions relating to the implementation and monitoring of the National Action Plan. He said he was confident that the ambitious solar power initiative could be implemented effectively, beginning with property owned by the public sector, where as much as 50% of available roof space may someday be used for solar panels. Yet many details of the NAP missions are still in the works; at present, the Prime Minister's office is holding a series of brainstorming sessions to seek input on the NAP from businesses, industry leaders, NGOs, academics, and science and technology experts.

A trading scheme for Energy Efficiency Certificates is also in the development stage. The government is looking for a way to incentivize efficiency without ignoring the fact that some plants and factories already have much greater energy efficiency than others. After ironing out these details, monitoring the progress of all these initiatives will pose the next big hurtle. For help with this, the Indian government plans to draw on local and regional networks, which has been a successful strategy in past monitoring efforts.

Finally, several questions addressed India's future energy prospects, ranging from conventional fossil fuels to nuclear energy and renewables. Saran explained that India does not believe carbon capture and sequestration is an economically viable solution; instead, India hopes to continue collaborating with the U.S. on other technology to reduce coal emissions, such super-critical power plants. Cleaner coal is especially important, he said, because at least 50% of the country's electricity needs will still be met by coal in the coming decades. Similarly, India will continue to rely heavily on petroleum in the next few decades, particularly because biofuels are an unlikely and unpopular substitute in a country with many people on the brink of starvation.

But even as fossil fuels continue to play an important role, nuclear power will provide an increasing share of India's energy. Saran, as a key negotiator in the U.S.-India civil nuclear deal, expressed his hope for a rapid expansion of nuclear power. With the door opened for nuclear energy commerce, India hopes to reach 60,000 megawatts by 2030 and perhaps as much as 250,000 megawatts by 2050. On nuclear energy as well as on other low-carbon energy sources, Saran concluded, India looks forward to working with the U.S. to find solutions that benefit both countries.

INDIA PLANS ENERGY TRADING SCHEME TO BOOST RENEWABLE RESOURCES NEWS

India is planning an energy trading scheme to allow businesses that need more energy to be able to buy energy certificates from those using less energy or using renewable energy.[8]

According to the prime minister's special envoy on climate change Shyam Saran this could expand the domains of renewable energy.

Speaking at a seminar on 'Business Response to Climate Change' organised by the Confederation of Indian Industry-ITC Centre of Excellence for Sustainable Development, Saran said, the government was setting up energy benchmarks for each industry sector.

Those companies that do not meet the benchmarks would have to buy these certificates under a reward and penalty system, which could perhaps even be linked with the concept of renewable energy certificates. Saran said if this link could be established, the country could have a very fast growing market for energy efficiency and renewable energy certificates, which would be a major innovation.

"We are looking at trading mechanisms so if you are more efficient you get a certain credit, if you are less efficient you have to buy it," Saran said.

India has identified energy efficiency as one of the major aspects in its national climate change policy last year. It hopes to reduce energy consumption by at least 25 per cent in energy-intensive sectors such as power and cement.

However, most Indian businesses have yet to plan for the impact of climate change.

According to a study, India, accounts for four per cent of global emissions, compared to 20 per cent by US and 16 per cent by China. India emits about 1.1 tonnes of carbon per capita while the corresponding figure for US is more than 20 tonnes.

"Science suggests the current climate change is due to accumulated. emissions of over 200 years of industrialisation. The world, therefore, should work together to achieve sustainability," Saran opined.

"If India has to continuously grow at eight to nine per cent, then it should reduce dependence on fossil fuels. According to Indias Integrated Energy Policy, by 2030 India will be importing more than 90 per cent of oil and about two-thirds to three-fourths of coal, and the energy cost will increase."

He said, "The clearance of civil nuclear energy agreement (with the US) will help India to have better energy security. The current economic downturn has turned to India's advantage as the cost of equipment and fuel have come down considerably."

"In international negotiations we have taken the position that climate change is a challenge which must be dealt on its own and through supportive global regime," Saran said while indicating India's stand to be taken at Copenhagen at the end of the year when countries will meet to discuss a global policy on climate change.

Weekly Climate Change Policy Update—March 9, 2009

KYLE DANISH, SHELLEY FIDLER, KEVIN GALLAGHER, MEGAN CERONSKY, TOMÁS CARBONELL

March 9, 2009

Commentary

In international news, the EU Environment Ministers reaffirmed their call for a mid-term emissions target for developed countries of 25-40 per cent below 1990 levels by 2020. However, State Department Climate Envoy Todd Stern made clear that the United States would not support such a proposal . . . Senate Majority Leader Reid and House Speaker Pelosi now have the same basic game plan: Develop legislation that combine cap-and-trade with energy policy, including a renewable electricity standard and transmission reform . . . The House Subcommittee on Energy and Environment held a hearing on offsets in cap-and-trade legislation. The discussion suggested that, for the Democrats, the issue is not "whether" but "how."

Executive Branch

Climate Envoy Dismisses EU-Proposed Mid-term Targets. State Department climate change envoy Todd Stern said that he opposes a European proposal for developed nations to reduce greenhouse gas (GHG) emissions by 25-40 per cent below 1990 levels over the next decade. Stern argued that such reductions were not scientifically necessary and that he did not want to bring Congress a "dead-on-arrival agreement. We tried that. It didn't do the world a lot of good." Stern also said it would be optimal if Congress could pass cap-and-trade legislation before the next major round of international negotiations in December, but acknowledged that this was "an extremely tall order." Stern confirmed that President Obama would continue to engage with leaders of major economic powers through a forum distinct from the U.N.-led climate change discussions, an initiative begun by the prior administration. (For further details on the EU-proposed targets, see the discussion under "International" below).

Chu Responds to CCS, Nuclear Waste Controversies. Energy Secretary Steven Chu said that DOE is taking a "fresh look" at FutureGen, a federal-industry collaboration to build a coal-fired power plant with carbon capture and sequestration (CCS). FutureGen was abandoned by the Bush Administration because of cost increases. Chu also said he wants to coordinate with other international CCS technology development initiatives in order to increase the efficiency of technology development and testing. In response to GOP criticism of the abandonment of the Yucca Mountain nuclear waste repository, Chu commented that the Obama Administration was considering distributing the waste to multiple repositories.

President Announces Science Advisor Pick. President Obama announced that Sherburne "Shere" Abbott will be his nominee for associate director of environment at the White House Office of Science and Technology. Abbott is currently serving as director for the Center for Science and Practice of Sustainability at the University of Texas at Austin. Abbot previously worked at the American Association for the Advancement of Science and at the National Academies' National Research Council, and has consulted widely on sustainable development issues.

Jackson Considering Environmental Justice and Climate Change. In determining whether GHG emissions from vehicles endanger public health and welfare, as required by the Supreme Court in *Massachusetts v. EPA*, EPA Administrator Lisa Jackson said she will consider the effects of climate change on disadvantaged individuals and communities, especially those disproportionately impacted by other sources of pollution. An affirmative endangerment finding would trigger CO_2 regulation under the Clean Air Act.

OMB Director Orszag Defends Obama Cap-and-Trade Plan Before House. During testimony in support of President Obama's proposed budget before the House Budget Committee, Office of Management and Budget (OMB) Director Peter Orszag defended the President's plan for a 100% auction of carbon allowances. Orszag stated that a free allocation of emission allowances would amount to "corporate welfare," which the recipients would use to increase profits rather than pass savings on to consumers. By contrast, a full auction would generate significant revenues which could be used to "cushion" impacts on consumers and invest in energy efficiency improvements. Commenting on the Obama Administration's position on nuclear power, Orszag acknowledged that nuclear power has lower GHG emissions than coal-fired power plants and stated that "discussion would occur" on the role of nuclear power as climate change legislation is crafted.

Congress

House and Senate to Combine Energy and Climate Legislation. Both House Speaker Nancy Pelosi (D-CA) and Senate Majority Leader Harry Reid (D-NV) announced that they intend to produce a single energy and climate change bill in each legislative chamber this year, integrating cap-and-trade legislation with a renewable electricity standard and transmission grid reform. Legislative drafting efforts are moving forward:

- Sen. Reid introduced The Clean Renewable Energy and Economic Development Act this week. The transmission legislation would create renewable energy zones in areas with significant generation potential and give FERC the authority to site transmission lines to transport electricity from those zones to load centers if state and regional transmission development efforts stall. The "green" transmission lines built using the federal backstop authority would be required to devote 75 per cent of their capacity to renewable energy, or as much as possible while also preserving grid stability. FERC would also have the authority to spread costs of transmission development across rate payers in the absence of a local cost allocation plan, and the agency would be given full control over review of environmental impacts of "green" transmission lines on federal lands.
- House Energy and Commerce Chairman Henry Waxman (D-CA) said he hopes to have a draft of climate change legislation this month, which staff have begun writing. Rep. Ed Markey, Chairman of the Energy and Environment Subcommittee of the House Energy and Commerce Committee, said he believes the Federal Energy Regulatory Commission will be the proper agency to oversee the new carbon market.
- On the Senate side, Energy and Natural Resources Chairman Jeff Bingaman (D-NM) said he is "optimistic" that energy legislation will be reported out of committee within a month, and plans to circulate draft legislation to provide financial support for clean energy projects "as early as next week."
- Rep. John Larson (D-CT), who opposes the cap-and-trade framework, reintroduced his carbon tax bill. The legislation proposes an upstream $15 per metric ton of carbon tax to ratchet up by $10 each year until U.S. emissions are 80% below 2005 levels. Revenues generated by the tax would be dedicated to reducing payroll taxes, investing in clean energy initiatives, and providing "transition assistance" to carbon-intensive industries.

Congress Hearing Plenty on Climate Change. A number of Congressional committees held hearings on climate change and related issues this week, including:

- The Subcommittee on Energy and Environment of the House Committee on Energy and Commerce convened a hearing on the use of offsets within a cap-and-trade program. Although a number of Republican Representatives indicated skepticism about offsets, in general Sub-committee members expressed support for an environmentally rigorous offsets program as a method of reducing emissions while producing cost-containment, ancillary environmental benefits, and opportunities for their constituents. Sub-committee Chairman Ed Markey (D-MA) and other members showed interest in establishing a scientific advisory board to advise the EPA in developing an offsets program.
- The Senate Energy and Natural Resources Committee heard from DOE Secretary Steven Chu on reform to DOE's R&D programs. Chu described the challenge as bridging the gap between basic science research by government and universities and technology deployment, and said his goal is to build research networks within government, the U.S., and internationally to integrate research efforts. The Committee published a draft of legislation to expand R&D and science funding authorizations for DOE.
- The National Parks, Forests and Public Lands Subcommittee of the House Natural Resources Committee held a hearing on natural resource management in the context of climate change, including the possibility of reform to the National Environmental Policy Act and using public lands to mitigate climate change. Barton Thompson, director of the Woods Institute for the Environment at Stanford University, advised incorporating climate change considerations into resource management plants.

States and Cities

New York Governor Patterson to Consider Increase of Free Distribution of RGGI Allowances. New York Governor David Patterson (D) will reconsider State Department of Environmental Conservation regulations that mandate the auction of most of the state's annual allocation of 64.3 million Regional Greenhouse Gas Initiative (RGGI) CO_2 emission allowances. Under those regulations, the state currently auctions 62.8 million allowances and distributes the remaining 1.5 million allowances for free to regulated entities in the energy sector. Intended to reduce compliance costs for the energy sector, the Governor will consider amending the regulations to increase the number of allowances distributed for free, although the exact amount of the proposed increase has not been announced. The change comes in response to complaints about compliance costs from regulated utilities that, due to long-term power purchase agreements that do not account for the cost of CO_2 emission allowances, are unable to pass through the cost of allowances. Indeck Energy, an independent power producer in upstate New York that operates under such an agreement, recently brought a lawsuit against Gov. Patterson and several state agencies challenging those agencies' authority to promulgate regulations implementing RGGI. RGGI is a regional GHG cap-and-trade program comprised of ten northeastern states.

Maryland Senate Passes GHG Targets. The Maryland Senate passed legislation that would cap the state's GHG emissions at 25 per cent below 2006 levels by 2025. The bill, the GHG Reduction Act, would give the Maryland Department of Environment until 2012 to draft regulations to meet the target, although it exempts the state's manufacturing sector from emission restrictions. The Maryland House must now pass the legislation before it can be sent to Governor Martin O'Malley (D), who considers the legislation a priority for this legislative session. Maryland is currently a member of RGGI.

California Air Resources Board Issues Rules Limiting Fluorinated Gases. In an effort to meet the GHG emission targets imposed by California's A.B. 32 legislation, the California Air Resources Board issued two measures aimed at reducing emissions of fluorinated gases, a family of potent GHGs. The regulations control the emissions rather than the production of the gases. The first rule sets performance-based fluorinated gas emission standards for semi-conductor manufacturers that use fluorinated gases in amounts above a specific threshold. The rule, which supplements existing voluntary reduction programs for semiconductor manufacturers, will be phased in between 2012-14. The second rule will phase out the use of sulfur hexafluorocarbons (SF_6) in non-utility, non-semiconductor applications. Fluorinated gases include sulfur hexafluoride (SF_6), nitrogen trifluoride, perfluorocarbons, and hydrofluorocarbons, among others. SF_6 is the most potent of the six major GHGs, with each ton having a climate impact (or global warming potential) equal to 23,900 tons of CO_2. The global warming potentials of other fluorinated gases range between 6,500-17,200 CO_2-equivalent tons.

California Delivers Climate Recommendations to U.S. EPA. California Environmental Protection Agency Secretary Linda Adams delivered to U.S. Environmental Protection Agency (EPA) Administrator Lisa Jackson a letter recommending design options for a federal climate program. In the letter, Secretary Adams recommended that a future federal program preserve state programs that are in place prior to implementation of the federal program, permit use of federal allowances for compliance with state program obligations, allow states to retire federal allowances, link to emission trading programs outside North America, accept international offset credits, distribute the majority of allowances through auction, and set GHG emission caps at between 50 and 85 per cent below 2000 levels by 2050. The letter also recommended that EPA use The Climate Registry to register, track and retire emission allowances. The Climate Registry is a voluntary GHG registry whose members include 40 U.S. states, all 10 Canadian provinces, and 6 Mexican states.

Wyoming Governor Signs Carbon Sequestration Bills. Wyoming Governor Dave Freudenthal (D) signed into law two bills that will regulate carbon capture and sequestration (CCS) activities in the state. The first bill grants resource mining or drilling rights precedence over underground storage rights. The second bill states that whoever sequesters CO_2 underground remains legally responsible for the sequestered gases. The two bills follow a bill passed last year that gave land owners rights to underground storage space.

Utah House Approves Resolution Seeking Withdrawal From WCI. The Utah House passed a non-binding resolution urging Governor Jon Huntsman (R) to withdraw the state from the Western Climate Initiative (WCI), a regional GHG cap-and-trade program. The resolution cited the lack of legislative consultation or public input, as well as economic concerns, as reasons for opposing participation in the WCI. WCI members include Arizona, California, Montana, New Mexico, Oregon, Utah and Washington and the Canadian provinces of British Columbia, Manitoba, Quebec and Ontario. The unicameral measure will not be voted on by the state Senate and Gov. Huntsman has stated he will not withdraw Utah from the WCI.

Industry

Utilities Disclose RGGI Compliance Costs. Mirant Corp., which owns generating stations in Maryland, Massachusetts, and New York, revealed that its plants would emit approximately 16.6 million tons of CO_2 in 2009. At an expected allowance price of $3.48, Mirant forecasted a total Regional Greenhouse Gas Initiative (RGGI) compliance cost of $43 million in 2009. By contrast, Calpine Corp. announced that RGGI would have a neutral or even positive financial impact, since its combined-cycle gas-fired generators in Maine, New York and New Jersey emit CO_2 at less than half the rate of traditional coal-fired power plants.

Secondary RGGI Allowance Market Growing Quickly. Potomac Economics, RGGI's independent market monitor, reported that RGGI futures trading has grown 113% since September 2008. An average of 330,000 futures contracts were traded daily in January. Over three quarters of RGGI options between August 15, 2008 and January 30, 2009 took the form of "puts," suggesting that most options traders expected allowance prices to decline over time. In addition, the report found no evidence of anti-competitive conduct during the first few months of secondary market trading and noted increased market stability over recent months. The next RGGI allowance auction is scheduled to take place March 18, 2009.

Duke CEO, Rural Electric Cooperatives Critique President Obama's Proposed 100 Per cent Auction. Duke Energy CEO Jim Rogers stated that President Obama's proposal to auction 100 per cent of emission allowances in a future federal cap-and-trade program would constitute a "cap-and-tax" program whose financial burden would fall disproportionately on Mid-western states that depend on coal as a power source. Rogers estimated that electricity rates would increase by as much as 40 per cent if utilities had to operate under such a system. Citing the Clean Air Act's sulfur dioxide trading program, Rogers recommended that no more than 20% of allowances in a federal climate program be auctioned. Similar criticisms were raised in a letter from the National Rural Electric Cooperatives Association to President Obama, claiming that cooperative customers would see a rate increase of 15% under the proposed plan.

Global Economy Hurting Investment in Renewables, Energy Efficiency, and Carbon Sequestration. A report by the British firm New Energy Finance estimated that global investment in renewable energy, energy efficiency, and carbon sequestration projects totaled $150 billion in both 2007 and 2008, a dramatic increase from the $34 billion invested in these "cleantech" industries in 2004. However, the report found that investment growth in cleantech industries has stalled, and forecasted that investment levels would stay constant at about $150 billion per year until at least 2011. The report, titled "Global Futures 2009," predicted that investment growth in the cleantech sector would resume after 2011, and reach $350 billion in 2020.

Studies and Reports

U.S. Emissions Up 1.4% in 2007. A draft annual report issued by the EPA found that U.S. GHG emissions increased by 17.1% between 1990 and 2007, and increased 1.4% in 2007 alone. The EPA attributed the 2007 numbers to a colder winter and a warmer summer than in 2006 as well as to a decrease in the availability of hydropower generation. Fossil fuel combustion was the source of 94.4% of U.S. CO_2 emissions in 2007.

Study Says President's Cap-and-Trade Program Will Not Raise Taxes. According to a report by the Center on Budget and Policy Priorities, claims that President Obama's proposed cap-and-trade program is a tax increase for consumers are misleading. Because most of the revenues from the auction of emissions allowances would be returned to consumers to offset the increases in energy costs under the President's plan, no significant tax increase would occur.

Corn Ethanol Benefits Delayed. A new study published in the journal *Ecological Applications* found that when land under a conservation program is plowed to grow corn for ethanol production, the carbon releases from the soil that result may offset carbon gains from biofuel production for at least half a century. Cellulosic ethanol was projected to produce the greatest sequestration gains—although conventional corn production can release 30-50% of the carbon stored in the soil, plants used for cellulosic ethanol could increase soil carbon levels by 30-50%, because they do not require annual plowing and planting. The authors concluded that climate change policies should not encourage the conversion of CRP or other set-aside lands to corn ethanol production, and that setting aside agricultural lands for conservation may be a more cost-effective means of sequestering carbon than using that land to produce corn-based ethanol for at least 100 years.

International

EU Seeks 30 Per Cent Reduction from 1990 Emission Levels by 2020 for Developed Countries. Meeting at the EU Council in Brussels, Belgium, EU environment ministers called on developed nations to adopt by mid-2009 an emission-reduction target of 30 per cent from 1990 levels by 2020. The ministers urged the early acceptance of mid-term targets as part of preparations for the Conference of the Parties to United Nations Framework Convention on Climate Change, which will be held in Copenhagen, Denmark this December. The ministers' recommendations sought commitments for €175 billion ($221 billion) in climate change mitigation funding annually by 2020 from developed nations as a group. The EU ministers also called on developing countries to adopt "low carbon development plans" by the end of 2011.

Indian Post-Kyoto Climate Position Calls for Focus on Historic Emissions. India's Special Envoy for Climate Change Shyam Saran, the country's lead climate change negotiator, released a document detailing the country's positions for a post-Kyoto Protocol. The document said that the treaty should take into account historical emissions. In addition, the document noted that the nation will greatly resist a treaty that calls for binding emission caps for developing nations.

Notes and References

1. Business Desk (2009), "Climate Change and Development Imperatives", March 16
2. IANS (2009), "India and fossil fuels", March 16, New Delhi.
3. Sahil Nagpal (2008), "India and Global Climate Change Negotiations", April 21.
4. DC (2009), "Strategies for a Greener Future", March 24, Washington.
5. Bled Forum (2008), "Speech by Shyam Saran", September 1.
6. IST, PTI (2008) "Climate Change Plan to Focus on Sustainable Development", April 2, Mumbai.
7. William Chandler, (2009), MARCH 24.
8. William Chandler, Shyam Saran (2009), "India's Climate Change Initiatives: Strategies for a Greener Future", March 24.

CHAPTER

3

WATER FOR LIFE THROUGH SUSTAINABLE DEVELOPMENT OF RESOURCES

B.S. BHAVANISHANKAR

ABSTRACT

There is an acute shortage of water in almost all the Indian rivers because of poor management policies of the government. It is observed that there are a number of small river basins in the South, with no interstate disputes as in the Western Ghats, draining into the Arabian Sea.

While the tussle is on for Krishna and Cauvery waters due to the lesser and limited availability, practically all, the 2000 TMC of the Ghats Rivers flow down unutilized within the state.

Till today no serious thought seems to have been given or plans made to skim Western flow for use in the large eastern water deficit plains of Krishna and Cauvery basins, through any imaginative and economical engineering interventions.

A technology that was developed more than six decades in the Western Countries, can be applied for our specific requirement to meet the water and peak power requirements of the State. Incidentally the strategy will also reduce floods in the west flowing rivers and the damage in low-lying coastal areas as in the case of Mangalore.

If the three states, Karnataka, Maharashtra and Kerala join along with Andhra Pradesh and Tamilnadu to form a Water and Power Council to optimize their abundant natural resources particularly in the water and power sectors, there will not be any shortage for long years to come. Some waters can even be spared from the surplus to other States as well.

The strategy for Northern India comprises in understanding the entire Gangetic plain below the Himalayas from West to East as a large continuous deep aquifer that has an inexhaustible ground water potential.

The strategy is required for Central India, comprising portions of the states of MP, Maharashtra, Gujarat, Andhra Pradesh, Orissa and Southern UP, that have less rain fall and few aquifer zones for ground water tapping is different.

A bolder vision is needed in the present context to develop the Nation, holistically supported by integrated water, power and land resource management.

PREAMBLE

The concept described in the paper is an alternative to the government's proposal to interlink the rivers in the country as per the National Water Development Agency's plan that is on the anvil for more than two decades. Its basic premise is that we can create energy to the extent desired but not fresh water that is finite. This concept envisages least involuntary resettlement and rehabilitation, few major dams and negligible submersion of lands, least disturbance to ecology and environment. Further it is costs least, involving participation of people and private sector that is controlled and regulated by the government. The cost to the public exchequer will be least and major investment comes from private sector and through public participation.

The whole project can be taken up in several stages depending upon the priorities, funds availability and logistics. As there will be least disturbance to environment and ecology, sustainability is built-in at every stage of development. A unique feature is that the Northern Himalayan Rivers will be resurrected restoring the post monsoon flows as in the past centuries before dams and diversions while the peninsular rivers made perennial with flows throughout the year.

The paper deals with three strategies one for Southern peninsula where droughts recur and on account of which, the thinking to divert waters of Northern Rivers to South was conceived in the past and being pushed in the present as well, and the second for the Northern plains where recurring and increasing floods are a bane. The third is the limited rivers linking, carved out of the government's proposal for the Central India, which is different from either the Southern Peninsula or the Northern Indian Gangetic plains.

THE STRATEGY FOR THE SOUTHERN PENINSULA

Before spelling out this strategy, as an example, the vision for Karnataka State that has maximum and serious problems with its neighbors Tamilnadu, Andhra.

Figure 1: Map of Karnataka Pradesh and to some extent with Maharashtra is illustrated. Thereafter, broaden it to cover the rest of the States of the peninsula to develop the total vision.

Karnataka has a geographical area of 1,90,498 sq. km. about 5.8% of the country. The major river basins in the State are the Krishna, which originates in Maharastra, flowing down to Andhra Pradesh and the Cauvery originating in the State to go into Tamilnadu. Both ultimately end

FIGURE I

Map of Karnataka Pradesh

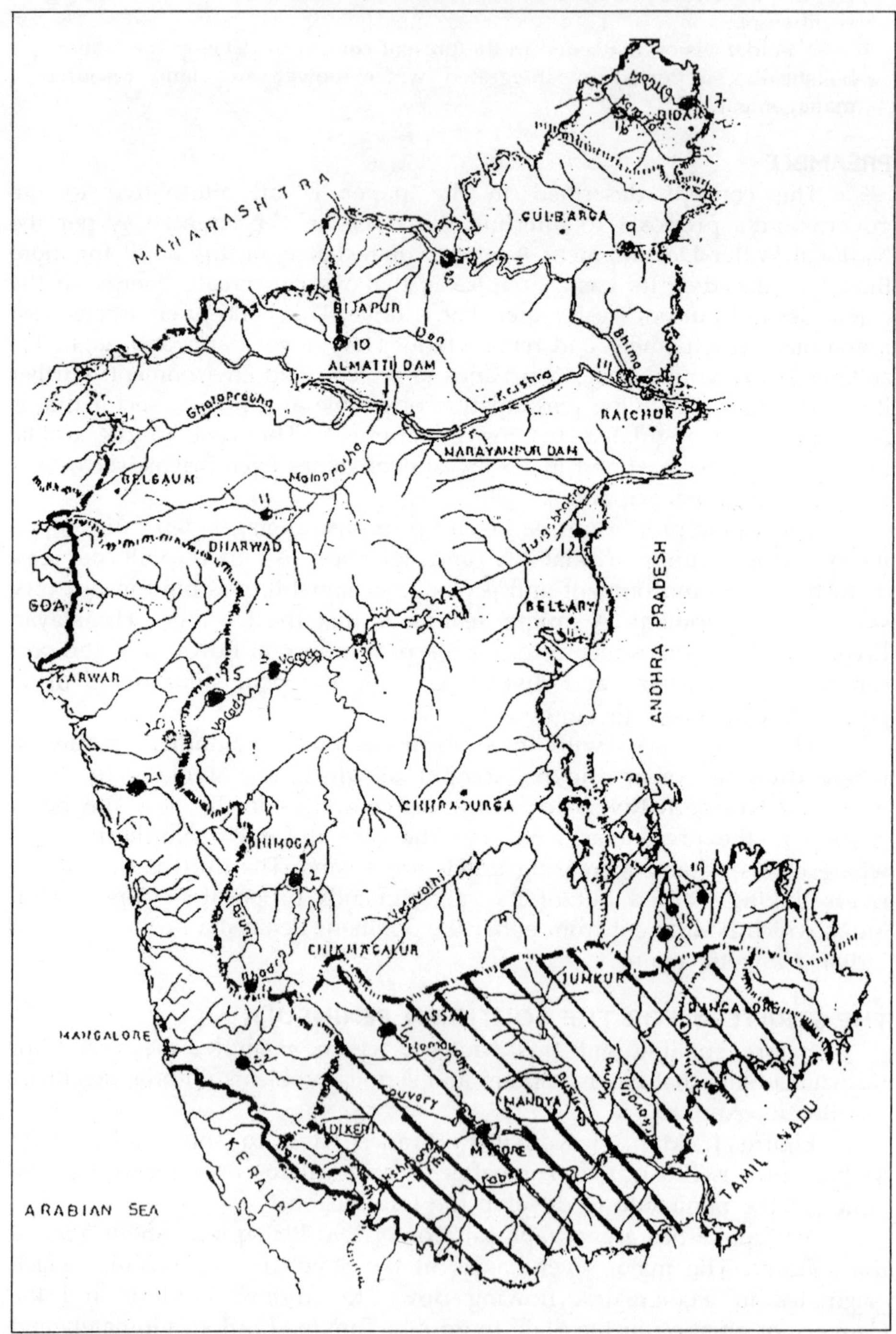

in the Bay of Bengal. Godavari, Palar and Pennar have negligible portions of their basins in the State (Figure 1).

It is observed that there are a number of small river basins, with no interstate disputes, entirely within the State, as in the Western Ghats, draining into the Arabian Sea. The State receives maximum rainfall from the Southwest Monsoons most of which precipitates up to 6,000 -10,000 mm annually on the seaward slopes of Ghat areas (Figure 2).

FIGURE 2

Sketch of a Typical Pumped Storage Scheme

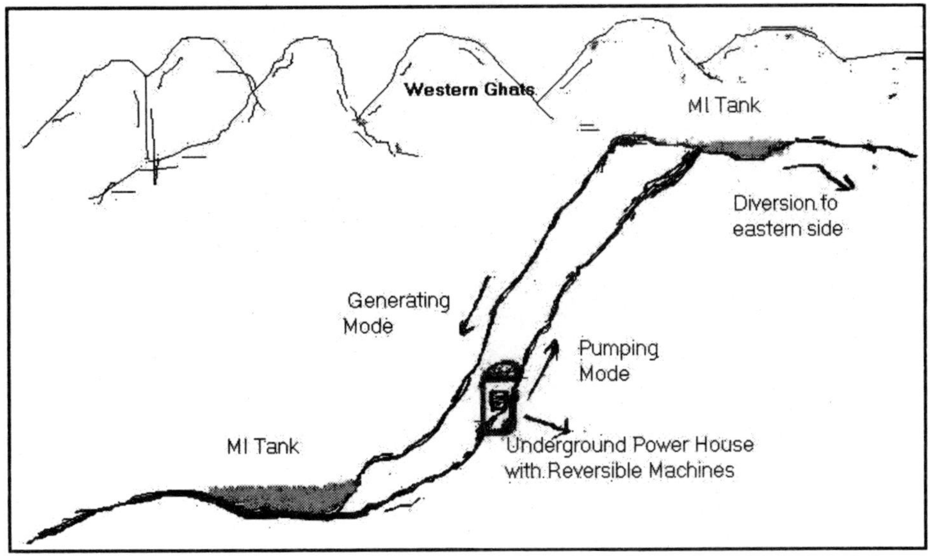

The monsoon clouds after crossing the Ghats carry residual moisture towards the Eastern plains; comprising the Krishna and Cauvery basins, precipitate rainfall varying 600-1000 mm annually. As per the Central Water Commission Report, GOI, Report (1982), the State has the highest per centage of drought prone area of 79 % of its geographical area in the Krishna and Cauvery basins (See Statement I). It is in these plains that there are not only large urban agglomerations but also high intensity of agriculture by its farming community.

Thus the demand for water and power is correspondingly high causing stress to the populace, resulting in conflicts and disputes with the neighboring States for sharing the interstate river waters. With the rising population and expanding demands for food and fiber, as also the need of water for sustenance of life, coupled with the concomitant increasing pollution of the natural sources, due to various industrial and agricultural activities, the scarcity of the finite water resource is getting worse day-by-day. At times, the conflicts in drought years becomes so serious as to cause violent agitations against each other, inciting people to bloodshed, as had happened in the past on the Cauvery issue of sharing limited waters.

STATEMENT I

Statement Showing the Per centage of Geographical Area Affected by Drought

(Statewise)

Sl. No.	State	Total Geographical Area (in Hectares)	Geographical Area Affected by Drought	%age
1.	Tamil Nadu	1,30,07,000	83,27,619	64
2.	West Bengal	87,85,000	26,74,630	30
3.	Uttar Pradesh	2,94,41,000	43,74,065	15
4.	Bihar	1,73,88,000	42,80,772	25
5.	Rajasthan	3,42,22,000	2,14,08,800	63
6.	Andhra Pradesh	2,76,82,000	1,25,62,382	45
7.	Karnataka	1,91,77,000	1,52,40,095	79
8.	Maharashtra	3,07,76,000	1,24,18,056	40
9.	Jammu and Kashmir	2,22,24,000	8,41,318	3
10.	Haryana	44,22,000	16,79,845	38
11.	Madhya Pradesh	4,42,84,000	86,48,869	20
12.	Orissa	1,55,78,000	22,90,000	15
13.	Gujarat	1,95,98,000	1,20,91,618	62
	Total	28,65,84,000	10,68,39,069	37

The innovative way it appears, that could be directed to reduce the interstate tensions, apart from such measures as demand management, recycling, etc which may mitigate the problem to a limited extent, is to look for tapping the large quantity of fresh water that goes wasting down the Western Ghats to the Arabian Sea. The geographical area of the Ghats is only 13 % of the State (Figure 1). But as assessed by the Water Resources Development Organization (WRDO) of the government, it has about 2000 TMC of annual average surface water flow. In contrast, the Krishna and Cauvery basins constituting nearly 80% of the State's area has only about 1350 TMC comprising 950 TMC in the former and 500 TMC in the latter.

While the tussle is on for Krishna and Cauvery waters due to the lesser and limited availability, practically all, the 2000 TMC of the Ghats Rivers flow down unutilized within the state (See Statement-II). Even after generating some hydroelectric power in the Kalinadi and Sharavathi basins, the tailrace waters have not been put to consumptive use.

Till today no serious thought seems to have been given or plans made to skim this Western flow for use in the large eastern water deficit plains of Krishna and Cauvery basins, through any imaginative and economical engineering interventions. The daunting task appears to have been the high lifts up to 2000 feet involved and the likely damage to the

STATEMENT II

West flowinng rivers in Uttara Kannada and Dakshina Kannada District have a atal drainage area of 24,530 sq. km. Constituting 12.79% of the total drainage area in Karnataka (Annexure II).

The Estimated average yield from the West flowing rivers is 57,489 M. Cum (2000 TMC) constituting 58.14% of the total water Resources of Karnataka.

There are 13 Sub-basin under the west flowing rivers as detailed below:

Sl. No.	*Sub-basin*	*Catchment area (in sq. km.)*	*Average Yield (M.Cum)*
1.	Kalinadi	412	934
2.	Sharavathi	3532	8816
3.	Chakra River	336	991
4.	Nethravathi	3222	9930
5.	Varahi	759	2265
6.	Mahadayi	412	934
7.	Bedthi	3574	5040
8.	Independent Catchment between Bedthi and Aghanashim	401	906
9.	Aghanashim	1330	3058
10.	Independent Catchment between Sharavathi and Chakra River	1041	3086
11.	Independent Catchment between Varahi and Nethravathi	3067	9457
12.	Independent Catchment between Nethravathi and Barapole	1320	4474
13.	Barapole	560	1274
	Total		57489 M.Cum = 2000 TMCFT

fragile forest environment of the Ghats, by creation of a number of large storage reservoirs to tap the monsoon flows and the huge energy required for large lifts, particularly in view of the serious shortages already being experienced. Coupled with this, is the vocal opposition by environmentalists rightly, against displacement of population due to submersion of lands and habitats and likely damage to the ecosystem.

These stated problems can however be overcome, if Pump Storage schemes are thought off, and planned for implementation, appropriately suited to such situations as the Ghats. Basically, a pump storage scheme with reversible turbines, consists of two small pools of water, one situated at a high elevation and another at the lower level connected by penstocks with reversible machines in an underground powerhouse (Figure 2). Operating the powerhouse, in dual modes, alternates water in the pools at any given time. In one mode, water is let down from the upper pool to the lower pool through the penstocks, to generate hydroelectric power and in the other mode water is pushed up by reversing the operation of the machines working as pump turbines into the upper pool when power from external source is supplied. The operations in the generating and the pumping modes are done diurnally in 24 hours of the day, the length of each mode depending on the requirement of a particular mode.

To minimize environmental and ecological damage, the powerhouse and the penstocks would be underground in tunnels with only small pools seen in the surface. The pools are like small minor irrigation tanks with little or no displacement of population or submersion of cultivated lands. Nor they can pose any appreciable threat to Environment and Ecology. Since the Ghats, being generally of rocky formations, are amenable for underground constructions and installations. As the Western Ghats receive the highest rainfall during the monsoons, causing torrential flows in those rivers (Statement-II), the duration of pumping mode can be longer to divert part of the flows to the eastern side. A small portion of the flow can be utilized in the generating mode to meet peak power requirements of the region.

The large power requirement for the pumping mode in such a typical pump storage scheme, needed during nights can be met as follows. It is well known now-a-days and in future that most of the new power stations are of the thermal or the atomic energy type since large new reservoirs across major rivers are not favored for power, due to environmental damages and moreover most of the easier and economical sites have already been tapped. Karnataka prided on hydroelectric generation, some five decades back but not presently. But it is now forced to look for thermal generation more and more as evidenced by such as Cogentrix, the Bidadi, the expansion of Raichur thermal station, the planned Vijayanagar and the recently commissioned Kaiga atomic power plant, etc. Even in the country as a whole, nearly 70-80% of power generation is coal based thermal type. A characteristic of thermal station with steam turbines is that the level of generation during the 24 hours of the day remains more or less uniform and it cannot be varied quickly unlike hydroelectric stations to match the varying demand in a day. It takes a number of days to fire the boilers or to bring the atomic power station to criticality for generation.

It is easily seen that the power demand in a day of 24 hours is never uniform anywhere. The demand is very high during day time, starting from about 6 AM in the morning with agricultural pumping operations (agriculture energy consumption alone in the State is reported to be about 40-50%), increasing further Figure 3: Energy Demand curve when the industries commence to work 8 AM onwards, coupled with the running of the domestic and office appliances. The peak period will be from 9 AM to about 5 PM. From 6 PM onwards the demand tapers down with the stoppage of agricultural pumping and closing down of major industries. There after, it becomes minimal and lowest after about 10 PM when even the domestic lighting and other appliances stop. Excepting the street lighting, a few odd industries and some essential services, the demands are the lowest for about 8 hours in the night.

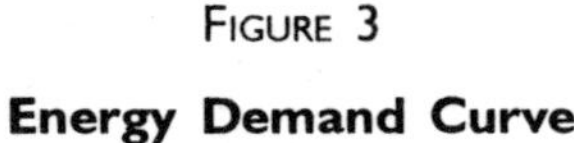

FIGURE 3

Energy Demand Curve

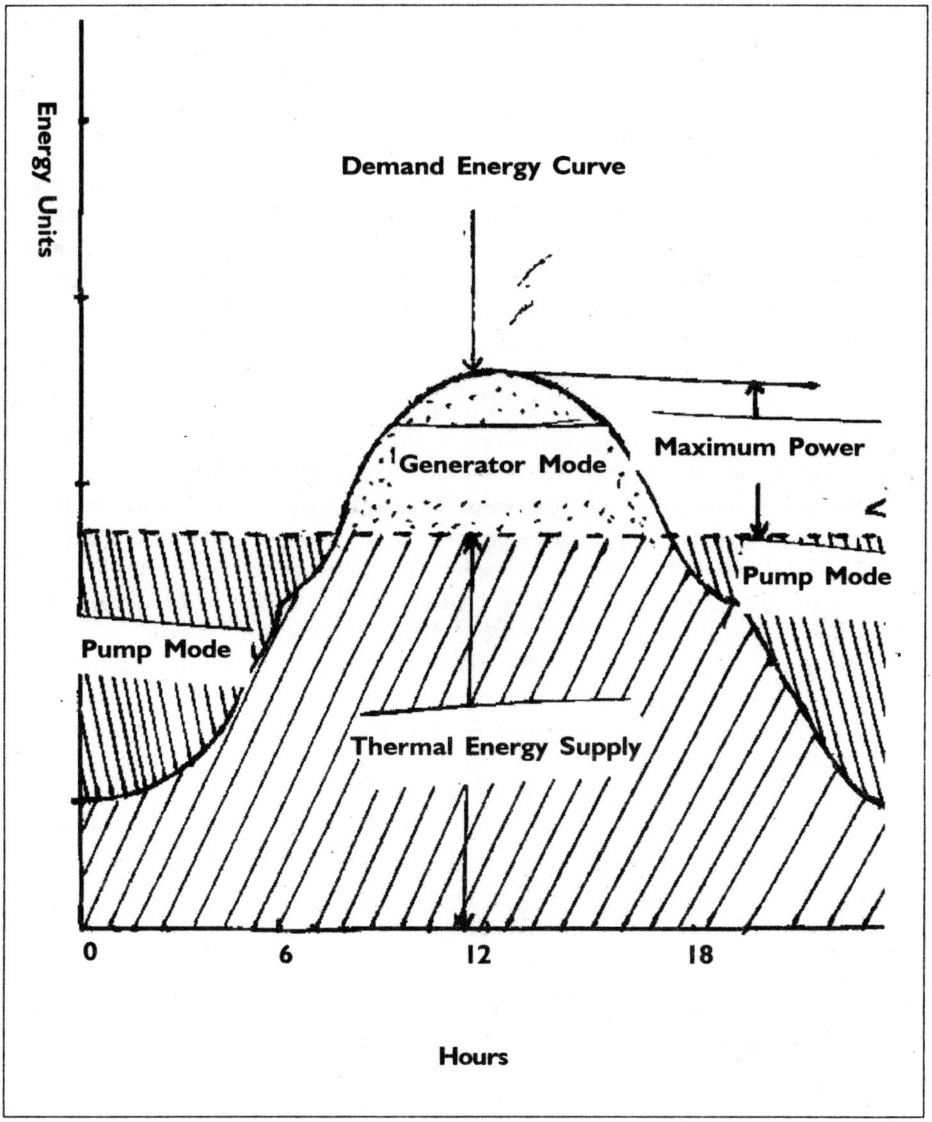

In that period, the thermal generation cannot be cut down of its power generation and there will be considerable surplus power getting wasted as spin off power or low heat in the transmission and distribution lines. It is this wasted surplus power that can be put to use to pump water in the underground pump storage schemes, if put in place across the numerous west flowing streams and rivers. Normally, during monsoons the lower pool gets filled up faster than the upper, as much of the water bearing clouds shed water on the slopes before crossing over the ridge of the Ghats (Figure 2). Since the Western Ghats have thick forests, the considerable post-monsoon waters of the rivers, while safeguarding the rights and requirements of the people including the ecological flows, can be skimmed considerably for use on the eastern plains. During day time, when the power demand is high, the peak power requirements of the region can be met by operating the same stations in the generating mode for about 6-8 hours or as required.

It is recognized generally that for every 3.2 units of wasted night thermal power (at present supplied to farmers in the night mostly wasted by inefficient use) 2.8 units can be recovered back and put to use for peaking. For pumping the entire surplus can be utilized. The pump storage scheme is considered, as a way of storing electricity in the form of potential energy of water, when it is surplus and used when needed, as large blocks of electricity cannot be stored as such. It is this technology that was developed more than six decades in the Western Countries, which can be applied for our specific requirement to meet the water and peak power requirements of the State. Since we are already moving to the era of combination power generation such as hydroelectric, thermal and atomic in a mix compulsively, it is most economical to have hydroelectric stations converted as reversible pump storage schemes to meet peak loads. At the same time, use them as pumping stations to divert water to deficit areas using the thermal power in the night times during monsoons.

With such a blend, we can divert practically a sizeable quantity of water say at least about 200 TMC of water (10%) if not more, out of 2000 TMC of the wasted western waters to meet the shortages. We can also spare some extra to Tamilnadu and Andhra Pradesh on some agreed basis of selling or in lieu of getting surplus night thermal power from the Grid. Andhra Pradesh has coal based thermal stations while Tamilnadu has lignite based stations to provide night surplus power otherwise wasted through inefficient use.

On the top of the Western Ghats, a series of small tanks if constructed like the one described in the example as components of the pump storage schemes and corresponding small tanks at the bottom of the Ghats connected with the top tanks to skim a portion of the flood waters to the Arabian Sea, the whole of Western Ghats will be saturated with the tank seepage water from these upper tanks. These will rejuvenate a number of springs on the steep slopes of the Ghats as well as some new springs will sprout up, providing clean potable water to all the residents, rural and urban in the Western side of Ghats right up to the Sea shore. In some locations, there could be substantial flows, which could be used even for irrigation, adopting drip and sprinkler systems consuming least quantum of water to produce high value crops. Incidentally the strategy will also reduce floods in the west flowing rivers and the damage in low-lying coastal areas as in the case of Mangalore. The coastal zone suffers due to heavy down pour of rains concentrated in the monsoons, while droughts result in summer without adequate drinking water with the drying up of the rivers.

In addition, such schemes can be constructed across the Western rivers with small pools created by low ungated weirs to lift a portion of their flow while the major component flows towards sea, can be used to generate power to feed additionally the tank type pumped storage schemes in conjunction.

From the peaking energy developed in these several pump storage schemes, big and small, all along the Ghats including across the river courses suitably, power can be supplied during day time to the farmers for their agricultural operations with machines and sprinkler systems. Thus, not only the people living on the other side of the Ghats of the Coastal region as well as the people living in the large plains of Krishna and Cauvery basins, will get benefited with the much needed water and peaking power during day time. Thus the whole of Karnataka gets benefited by the envisioned schemes causing little or no damage to the environment and ecosystem, as there will be little or no submersion of cultivable or forests lands or displacement of any habitation.

SOUTHERN WATER AND POWER COUNCIL

Similar features are in Maharashtra and Kerala on their Western side. If the three states, Karnataka, Maharashtra and Kerala join along with Andhra Pradesh and Tamilnadu to form a Water and Power Council to optimize their abundant natural resources particularly in the water and power sectors, there will not be any shortage for long years to come. Some waters can even be spared from the surplus to other States as well. If the country's population stabilizes in the year 2050 as per current demographic projections, shortages will never be experienced any time in future with such a development.

A Southern Water and Power Council for the Southern peninsula may be formed comprising the five Chief Ministers of these States, chaired by the PM of the Nation to resolve any differences and to conduct business in the interest of all. This council may guide the River Basin Authorities or Boards for the South to manage the resources as conceived under the River Boards Act and avoid disputes and costly and unsatisfactory Tribunals under the Interstate Water Disputes Act (1956) so far witnessed.

FINANCIAL INVESTMENT PROPOSALS FOR PUMPED STORAGE SCHEMES

Since the governments do not have adequate budgets in the years to come, and also in keeping with the desired current trends to involve public-private participation and people oriented actions reducing governmental management,

Figure 4: Plan of Agumbe Ghat pumped storage scheme projects such as these can be thrown open to private investment and management. The attractive sites such as at Agumbe Ghat, Maidali in Nethravathi basin,

Kumardhara, Varahi, Aghanashini, etc. in Karnataka can each easily be tapped for such pump storage schemes and leased out for private enterprises for a period of 30-35 years. Only the potential can be indicated in the contract agreement. They will do the investigation, planning, implementation and commissioning the projects skimming the western water during monsoons and developing peak power throughout the year.

FIGURE 4

Plan of Agumbe Ghat

Under a power-*cum*-water purchase agreement, the government can purchase the water and power in bulk at unit rates, and retail it to water user's societies/federations though its existing dams and conveyance systems which can be augmented, as well as the peaking power to industries through the grid. It can charge higher rates to consumers particularly the peak power to industries, which is always costlier any where in the world and cross subsidize the poorer farmers.

The private enterprises which implement the projects should be made to taper down the charges for bulk purchase under the purchase agreement annually to zero at the end of 30-35 years, to the government. In this period the private parties would have made enough profits after covering their capital investment and can take over another similar project. At the end of the lease period, the created facilities will be transferred free to the government for operation and management in future. The government may either manage itself such facilities or appoint management organizations under a commission agreement.

The government should all through exercise regulatory control to protect environment and ecology and prevent damages through safety enforcement and other control measures. It will be somewhat like build-operate-lease and transfer (BOLT). Ghatgarh pumped storage project in the Ghats under implementation and the completed Bhira pumped storage plant in Maharashtra are examples of this kind for serious consideration. In Yugoslavia, Japan and many other countries, the technology of pump storage scheme has been adopted to transfer water from water surplus a low level to higher level water deficit areas and at the same time to develop peaking power which has a high price as and when countries get industrially developed. At present China is leading in implementing the World's largest pump storage schemes. Recently the Palmett Pumped storage scheme of about 400 mW near Cape Town, in South Africa to supply water to the deficit area in the upper plateau and at the same time stabilize the power grid with the peaking power generated won the International Hydrological Association award of 2003 recommended by UNESCO for excellence in engineering technology taking care of environment and ecology

STRATEGY FOR NORTH INDIA

The strategy for Northern India comprises in understanding the entire Gangetic plain below the Himalayas from West to East as a large continuous deep aquifer that has an inexhaustible ground water potential. It is not an exaggeration to state that this is one of the largest aquifer plains in the World, without any comparison. It is known that in most of its area, the aquifer goes more than a mile deep.

This large aquifer is continuously fed or recharged by the perennial Himalayan Rivers until they empty into the Bay of Bengal. It needs to be questioned when such is the potential, why should one continue to do surface irrigation by building barrages and storage dams with large canal systems that have resulted in salinity and water logging unabated, in practically wherever there is a surface irrigation system in this zone by putting more water from the surface. The concomitant deleterious and negative effect of surface irrigation in terms of water logging and salinity are glaringly visible and is increasing in the Gangetic plains. In Uttar Pradesh 75% of the irrigated lands are turning waterlogged and saline. This is a serious feature killing the productivity of the once fertile land now to reckon with irreversible damage in many locations.

About 150 years back, when the country was visited by large-scale famines, the British continued and enlarged the practice of surface irrigation system initiated by the Moguls. In those days, the ground water table was considerably lower and surface supplies by gravity, did provide a positive insurance against famine effects by increased production in the fertile plains. However, this continuing practice over the years has become a bane, presently putting the lands out of productivity due to the effects of salinity and water logging due to saturation by surface system.

It is felt that this traditional strategy should be revisited and if it can be helped must be completely stopped. On the other hand, it is felt that we should in future, resort only to ground water irrigation exploiting the aquifer characteristic of the huge Gangetic plains. This drastic change needs to be done recognizing that a strategy that was good at a particular time range cannot be effective for all times to come. The surface irrigation in Gangetic plains needs to be gradually erased out giving way to ground water exploitation fully. It should be realized that this large aquifer is recharged continuously by the Himalayan Rivers through surface and subsurface flows and will never get exhausted by ground water tapping.

In order to control the water table at a reasonable depth below the ground everywhere, a combined operation of ground water extraction and simultaneously assisted recharging through injection in reverse tube wells, whenever and wherever water table goes deeper, has to be devised all along the Gangetic plains. There could be a defined zonal strip at the Gangetic aquifer fringe line all along the foot of the Himalayas having a number of large diameter (say, 1 mtr. diameter) reverse tube wells running the entire width from East to West. These wells could be crowded on both banks of each of the Himalayan Rivers from whose waters, portions could be led into detention basins on the banks by means of bed-dams and small diversion structures, to recharge the aquifer in a controlled manner (Figure 5)

Such an arrangement will quickly draw down much water including part of the floodwaters into the reverse tube wells and recharge practically the entire Gangetic plains. The aquifer potential thus recharged could be exploited continuously for irrigation, drinking water supply and industrial needs practically anywhere in the entire length and breadth of the Gangetic plains. The present surface systems of canals should then be gradually eliminated making available considerable chunks of fertile land available for increased crop production for the expanding population. Even the surface storages can be gradually de-commissioned

Figure 5: Map of India showing Gangetic plain with reverse tube wells at the foot of the Himalaya leaving a minimum for emergency use during droughts making the submerged land available for production

FIGURE 5

Map of India

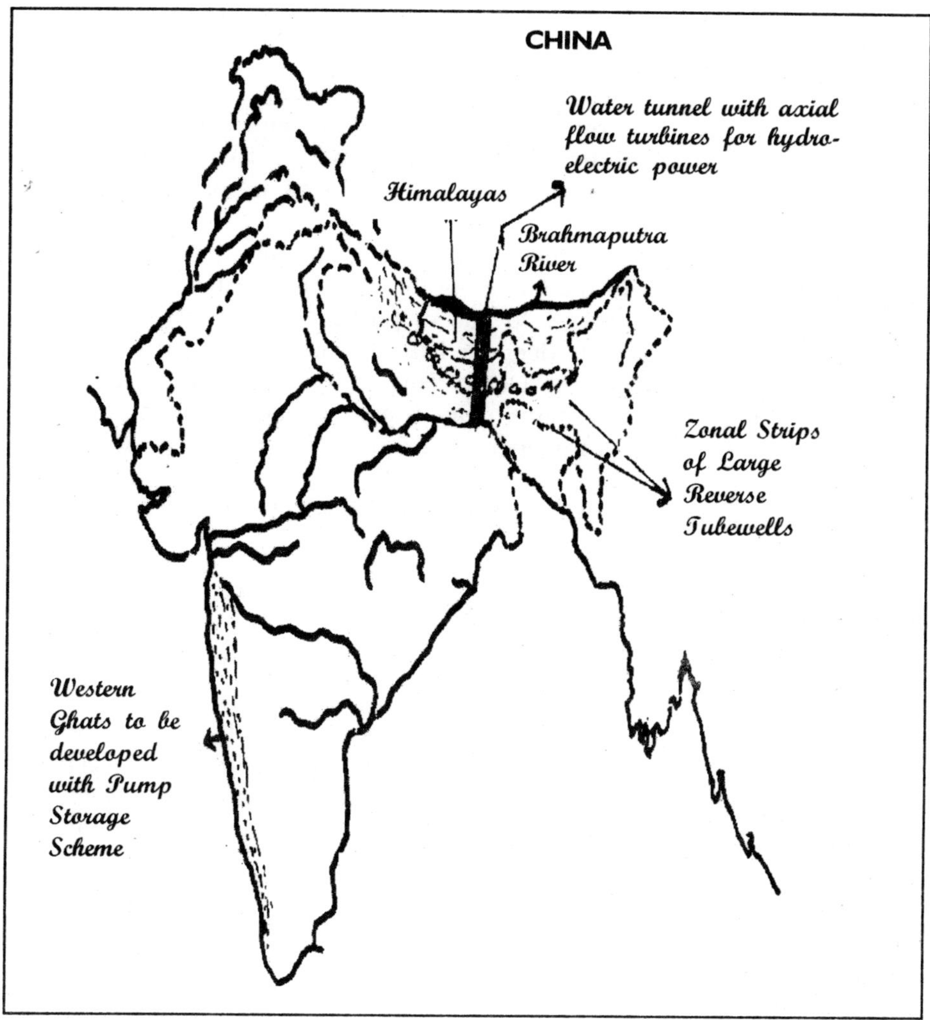

In order to further reduce the flood flow effects, a study of satellite imagery of the Himalayan rivers both during the dry weather season and the flood season will indicate the behavior of the silt laden flows as well as the formation of the delta, when they meet the still waters of the Bay of Bengal. The delta formation is caused due to dropping and deposition of silt and debris when the velocity is killed at the confluence. Year after year these deposits increase and the delta formation also expands with a number of channels. This deposition of the silt at the deltaic zone causes gradual aggradations of the silt deposits upstream moving towards the source of the river. This causes gradual and imperceptible rises in the bed level of each of the Himalayan Rivers causing floods to overtop and break the protective embankment or levees that are being constructed year after year by the governments. This phenomenon is clearly experienced in the state of Bihar, where a number of levees have been constructed to contain the floods.

However, these flood protection levees have never provided any permanent relief. Thousands of crores have been spent in all such States in the Gangetic plains. It is reported that since independence, nearly 60,000 Crores have been spent in the flood protection and relief works. Despite this large expenditure so far, it is experienced that floods are observed to be on the increase.

If a strategy could be developed to clear the mouths of these rivers at the delta particularly of the Ganga-Brahmaputra-Meghna, the process of aggradations can be reversed into that of retrogression moving upstream. This will make the riverbeds deepened by the natural forces of the flood flows with higher velocity at Delta. This is similar to the clearing of blockages at the outfall of man-made drains. If such a phenomenon is stimulated, the channels get deepened and most probably the flood could be contained in the natural channel of the river valley reducing the overtopping and breaking of the banks. Thus, there is a scope to positively minimize the flood effects.

The question is how to clear the large blockage at outfalls of the rivers at the confluence in the delta zones. One unconventional way could be to use directed explosion of the deposits in the delta during the flood period of the rivers moving the deposits deeper into the Bay of Bengal. On the basis of satellite imagery studies, both during the lean season and the flood season, explosive devices can be strategically located when the flow is lean in the delta zone and exploded during floods with an electronic device simultaneously and serially, to effect the loosening and force the movement of the silt and debris to get lodged by pushing deeper into the ocean.

The objective is to push the silt and debris deeper into the Bay of Bengal clearing the outfall or the mouths of these rivers. This of course, needs to be done in a gigantic magnitude depending upon the size of the river and the delta formation in the channels leading to the sea. A pilot experiment on a small river preceded by model studies in a hydraulic laboratory will give clues as to how the strategy can be scaled up and developed for large rivers and their deltas. This activity is not a one time operation but will be spread over a number of years in stages getting positive results in each stage getting accumulated until a stable regime for these rivers is achieved to clear the floods fast enough into the Bay

The second prong of the strategy to reduce the floods would be, to look at the critically erodible zones on the banks of these rivers and the tributaries in the Himalayas, through aerial photographs and satellite imageries. After identifying their extent through proper interpretation, a technique needs to be developed to prevent the erosion of the loose soil in the fragile mountainous slopes that feed the rivers with silt and debris. One way could be to spray these zones through helicopters with special vegetation seeds recommended by Forest Academies as a result of research. These seeds should provide a tough vegetative cover binding the soil, on catching a hold in the soil. Since the slopes are steep, mere spraying of the seeds expecting to sprout in the rains will be futile, as they get washed down into the streams.

In order to hold the seeds on to the soil, a special synthetic film needs to be developed that could be sprayed by helicopters on to the critical areas immediately after these seeds are scattered. The idea is to prevent the seeds getting washed down during the rains and at the same time allow the moisture to permeate through the film to enable the seeds to sprout taking roots binding down the soil and puncture the film to come out of the surface to grow into a thick vegetative cover above the ground. This of course needs relevant research and development to devise the appropriate technique.

Thus, for Northern India, the three pronged strategy, i.e. (1) eliminate the surface irrigation, to be replaced by ground water extraction supported by the recharging zonal strip of tube wells at the foot of the Himalayas; (2) to clear the outfalls of the rivers by the directional explosion to reverse the process of aggradations into retrogression; and (3) the stabilization of the critical zones in the Himalayas to reduce the feeding of the rivers with silt and debris, should be put in place. This will ensure sustainable development that will mitigate the water logging and salinity effects, flood effects and at the same time provide adequate fresh water in the entire Gangetic plains everywhere. However, this requires considerable energy or power for ground water extraction that could be either by atomic energy of which India has developed considerably safe techniques as compared to the earlier atomic plants in the West where the techniques were not so well developed or by thermal energy. Till this becomes adequate since the existing rivers get resurrected with their earlier post-monsoon flows prior the large scale diversions for the surface irrigation systems, considerable water flow will be available for the existing hydel power stations for increased power supply to the tube wells of the farmers.

A further supplement could be to short-circuit the big loop of the Brahmaputra river in Tibet at an elevation of about 15,000 ft above MSL by tapping it though diversions from the other side of the Himalayas and leading part of the base flows vertically Southwards North of Bihar through inclined shafts bored using tunnel boring machines (TBMs) through the Himalayan ranges at several points connecting the tributaries to Ganga leading directly to the Ganga in the plains flowing at an elevation of about 300 ft. above MSL. (Figure 6). The large difference in elevation between the intake and outfall will provide enormous cascade of hydroelectric energy by using axial flow turbines. This of course could be a long-range plan that would need the international cooperation of Nepal, Bangladesh and China who could of course share a part of the enormous energy benefits on a mutually agreed basis.

FIGURE 6

Diversion of Brahmaputra to Ganges through its Tributaries

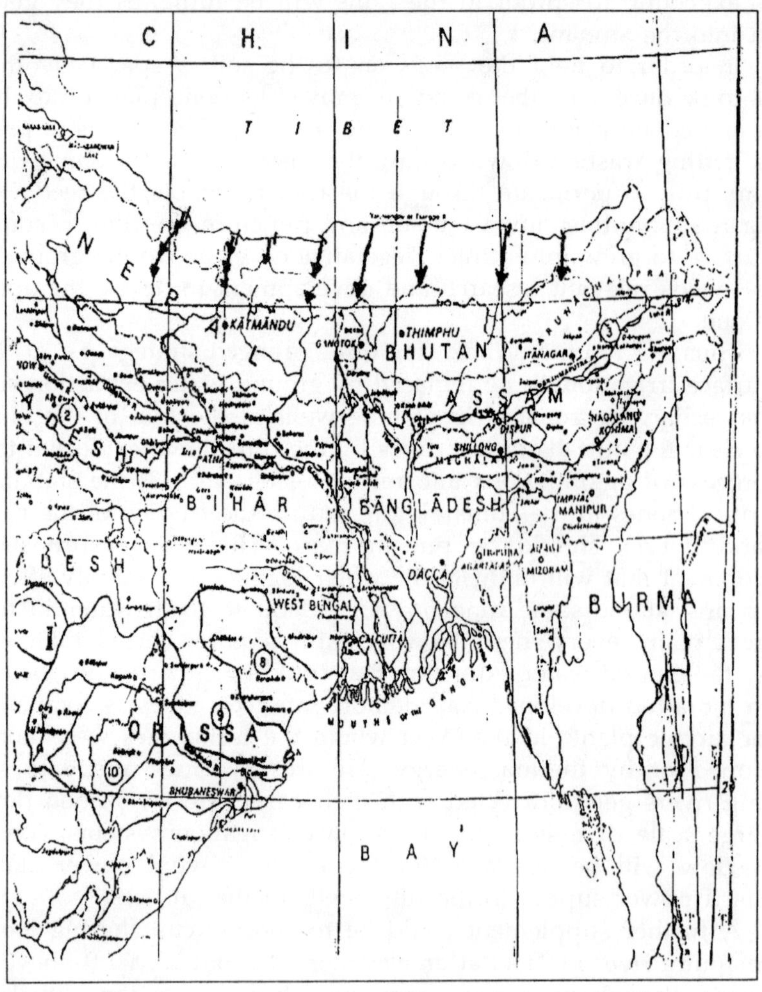

Thus, apart from developing considerable hydro-electric energy, appreciable flow will go into Ganges without submerging any land or surface diversions in order to keep the flows of the Ganges to Calcutta flushing the channel and at the same time provides adequate flows to Bangladesh. There would be benefits to both these countries avoiding the present recriminations in sharing Ganges water. These are of course unconventional ideas, but could be given a serious thought for pilot projects, preceded by model studies and later expanded to full scale gradually over a number of years. In this strategy, there is a large scope for the private industries to play an effective role in both the sinking of large diameter reverse tube wells and the development of hydro-electric power, with least disturbance to environment and ecology. The project could be done in a number of phases with commensurate benefits accruing in each phase.

Strategy for Central India

The strategy for Central India, comprising portions of the states of MP, Maharashtra, Gujarat, Andhra Pradesh, Orissa and Southern UP, that have less rain fall and few aquifer zones for ground water tapping is different. In this area, storage dams with limited linking of rivers such as Ken, Betwa, Chambal, Kalisindh, etc as proposed by the government is retained. A typical interlinking of rivers between Betwa and Chambal known as water grid with storages and links, in the Gwalior region that is nearing completion is an example. (see Figure 7)

FIGURE 7

Water Grid in Gwalior Region

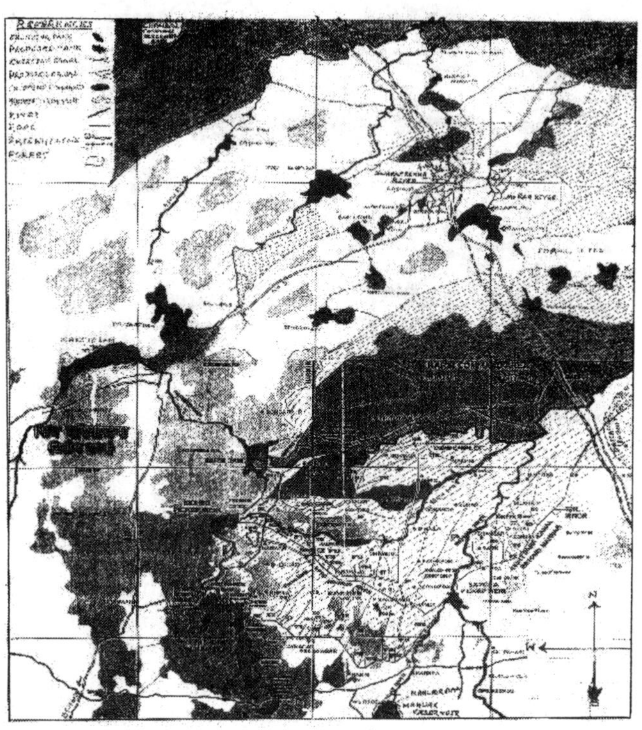

CONCLUSION

On the basis of geo-morphological characteristics, the country is divided into three zones.

(1) The Northern Indian Gangetic plans of aquifer zone.
(2) The Central Indian zone in hard rock areas with few aquifers.
(3) The Southern Indian peninsular zone south of Tapti and Satpura ranges, comprising the hard rock areas with high intensity of rainfall in the narrow coastal strip in the West. (see Figure 8)

FIGURE 8

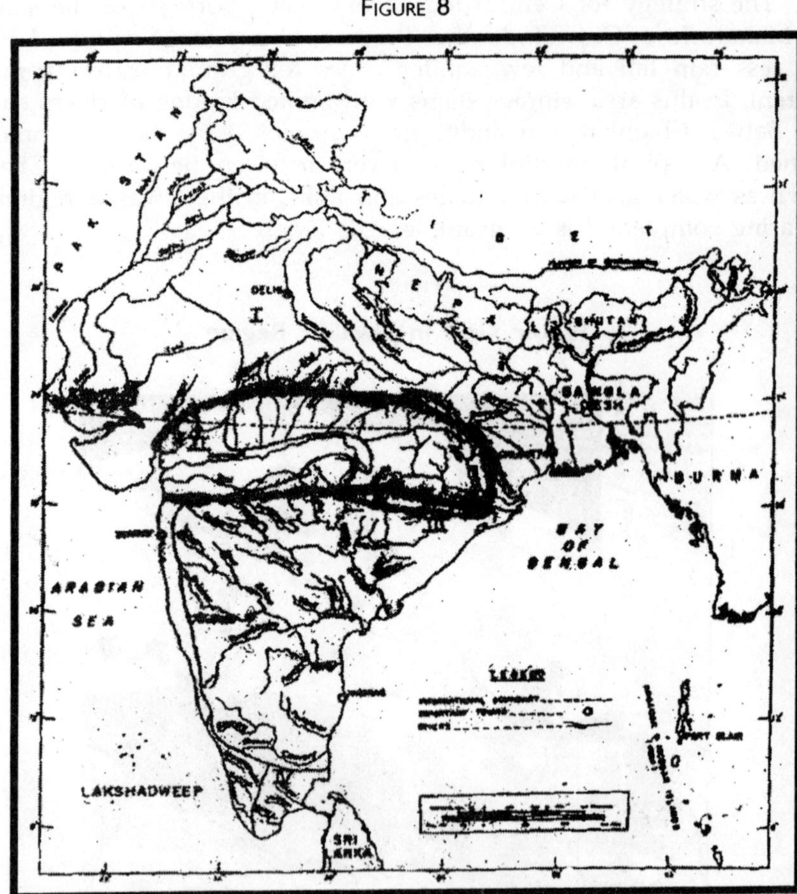

For each Zone a different strategy is conceived taking into consideration site natural and location specific character and tailored to harness the water resources best fitting with the ecology and environmental conditions

In the three strategies (termed Hybrid) for the South, North and the central, there will be least disturbance to ecology and environment. The need for stupendous effort of massive interlinking rivers with innumerable hurdles and controversies, as is being seriously thought off and that would disturb environmental and ecological balance may be avoided altogether for a long time to come.

For the Country as a whole, an appropriate integration of land, water and energy policies with differential tariff structure needs to be developed for sustainable growth, with creative imagination and innovative technologies eschewing the outworn and obsolete traditional techniques. A bolder vision is needed in the present context to develop the Nation, holistically supported by integrated water, power and land resource management.

References

K.L. Rao (1975), India's Water Wealth, its assessment, uses and projections, Published by Orient Longman.

Task Force (2003), Inter Basin Water Transfer Proposals, Interlinking of Rivers, MOWR, GOI Publications.

Interlinking of Rivers, National Water Development Agency, MOWR, GOI Publications.

Study on Drought Prone Area in India (1982), Central Water Commission, GOI Publications.

INCLUSIVE SUSTAINABLE DEVELOPMENT: THE CONCEPT AND ISSUES

B.B. TANDON AND ARUNESH GARG

ABSTRACT

Man has always strived to meet his present-day requirements by utilising the available resources in new and different ways. Sustainable development implies providing for the requirements of the present generations without compromising the ability of future generations to meet their own needs. The United Nations and the international community have taken some two generations to reach to the current stage of discussion on global warming and sustainable development. The idea of sustainable development has been evolving since 1970s. In 1972, the United Nations Conference on Environment was held in Stockholm. Since the 1972 conference, there have been many international environmental agreements. The World Commission on Environment and Development in 1983, Intergovernmental Panel on Climate Change (IPCC) in 1988, Montréal Protocol in 1987, United Nations Conference on Environment and Development (Earth Summit) in 1992, Kyoto Protocol in 1997, World Summit on Sustainable Development in 2002, the United Nations Climate Change Conference in 2007, etc. are some of the important initiatives by International Community to address issues of climate change and sustainable development. All the countries are scheduled to meet again in Copenhagen in December 2009 to take the discussions further and ensure cooperative action among them in future. It has been seen that mankind, in general, has made economic progress and accumulated various forms of capital. However, this has led to decline in natural capital. Rising population and industrial development have strained the availability of natural resources. There has been release of major pollutants and quality of environment has deteriorated. Further, the physical wealth that has been accumulated has not found equal distribution. Only a few sections of the society have actually bagged the fruits of economic development. Economic development of man has also resulted in poor quality of environment. This entails that sustainable development is required to be revisited in terms of inclusiveness. In general, inclusive sustainable development as a concept involves three dimensions, viz., social, economic and environmental sustainability. The present paper tries to address all these issues. Further, some suggestions have been given to facilitate inclusive sustainable development.

INTRODUCTION

Sustainable development implies development that meets the needs of the present without compromising the ability of future generations to meet their own needs (World Commission on Environment and Development (Bruntland Commission, 1987). Man has always strived to meet his present-day requirements by utilising the available resources in new and different ways. The growth and development that has been seen today is the result of ability and willingness of the man to evolve continuously. However, it has been observed that all these efforts aimed at development of mankind are not without pitfalls. In fact, it is being said that man is attempting to meet his own needs at the cost of the future generations. Inclusive sustainable development is aimed at addressing this issue.

SUSTAINABLE DEVELOPMENT—THE HISTORICAL BACKGROUND

The United Nations and the international community have taken some two generations to reach to the current stage of discussion on global warming and sustainable development. Environmental issues were never a major concern of the United Nations in the period immediately following the Organization's creation. In the first 23 years of its existence, UN was basically involved in highlighting the operational activities associated with natural resources, mainly through the World Meteorological Organization (WMO). The attention was paid to the natural resources within the context of adequacy of known natural resources to provide for the economic development of a large number of UN members or the "underdeveloped countries", as they were then termed. In 1949, the UN Scientific Conference on the conservation and utilization of resources was held in Lake Success, New York from 17 August to 6 September. It was the first UN body to address the depletion of those resources and their use. The focus, however, was mainly on how to manage them for economic and social development, and not from a conservation perspective. It was not until 1968 that environmental issues received serious attention by any major UN organs. The Economic and Social Council on 29 May was the first to include those issues in its agenda as a specific item. It was later endorsed by the General

Assembly to hold the first United Nations Conference on the Human Environment (Jackson, 2007). The idea of sustainable development has been evolving since 1970s. In 1972, the United Nations Conference on Environment was held in Stockholm. This was the first major international meeting to discuss the harmful affects of human activity on environment, and as many as 113 governments and two heads of state (Olaf Palme of Sweden and Indira Gandhi of India) participated in this. Mrs Gandhi explained the conditions of poverty in developing and under-developed countries and its relationship with environmental problems. Mrs. Gandhi in a way set the stage for international deliberations on these issues, which are continuing even today. Perhaps, she was referring to what is now widely known as relationship of social and economic growth with environment. The Stockholm conference secured a permanent place for the environment on the world's agenda and led to the establishment of the United Nations Environment Program (UNEP). Since the 1972 conference, there have been many international environmental agreements which include the 1978 Great Lakes Water Quality Agreement; the 1979 Geneva Convention on Long-range Transboundary Air Pollution; the 1985 Helsinki Agreement which is a 21-nation commitment to reduce sulphur dioxide emissions; the 1988 Montreal Protocol on Substances that Deplete the Ozone Layer; the 1989 Basel Convention on Transboundary Movements of Hazardous Wastes; etc (http://dsp-psd.tpsgc.gc.ca/Collection-R/LoPBdP/BP/bp317-e.htm).

In 1983, the World Commission on Environment and Development was appointed by the United Nations under the chairmanship of Mrs. Gro Harlem Bruntland, the Norwegian Prime Minister. The Commission aimed to link environmental issues to the findings of the 1980 Brandt report on North-South relations. In 1987, this commission released a report titled 'Our Common Future', which emphasised the need for development along with environmental protection. The report stressed that human development must change course to fit within the planet's ecological limits. The commission coined and popularised the term 'Sustainable Development'. It was emphasised that sustainable development has to be the way to ensure that economic development would not endanger the ability of future generations to enjoy the fruits of the earth (World Commission on Environment and Development (Bruntland Commission), 1987).

Intergovernmental Panel on Climate Change (IPCC) was set-up in 1988. The IPCC has been established to provide the stakeholders with an objective source of information about climate change. The IPCC is a scientific body. The IPCC is not mandated to conduct any research nor it is supposed to monitor climate related data or parameters. Its role is to assess on a comprehensive, objective, open and transparent basis the latest scientific, technical and socio-economic literature produced worldwide relevant to the understanding of the risk of human-induced climate change, its observed and projected impacts and options for adaptation and mitigation. IPCC is supposed to come out with reports that should be neutral with respect to policy, although they need to deal objectively with policy relevant scientific, technical and socio-economic factors. They should be of high scientific and technical standards, and aim to reflect a range of views, expertise and wide geographical coverage.

Montréal protocol, an international treaty was first signed in 1987 by 24 developed countries and subsequently ratified by 180 countries. The treaty aims to protect the ozone layer by phasing out the production of a number of substances believed to be responsible for ozone depletion. Ban on chlorofluorocarbons (CFCs), which deplete the ozone layer was achieved with this treaty. The treaty came into force on January 1, 1989 followed by a first meeting in Helsinki, May 1989. Since then, it has undergone seven revisions, in 1990 (London), 1991 (Nairobi), 1992 (Copenhagen), 1993 (Bangkok), 1995 (Vienna), 1997 (Montreal), and 1999 (Beijing). It is believed that if the international agreement is adhered to, the ozone layer is expected to recover by 2050.

In 1992, United Nations Conference on Environment and Development in Rio de Janeiro, Brazil brought together more than 170 governments for the first international 'Earth Summit'. An attempt was made to address problems of social and economic development, and environmental protection. The Earth Summit influenced all subsequent UN conferences, which have examined the relationship between human rights, population, social development, women and human settlements — and the need for environmentally sustainable development. The issues addressed at the summit included systematic scrutiny of production patterns especially toxic ones; alternative sources of energy to replace fossil fuels; new means of public transportation in order to reduce traffic congestion, vehicle emissions and health problems caused by smog and pollution; and the ever increasing growing scarcity of water. At that meeting, leaders created the United Nations Framework Convention on Climate Change (UNFCCC), which set a non-binding goal of stabilising emissions at 1990 levels by 2000. All subsequent multilateral negotiations on different aspects of climate change are being held based on principles and objectives set out by UNFCCC. The Rio declaration has defined rights and responsibilities of states regarding development and environment and insisted that developed countries should recognise their responsibility in pursuit of sustainable development. The Rio Summit came out with global document 'Agenda 21' as a plan document for sustainable development in the 21st century. It calls on governments to preserve natural resources, and prevent emissions and pollution. The signatory countries to 'Agenda 21' have committed to collect data on their national greenhouse gas emissions and come out with national strategies to ensure sustainable development. Governments who signed up 'Agenda 21' were not required to follow each of its recommendations, but rather adopt those that were most relevant to their own situation. It was believed that local-level governments are major players in local economy and are primary regulators of local environment. Hence, local-level governments were assigned the task of developing and delivering 'Agenda 21' programme. However, the efforts to switch to greener, practices mandated by the summit were voluntary. The Conference of Parties (COP conferences) that followed were marked by a lack of co-operation and consistent placement of national interests over global ones. One of the remarkable feats achieved by the summit was an agreement on the Climate Change Convention which in turn led to the Kyoto Protocol.

In 1997, COP3, a conference was held in Kyoto, Japan in which participating governments agreed to reduce greenhouse gas emissions to tackle the problem of global warming. The Kyoto Protocol was created as a result of the conference, which mandated that subject to ratification by signatory states, the developed countries would reduce their emissions. The Kyoto Protocol establishes legally binding commitments for the reduction of four greenhouse gases (carbon dioxide, methane, nitrous oxide, sulphur hexafluoride), and two groups of gases (hydrofluorocarbons and perfluorocarbons) produced by industrialized nations, as well as general commitments for all member countries.The detailed rules for the implementation of Kyoto Protocol were adopted at COP7 in Marrakesh in 2001, and are called 'Marrakesh Accords'. The Protocol came into force in 2005, when Russia ratified it. As of 2008, as many as 183 nations representing 60 per cent of the global emissions are cutting their emissions. Under the protocol, the developed countries are required to reduce emissions of green house gases by an average of 5.2 per cent below 1990 levels by 2012. National limitations range from 8% reductions for the European Union and some others to 7% for the United States, 6% for Japan, and 0% for Russia. The treaty permitted GHG emission increases of 8% for Australia and 10% for Iceland. The goal is to lower overall emissions of six greenhouse gases—carbon dioxide, methane, nitrous oxide, ozone, water vapours and halocarbons—calculated as an average over the five-year period of 2008-12.

The Kyoto Protocol is a protocol to the United Nations Framework Convention on Climate Change (UNFCCC or FCCC), an international environmental treaty produced at the United Nations Conference on treaty is intended to achieve "stabilization of greenhouse gas concentrations in the atmosphere at a level that would prevent dangerous anthropogenic interference with the climate system. As of 2008, 183 parties have ratified the protocol, which was initially adopted for use on 11 December 1997 in Kyoto, Japan and which entered into force on 16 February 2005. Under Kyoto, industrialized countries agreed to reduce their collective GHG emissions by 5.2% compared to the year 1990. National limitations range from 8% reductions for the European Union and some others to 7% for the United States, 6% for Japan, and 0% for Russia. The treaty permitted GHG emission increases of 8% for Australia and 10% for Iceland.

Kyoto includes defined "flexible mechanisms" such as Emissions Trading, the Clean Development Mechanism and Joint Implementation to allow Annex I economies to meet their greenhouse gas (GHG) emission limitations by purchasing GHG emission reductions credits from elsewhere, through financial exchanges, projects that reduce emissions in non-Annex I economies, from other Annex I countries, or from Annex I countries with excess allowances. In practice this means that Non-Annex I economies have no GHG emission restrictions, but have financial incentives to develop GHG emission reduction projects to receive "carbon credits" that can then be sold to Annex I buyers, encouraging sustainable development. In addition, the flexible mechanisms allow Annex I nations with efficient, low GHG-emitting industries, and high prevailing environmental standards to purchase carbon credits on the world market instead of reducing greenhouse gas emissions domestically. Among the Annex I signatories, all nations have established Designated National Authorities to manage their greenhouse gas portfolios; countries including Japan, Canada, Italy, the Netherlands, Germany, France, Spain and others are actively promoting government carbon funds, supporting multilateral carbon funds intent on purchasing Carbon Credits from Non-Annex I countries, and are working closely with their major utility, energy, oil and gas and chemicals conglomerates to acquire Greenhouse Gas Certificates as cheaply as possible. Virtually all of the non-Annex I countries have also established Designated National Authorities to manage the Kyoto process, specifically the "CDM process" that determines which GHG Projects they wish to propose for accreditation by the CDM Executive Board

World Summit on Sustainable Development, organized by the United Nations, took place from 26 August to 4 September 2002, at the Sandton Convention Centre in Johannesburg, South Africa. The summit marked the 10th anniversary of the United Nations Conference on Environment and Development (UNCED) which took place in Rio de Janeiro, Brazil in 1992. The 2002 summit is also informally known as "Rio+10". The summit has attempted to assess world developments in sustainability since the 1992 Earth Summit, and to evaluate the effectiveness of Agenda 21 and other agreements reached at the 1992 meeting. Attendees assessed the effectiveness of Agenda 21, to what extent countries had kept up their commitment to the agenda, how challenges to sustainability had changed, and how to properly address new challenges. Kofi Annan, UN Secretary-General, outlined five topic areas which were to be the key points of discussion at the summit: (1) Water and sanitation, (2) Energy, (3) Human health, (4) Agricultural productivity, and (5) Biodiversity and ecosystem management. The summit identified that the World was on crossroads as regards environmental cooperation the hope for which was ignited by Earth Summit, 1992. The industrialized countries of the north were reluctant to provide the developing countries of the south with the necessary support to overcome environmental challenges. In fact, Johannesburg summit has been marked with sour global mood followed after the tragic terrorist attacks on US. The summit did not end with optimism as had accompanied earlier summits on environmental issues. However, this summit could reveal that 'sustainable development' has become a political necessity. Johannesburg was viewed as an attempt to keep alive the agenda of 'Earth

Summit' held in Rio. The Summit has impressed upon the nations to commit for sustainable development and its implementation at local, national and international levels by fostering partnerships among governments, the private sector and civil society. The major result of Johannesburg has been the so-called 'Type 2' agreements. These are informal agreements involving non-state parties, sometimes amongst themselves and sometimes with individual governments. On the one hand, Type 2 agreements are a reflection of the massive change in landscape that had occurred over the previous 10 years, with NGOs and business taking a far more important role in international environmental affairs. At the same time, however, they are a reflection of the Johannesburg summit organizer's desperation and desire to get something memorable out of the summit. More than 220 Type 2 agreements were reached at Johannesburg, signifying around US$ 235 million in pledged resources; thirty-two of these Type 2 agreements related to energy, accounting for US$ 26 million in resources; the vast majority of these were programmes of technical cooperation in energy generation and conservation. However, a systematic accounting of these agreements has not yet been accomplished. Further, it is not yet clear how many of these agreements and how much of these resources are new and unique. The other contribution of Johannesburg, in comparison to previous summits, related to the fact that the Johannesburg Plan of Implementation sought agreement on actual targets and timetables rather than simple statements of intent. The Johannesburg Declaration is a key outcome of the Summit. The declaration was a collection of general political statements, reaffirming a commitment to agreements made at the Rio de Janeiro summit, 10 years before and at the Stockholm Summit on the Human Environment 30 years before. International cooperation, decreasing world poverty, special attention for developing nations, empowering women, and maintaining biodiversity, among other things, were outlined as key points to building a sustainable future. The document was meant to serve as a contract for the participants of the summit, binding them to the outlined agreements. A Plan of Implementation laid down more specific goals for the nations and organizations that participated in the summit. Some of these goals included:

- The establishment of a solidarity fund to wipe out poverty. This fund would be sustained by voluntary contributions; however, developed nations were urged to dedicate 0.7% of their national income to this cause.
- Cutting in half by 2015 the proportion of the world's population living on less than a dollar a day. This was a reaffirmation of a UN Millennium Summit goal.
- Cutting in half by 2015 the number of people who lack clean drinking water and basic sanitation.
- Substantially increase the global share of renewable energy.

- Cut significantly by 2010 the rate at which rare plants and animals are becoming extinct.
- Restore (where possible) depleted fish stocks by 2015.
- Halving the number of people suffering from hunger.

However, the outcomes of the Johannesburg Summit have been criticized in subsequent years as being too vague and for setting weaker goals than those agreed upon in previous summits. The resolutions passed at the summit also lack the provisions for substantial enforcement, making it difficult to assess what progress was actually made. NGOs such as the Global Peoples Forum and Friends of the Earth have set forth recommendations to strengthen the Johannesburg goals, and The Earth Charter Initiative has proposed an Earth Charter as a replacement for the current political declaration. Whether or not the UN decides to make changes to the original Johannesburg documents, the real impact of the 2002 summit should become clearer in the coming decade (Sibley, 2007).

The United Nations Climate Change Conference 2007 in Bali was held from Monday, 3 December to Friday, 14 December 2007. The first week involved negotiations among the Parties at the level of high-ranking government officials on a wide range of issues. On Wednesday, 12 December, the high-level segment started with addresses by the UN Secretary-General and the President of Indonesia. It was attended by 187 Environment Ministers and 11,000 participants in total. Bali Conference was considered to be an event great importance. The scientific report from the UN's Inter-governmental Panel on Climate Change (IPCC) for the year 2006-07 had stressed that climate change is a reality and can seriously harm the future development of our economies, societies and eco-systems worldwide. The report suggested immediate action in order to prevent the most severe impacts. It was recognized that since climate change is a global issue, tackling climate change and its impacts can only be successfully coordinated at the international level. The UN Framework Convention on Climate Change (UNFCCC) presented the appropriate forum to do this. It was expanded by the Kyoto Protocol which included emission reduction commitments for developed countries over the period 2008-12. International community accepted that a new international climate change deal must be put in place in time to ensure that necessary action is undertaken immediately after 2012 when the current phase of the Kyoto Protocol ends. Therefore, it was felt that comprehensive negotiations on a new climate deal needed to begin without further delay. This thinking formed background to United Nations Climate Change Conference 2007. The attendees of the conference agreed to launch negotiations towards a crucial and strengthened international climate change deal. The conference resulted in an agenda, given below, for the key issues to be negotiated up to 2009.

- Action for adapting to the negative consequences of climate change, such as droughts and floods.

- Ways to reduce greenhouse gas emissions.
- Ways to widely deploy climate-friendly technologies and financing both adaptation and mitigation measures.

It was further agreed that a new deal can enter into force by 2013, following the expiration of the first phase of the Kyoto Protocol. "This is a real breakthrough, a real opportunity for the international community to successfully fight climate change," said Yvo de Boer, Executive Secretary of the United Nations Framework Convention on Climate Change (UNFCCC). "Parties have recognized the urgency of action on climate change and have now provided the political response to what scientists have been telling us is needed," he added. Hence, a new global deal was envisioned for 2013. The participating countries also agreed on a number of steps that needed to be taken immediately to further implement the existing commitments of parties to the UNFCCC. For example, governments decided that funding for adaptation projects in developing countries, financed by the Kyoto Protocol's Clean Development Mechanism (CDM), would begin under the management of the Global Environment Facility (GEF). This would ensure that the Adaptation Fund would become operational in an early stage of the first commitment period of the Kyoto Protocol (2008-12). The fund was decided to be filled by means of a 2% levy on CDM projects. The Bali Conference also made progress on the issue of technology, one of the key concerns of developing countries. The participating countries agreed to kick start strategic programs to scale up the level of investment for the transfer of both the mitigation and adaptation technologies that developing countries need creating more attractive environments for investment, as well as to provide incentives to the private sector for technology transfer (http://www.un-ngls.org/spip.php?page=article_s&id_article=396). Hence, the Conference discussed the course for new negotiating process to be concluded by 2009 that will ultimately lead to a post-2012 international agreement on climate change, following the expiry of first phase of Kyoto Protocol. Further, the Conference came out with the launch of Adaptation Fund as well as decisions on technology transfer, and on reducing emissions from deforestation.

All the countries are scheduled to meet again in Copenhagen in December 2009 to take the discussions further and ensure cooperative action among them in future. The Kyoto Protocol to prevent climate changes and global warming runs out in 2012. In order to keep the process on the line, there is an urgent need for a new climate protocol. At the conference in Copenhagen 2009, the parties of the UNFCCC meet for the last time on government level before the climate agreement is to be renewed. Hence, the Climate Conference in Copenhagen is essential to make an effort towards saving global climate. The Danish government and UNFCCC are putting up hard effort in making the meeting in Copenhagen a success ending up with a Copenhagen Protocol to prevent global warming and climate changes. Governmental representatives from 170 countries are expected to be in

Copenhagen for the conference accompanied by other governmental representatives, NGO's, journalists and others. In total 8000 people are expected to Copenhagen during the period of the climate meeting. The conference in Copenhagen is the 15th conference of parties (COP15) in the Framework Convention on Climate Change (http://www.erantis.com/events/denmark/copenhagen/climate-conference-2009/index.htm).

SUSTAINABLE DEVELOPMENT—THE DIMENSIONS OF INCLUSIVENESS

Successful development can imply many things, such as (though not limited to):

- An improvement in living standards and access to all basic needs such that a person has enough food, water, shelter, clothing, health, education, etc;
- A stable political, social and economic environment, with associated political, social and economic freedoms, such as (though not limited to) equitable ownership of land and property;
- The ability to make free and informed choices that are not coerced;
- Be able to participate in a democratic environment with the ability to have a say in one's own future; and
- To have the full potential for what the United Nations calls Human Development:

> "Human development is about much more than the rise or fall of national incomes. It is about creating an environment in which people can develop their full potential and lead productive, creative lives in accord with their needs and interests. People are the real wealth of nations. Development is thus about expanding the choices people have to lead lives that they value. And it is thus about much more than economic growth, which is only a means—if a very important one—of enlarging people's choices."

—*What is Human Development*?, Human Development Reports, United Nations Development Program

At household, community, societal, national and international levels, various aspects of the above need to be provided, as well as commitment to various democratic institutions that do not become corrupted by special interests and agendas. Yet, for a variety of reasons, these "full rights" are not available in many segments of various societies from the richest to the poorest. When political agendas deprive these possibilities in a country, that country cannot develop (Shah, 2008).

It has been seen that mankind, in general, has made economic progress and accumulated various forms of capital. However, this has led to decline in natural capital. Rising population and industrial development have strained the availability of natural resources. There has been release of major pollutants and quality of environment has deteriorated. Further, the physical wealth that has been accumulated has not found equal distribution. Only a few sections of the society have actually bagged the fruits of economic development. Economic development of man has also resulted in poor quality of environment. Inclusive sustainable development seeks to attract attraction of mankind to all these issues. In general, inclusive sustainable development as a concept involves three dimensions, viz., social, economic and environmental sustainability.

Economic Dimension

Inclusive sustainable development involves poverty reduction and equal distribution of wealth among all sections of the society. Causes of poverty have been identified as:

- *Warfare*: The material and human destruction caused by warfare is a major development problem. For example, from 1990 to 1993, the period encompassing Desert Storm, per capita GDP in Iraq fell from $3500 to $761. The drop in average income, while a striking representation of the drop in the well-being of the average Iraqi citizen in the aftermath of the war, fails to capture the broader affects of damages to the infrastructure and social services, such as health care and access to clean water.
- *Agricultural Cycles*: People who rely on fruits and vegetables that they produce for household food consumption (subsistence farmers) often go through cycles of relative abundance and scarcity. For many families that rely on subsistence production for survival, the period immediately prior to harvest is a 'hungry period.' During these periods of scarcity, many families lack sufficient resources to meet their minimal nutritional needs. Being familiar with these cycles has enabled development practitioners to anticipate and prepare for periods of acute need for assistance.
- *Droughts and Flooding*: Besides the immediate destruction caused by natural events such as hurricanes, environmental forces often cause acute periods of crisis by destroying crops and animals.
- *Natural Disasters*: Natural disasters such as hurricanes and earthquakes have devastated communities throughout the world. Developing countries often suffer much more extensive and acute crises at the hands of natural disasters, because limited resources inhibit the construction of adequate housing, infrastructure, and mechanisms for responding to crises.

Certain other entrenched factors associated with poverty have been identified as:

- *Colonial Histories*: One of the most important barriers to development in poor countries is lack of uniform, basic infrastructure, such as roads and means of communication. Some development scholars have identified colonial history as an important contributor to the current situation. In most countries with a history of colonization, the colonizers developed local economies to facilitate the expropriation of resources for their own economic growth and development.
- *Centralization of Power*: In many developing countries, political power is disproportionately centralized. Instead of having a network of political representatives distributed equally throughout society, in centralized systems of governance one major party, politician, or region is responsible for decision-making throughout the country. This often causes development problems. For example, in these situations politicians make decisions about places that they are unfamiliar with, lacking sufficient knowledge about the context to design effective and appropriate policies and programs.
- *Corruption*: Corruption often accompanies centralization of power, when leaders are not accountable to those they serve. Most directly, corruption inhibits development when leaders help themselves to money that would otherwise be used for development projects. In other cases, leaders reward political support by providing services to their followers.
- *Warfare*: Warfare contributes to more entrenched poverty by diverting scarce resources from fighting poverty to maintaining a military. Take, for example, the cases of Ethiopia and Eritrea. The most recent conflict over borders between the two countries erupted into war during 1999 and 2000, a period when both countries faced severe food shortages due to drought.
- *Environmental degradation*: Awareness and concern about environmental degradation have grown around the world over the last few decades, and are currently shared by people of different nations, cultures, religions, and social classes. However, the negative impacts of environmental degradation are disproportionately felt by the poor. Throughout the developing world, the poor often rely on natural resources to meet their basic needs through agricultural production and gathering resources essential for household maintenance, such as water, firewood, and wild plants for consumption and medicine. Thus, the depletion and contamination of water sources directly threaten the livelihoods of those who depend on them.
- *Social Inequality*: One of the more entrenched sources of poverty throughout the world is social inequality that stems from

> cultural ideas about the relative worth of different genders, races, ethnic groups, and social classes. Ascribed inequality works by placing individuals in different social categories at birth, often based on religious, ethnic, or 'racial' characteristics. In South African history, apartheid laws defined a binary caste system that assigned different rights (or lack thereof) and social spaces to Whites and Blacks, using skin colour to automatically determine the opportunities available to individuals in each group.
>
> (http://www.gdrc.org/sustdev/causes-poverty.html)

It has to be noted that poverty has multi-dimensional effects. Poverty causes hunger and malnutrition. There is lack of access to education, adequate health services, and clean water and sanitation. Poverty makes people vulnerable to economic shocks, natural disasters, violence, and crime. According to new estimates, published in World Bank's World Development Indicators 2007, an estimated 985 million people- one fifth of the world's population—worldwide live in extreme poverty, earning even less than US$ 1 per day. Further, 2.5 billion people worldwide live on less than US$2 a day. This is despite the fact that poverty incidence has decreased from 29 per cent of global population in 1990 to 18 per cent in 2004, and developing countries have averaged a solid 3.9 per cent annual growth in GDP per capita a year since 2000. This means that in general, there has been betterment of the poor in absolute sense.

In case of many countries and regions, despite sustained economic growth, all segments of the population have not benefited. In these countries and regions, economic inequality has increased, as people living in extreme poverty have not been able to avail the desired benefits because of lack of job opportunities. Further, it is to be noted that poverty level has declined in many countries, but some of the least developed countries have been left behind on economic front. As per World Bank's World Development Report 2008, gross national income measured in US$ per capita varies from as low as less than US$ 200 in case of countries like Malawi, Burundi, Eriteria and Ethopia to as high as more than US$ 50,000 in case of countries like Denmark, Norway and Switzerland. According to International Monetary Fund's World Economic Outlook, 2007, in the current phase of globalisation, there has been a surge in income inequality in case of most of the countries and regions over the past two decades. It has been pointed out that income has risen at a faster pace for those who are already better-off. Technological development has contributed in the rising inequality among the rich and the poor in the recent times. It has led to a decline in the demand for low-skill workers and increase in the demand for the highly skilled workers; hence, there is more scope for rewards and opportunities in case of the highly skilled workers. Foreign direct investment also causes an increase in the relative demand for skilled workers and leads to rising income inequalities. Further, in addition, World

Economic Outlook, 2007 indicates that financial development contributes in rising inequalities as higher income groups are in a better position to exploit the increased opportunities to borrow. However, greater global trade integration by opening up of the trade barriers, and providing more opportunities to the under developed nations to export to the developed nations is expected to contribute in removing income disparities in case of different segments of the population. Lack of capability has prevented some of the least developed countries to take advantage of the available international trade opportunities. Persistence of trade barriers, and lack of access to markets for products from these countries by their developed counterparts has also aggravated the economic problems of the least developed countries.

Social Dimension

Poverty and income disparity are believed to be important factors among others, which lead to problems at the social front. Worldwide, governments are confronted with unemployment, and providing drinking water, health, primary education, sanitation and other basic amenities to their residents. Poor governments do not have the capacity to provide for, and guarantee health and education for their population. Lack of health and education limit productivity and income of the population, and hence, access to betterment in life. The quality of health care including lack of access to healthcare; incidence of diseases like HIV/AIDS, malaria, etc.; child mortality; death of pregnant women; malnutrition;, etc. is grossly uneven both within and across the countries. Better nutrition in early years of a child's life increases his prospects for finishing school and influences his chances of growing as a healthy, informed and productive citizen of his country. Worldwide, as compared to their urban counterparts, there is limited access to rural folk as far as education, health and other civic facilities are concerned. This is limiting the capability of rural population to earn and prosper; hence, widening the disparity between rural and urban residents. This gap may create unwanted rift between the two sections of the society. Many countries are facing the problem of increasing population. This is putting pressure on land, food, water, environment, etc. and straining the capacity of these countries. Those who are rich can have access to all the amenities of life. But, poor segments of the population are deprived of the right of respectful and fulfilling life. This breeds contempt and discontent among the deprived lot, and they may resort to unfair means to feed themselves. Increasingly, world is facing instances of crimes and thefts. Lack of access to education may impinge upon the ability of an individual to think and act rationally. There are incidences of gender disparity and racial discrimination. This is more pronounced in case of poorer and uneducated segments of the population including rural areas. Poor, illiterate and deprived lot is easily influenced by unscrupulous elements to carry out unlawful and anti-social activities. Inability to meet the aspirations of the various groups, uneven development, income disparity, lack of avenues to earn, lack of education, etc. are contributing to the problems of social unrest, terrorism, demands for separation, etc.

As per Global Monitoring Report 2008 of World Bank, worldwide notable progress has been made on various social fronts. Growth in developing countries has averaged over seven per cent in the last five years. The number of extreme poor—those living under US$1 a day—in the developing world declined by 278 million between 1990 and 2004. As compared to 1990, at present, about 40 million more children are in school; gender disparity in primary and secondary schools has declined by 60 per cent; 3 million more children survive every year; 2 million lives are saved every year by immunization; and 2 million people now receive AIDS treatment. However, about 75 million children of primary school age are still not in school. Every week, worldwide 10,000 women die from treatable complications of pregnancy and birth. More than 1,90,000 children under five die of disease every week. Unsafe drinking water and poor sanitation and hygiene account for around 90 per cent of diarrhea cases worldwide. As many as 33 million people are infected with HIV, with more than 2 million dying every year from AIDS. Further, every year more than 1 million people die of malaria, a preventable disease. The Report also points out that about half of the developing world lacks basic sanitation.

Environmental Dimension

The economic growth of man has exerted pressure on environment. The so-called developed countries, in a bid to develop their economies, used fossil fuels and poured thousands of tones of carbon dioxide into the atmosphere. The developing countries are also slowly following the same path. Natural resources are being continuously overused and degraded by man. Pollutants arising from industrial activity, energy consumption, transportation, agricultural activity, etc. are contributing in environmental degradation. Usage of coal and oil in coal-fired power plants and households is contributing emissions and concentration of carbon dioxide, sulphur oxides, nitrogen oxides and particulate matter in the environment. Industrial production, rising population, increasing affluence and shift to nuclear families are contributing in the growth of solid waste. Sources of organic pollutants include discharges of inadequately treated sewage from municipal treatment plants and household septic systems, runoff of fertilisers and animal waste from farms and deposition of air pollutants. Decrease in the forest cover, deterioration of river and lake water due to human and industrial waste, contamination of ecosystems, degradation of agricultural soil, and polluted industrial sites are aggravating the environmental degradation induced problems. There is growing concern about the widespread presence of chemicals like sulphur oxides, nitrogen oxides, ammonia, carbon dioxide, methane, etc. in the environment in terms of their potential effects on both ecosystems and human health.

Further, it is being increasingly believed that human-induced global warming is causing change in the climate and rise in the average temperature is a reality. As climate gets hotter, weather patterns are disrupted, glaciers retreat, polar icecaps melt, sea levels rise, rivers dry up, and bio-diversity is severely diminished. Global warming is linked to a range of human economic activities, particularly the burning and production of fossil fuels, converting forestland to other uses, unsustainable farming practices, disposing of waste in landfills, among others. Stationary fuel combustion is majorly responsible for greenhouse gas emissions, followed by transport, agriculture, industrial processes, waste, and fuel production. Carbon dioxide (CO_2) is the dominant greenhouse gas, followed by methane and nitrous oxide. The contribution of rise in absolute emissions is generally in case of the regions with high population and economic growth. Climate change may affect availability of food, fresh water and human health both directly and indirectly. Changes in temperature and precipitation may contribute in increased incidence of diseases such as diarrhea, malaria, cardiovascular diseases and respiratory infections. Extreme weather events—hurricanes, floods, and tornadoes—are likely to raise accidental deaths and injuries. The fertile areas on this globe may not remain fertile due to global warming, resulting in global food shortage. Increased evaporation and drier soils in some regions may result in prolonged draughts. Developing countries in general stand to loss more from the affects of global warming than do industrial countries. Most of the developing countries have less capacity to adapt. Most are in the warmer parts of the globe, where temperatures are already close to or beyond thresholds.

The Inter-governmental Panel on Climate Change, 2007 projects that in the absence of emission control policies, global temperature will increase on average by 2.8°C by 2100. It highlights that average earth temperature has risen by 0.74°C since the start of the industrial revolution in the mid-1800s. Further, eleven of the last years rank among the warmest years on record since 1850. There has been a consistent rise in global sea levels at an average rate of 1.8 millimeters a year since 1961. However, since 1993 the global sea levels have risen at an average rate of 3.1 millimeters a year. Average temperatures in the Arctic are rising twice as fast as elsewhere in the world. The Inter-governmental Panel on Climate Change, 2007 further states that polar ice cap as a whole is shrinking and area of permanent ice cover is contracting at a rate of 9 per cent each decade. If this melting continues, summers in the Arctic could become nearly ice-free by the end of the century. World Bank's Global Monitoring Report, 2008 reveals that more than 40 per cent of the global burden of malaria can be prevented through improved environmental management. An estimated 1.5 million deaths annually caused by respiratory infections are attributable to environmental pollution. More than 200 million people in developing countries live in potential impact zones where they would become refugees from coastal flooding at a three-meter sea level rise. During the 1990s, 200 million people per year, on average, were affected by climate-related disasters in developing countries, compared with about 1 million in developed countries. It is estimated that by 2100, globally crop productivity will increase with increases in local average temperature over a range of 1-3°C, but above this it is projected to decrease. In South Asia, the fall in crop yield could be as much as 30 per cent. In some countries, yields from rain-fed agriculture could be reduced by up to 50 per cent by 2020. Further, 75 to 250 million people exposed to increased water stress in 2020 in Africa. It is also projected that 20-30 per cent of plant and animal species at risk of extinction if increases in global average temperature exceed 1.5-2.5°C.

INCLUSIVE SUSTAINABLE DEVELOPMENT—THE ISSUES AND TASKS INVOLVED

Most countries have agreed in 2005 to set ambitious targets for sustainable development through eight development goals contained in United Nations Millennium Development Declaration. These goals range from halving extreme poverty to halting the spread of HIV/AIDS and providing universal primary education, all by the target date of 2015. In fact, inclusive sustainable development is not possible without reducing poverty, diseases and illiteracy. It demands bilateral and multilateral co-operation, co-ordination and partnerships among developed countries, developing countries, under-developed countries, and various stakeholders. Country-specific constraints have to be identified and global community and governments need to broad base processes so as to include poor sections of the society in the growth process. In light of the growing global integration of economic, social and environmental systems, international agreements are being discussed at various forums to tackle the issues confronting inclusive sustainable development. Developed countries need to support developing and under-developed countries by directing technology and resources. Removal of international barriers to trade and investment liberalisation are important for inclusive sustainable development. Trade and investment promotes employment opportunities, economic growth and overall development by diffusing knowledge, improving resource allocation, exposing producers to competition, and hence enabling the availability of quality product at affordable prices. International initiatives aimed at increasing the market access for products from least developed countries can help remove trade distortions and complement the process of inclusive sustainable development. In general, the world has seen many countries reducing their trade barriers owing to their commitment to many regional trading agreements and World Trade Organisation agreements. However, much is left to be done in this direction. This has to be backed by national policies to ensure social and economic benefits and economic growth. Further, one of the most critical issues faced by the world community is developing quantitative measure of sustainable development. United Nations Division for Sustainable Development has recently come out with a list of 96 indicators of sustainable development, out of which 50 are core indicators. Monitoring the progress across indicators of all the three dimensions of inclusive sustainable development is an enormous challenge.

At national level, government, private sector and civil society—all need to play an active role in creating social infrastructure. Assets may remain with government. However, private sector should manage these assets and civil society has to ensure equity and fairness. Each government should aim at developing policies targeted at inclusive sustainable growth at national level so as to ensure good governance, transparency, living conditions, and appropriate environmental and social conditions. Investments in health, housing, anti-poverty programmes, sanitation and education will contribute to human productivity. The resources are required to be diverted to ensuring adequate food and drinking water supply. The governments have to be instrumental in ensuring sustainable agriculture. It involves promotion and establishment of appropriate eco-systems specific agricultural systems and technologies, diversification of production to cash crops and production of raw materials for processing to strengthen agricultural sector as a viable base for industrialisation. Rural industrialisation and eco-system specific community-based natural resource management at local levels will contribute to improve the lot of the masses. The government decision-making process has to change to ensure more integrated approach towards inclusive sustainable development and for the purpose, business and civil society should be given an increased chance to interact with the government policy-makers. Sufficient investments are needed in intellectual, human and natural capital to ensure sustained economic growth with less pressure on environment. Nation-wide campaigns have to be carried to create awareness regarding environmental and social pressures exerted as a result of actions of producers and consumers. The science and technology needs to be harnessed to cause decoupling of environmental strains from economic development. More intense efforts are to be directed to create alternative and renewable sources of energy, affordable drugs to combat diseases, efficient water purification systems, fertilisers to ensure fertility of agricultural land, and an enhanced understanding of ecosystem so as to preserve it.

There has to be decoupling of environmental pressures from economic growth. Some of the damage done to environment is irreversible. But, much can be done to prevent it from further damage. In order to address environmental externalities, market instruments like environmental taxes and permits should be engaged more intensely. Industries and households should be encouraged to switch from coal and heavy oils towards cleaner fuels such as natural gas. Governments should ensure increase in area under forests. Water resources need to be managed more judiciously. Heavy investments are required in sewage and industrial wastewater treatment facilities. The quality of river and water lakes needs to be improved. Technologies are required to be developed to ensure waste decomposition and recycling. Countries need to take action to decouple pressures on critical ecosystems and biodiversity from economic growth. Endangered species and their habitats are required to be protected. Global environmental change affects everyone regardless of the place or the country of residence. Many developing and under-developed countries face a great strain on their resources due to population growth, economic development and climate change. Global community needs to pledge support to such countries to ensure environment protection. Mechanisms like Global Environment Facility and Montreal Protocol Multilateral Fund provide financial support to enable countries to comply with multilateral environmental conventions. However, more of commitments are required from developed countries to support environment in developing countries.

World is recently seeing the changing consumer trends and policy incentives that promote low energy products, renewable energy generation, and cleaner industrial processes. There is a need for greater promotion of use of renewal sources of energy such as wind, water and sun energy. The organisations need to work towards saving our environment and make this world a better place to live in. The problem of energy efficiency is common with almost all the industries across the globe. The industry needs to be made energy aware and energy efficient. The industry should adopt appropriate strategies like benchmarking, sharing best practices and greater managerial attention to energy efficiency. They should adopt the concept of corporate social responsibility, which states that organisations commit their resources to the interests of the society and take initiatives to contribute towards upliftment of their community in terms of health, education, sanitation, environment, etc. The industry should learn how to improve their environment performance and run sustainably. It should collaborate in new ways with government and civil society.

One of the major development challenges confronting inclusive sustainable development is to make growth more participatory and inclusive. For the purpose, significant acceleration in employment situation is imperative. This requires initiatives to build capabilities of the poor, especially in the under-developed countries. Effort is required to create mechanisms and institutions that encourage innovations and creativity, provide equal growth opportunities to everyone, and a framework for all citizens to contribute and achieve to their potential. The governments should facilitate participation of general public to contribute to inclusive sustainable development. There is a need is to create general awareness to change our lifestyle and value system so as to incorporate the concept of sustainability into our daily life. The global community should take a pledge to choose an environmentally sustainable lifestyle. A lot of contribution may be made at individual level by judicious energy consumption. One should use TV, computer, lights, etc. to the minimum possible extent. More vehicles on the road mean more greenhouse gas emissions. Mass transportation and vehicle pooling should be used whenever possible. Efforts like keeping electrical appliance, vehicles, etc. in good condition; having air filters on air conditioners clean; ensuring fridge coils and tube lights dust free; more dependence on sunlight and natural ventilation; buying seasoned foods; avoidance of packaged, preserved and imported foods; choosing environment friendly products like solar cooker or water heater; tree planting;, etc. may go a long way in facilitating inclusive sustainable development.

References

Adam Simbley, (2007), "International Environmental Issues, Sustainable Development and Environmental Decision", http://www.eoearth.org/article/World_Summit_on_Sustainable_Development_(WSSD),_Johannesburg,_South_Africa, Last accessed on: Jul 28, 2009.

Anup Shah, (2008), "Poverty around the World", http://www.globalissues.org/print/article/4, Last accessed on: May 17, 2009.

International Monetary Fund (2007), World Economic Outlook, Washington DC: IMF.

IPCC (Inter-governmental Panel on Climate Change) (2007), Climate Change 2007: The Physical Science Basis, Contribution of Working Group I to the Fourth Assessment Report of the Inter-governmental Panel on Climate Change, Cambridge University Press: Cambridge and New York.

Peter Jackson, (2007), "A Brief History of Climate Change", http://www.un.org/Pubs/chronicle/2007/issue2/0207p06.htm, Last accessed on: Jul 18, 2009.

Kyoto Protocol to the United Nations Framework Convention on Climate Change, http://unfccc.int/resource/docs/convkp/kpeng.html, Last accessed on: Jun 20, 2008.

The United Nations Climate Change Conference in Bali, http://unfccc.int/meetings/cop_13/items/4049.php, Last accessed on: Jun 20, 2008.

Towards Earth Summit 2002, http://www.earthsummit2002.org/Es2002.pdf, Last Accessed on: Jun 21, 2008

United Nations Conference on Environment and Development (UNCED) (1992), Earth Summit, Rio de Janeiro, June 3-14, http://www.un.org/geninfo/bp/enviro.html, Last accessed on: Jun 23, 2008.

United Nations Environment Programme (1972), Declaration of the United Nations Conference on the Human Environment, Stockholm, June 5-14, http://www.unep.org/Documents.Multilingual/Default.asp?DocumentID=97&ArticleID=1503, Last accessed on: Jun 21, 2008.

United Nations General Assembly (2000), United Nations Millennium Declaration, Resolution 55/2 adopted by the General Assembly at 55th session, September 6-8, http://www.un.org/millennium/declaration/ares552e.pdf, Last accessed on: Jun 23, 2008.

World Bank (2007), Global Monitoring Report, Washington DC: World Bank.

_______(2008), Global Monitoring Report, Washington DC: World Bank.

World Commission on Environment and Development (1987), "Our Common Future". Published as Annex to General Assembly document A/42/427, Development and International Co-operation: Enviornment, August 2, http://www.un-documents.net/a42-427.htm, Last accessed on: Jun 23, 2009.

http://www.un-ngls.org/spip.php?page=article_s&id_article=396, Last accessed on: Jun 21, 2009.

http://www.erantis.com/events/denmark/copenhagen/climate-conference-2009/index.htm, Last accessed on: Jul 7, 2009.

http://www.gdrc.org/sustdev/causes-poverty.html, Last accessed on: Jun 23, 2009.

CHAPTER

5

INCLUSIVE GROWTH AND SUSTAINABLE DEVELOPMENT: THE ROUTE TO INDIA'S GROWTH

P.K. Vasudeva

ABSTRACT

The sustainable inclusive growths for any country come through skills and knowledge which are the driving forces for socio-economic development. Merely 5.0 per cent youth of India are single skill vocationally trained as compared to 95.86 per cent in South Korea.

The only saving grace for India is the unique opportunity to provide workers to an aging world. India has the youngest population in the world. In the year 2000 median age of India was 23.7 years whereas incase of China, Europe and Japan the corresponding figure was 30.2, 37.7 and 41.2 years respectively.

In order to promote inclusive growth there is an urgent need to address the issue of skilled development and employed ability for which National Skills Development Counsel with the able leadership of Prime Minister Dr. Manmohan Singh should create a movement like National Literacy Mission to engage the country in skills development and employment.

The private sector is also making great strides through microfinance, providing rural development capital while freeing many rural people from the grip of moneylenders. To realize the potential microfinance has tapped, however, India needs greater deregulation.

Business leaders observe that far reaching changes are imperative order for India's cities to achieve sustainable development and provide inclusive growth for its citizens. India should take initiative in a global partnership of leading city mayors and private sector board executives, supported by the World Bank, the International Energy Agency, UH-Habitat and ICLEI.

India's recent growth rate has been impressive, with real GDP rising by over 8 per cent a year since 2004. To sustain competitiveness, economic growth, and rising living standards over the long-term, India needs to aggressively harness its innovation potential. Unleashing India's Innovation: Toward Sustainable and Inclusive Growth provides national and local policy-makers, private sector enterprises, academic and research institutions, international organizations, and civil society with a better understanding of the power of innovation to fuel economic growth and poverty reduction.

The present international economic crisis poses both challenges and opportunities in terms of realising the potential for sustainable and inclusive growth in Asia.

INTRODUCTION

India is one of the fastest growing economies in the world having remarkable acceleration in economic growths within average growth rate of more than 7 per cent over the past decade since 1997 (except 2008-09 when India's economic growth fell short of 6.7 per cent due to global economic downturn) reducing poverty by about 10 per centage points, yet 25 per cent of the India's population is below poverty line, i.e. 287.5 million.

Inclusive Growth Through Skills and Knowledge

The sustainable inclusive growths for any country comes through skills and knowledge which are the driving forces for socio-economic development. The countries with better levels of skill are well equipped to address the opportunities in the world of work and capable of addressing the ever growing challenges of technological innovations and meeting the requirements of modern Hi-tech industries and services sectors. However, in India more than 70 per cent of the work force combined, organized and un-organised sector is illiterate or educated below primary level. Merely 5.0 per cent youth of India are single skill vocationally trained as compared to 95.86 per cent in South Korea. The corresponding figure for Botswana, Colombia, Mexico and Mauritius is 22.42, 28.06, 27.58 and 36.08 per cent respectively. Beside 2.5 million graduates passing out each year without skills connected to employment, hence remain un-employed.

The only saving grace for India is the unique opportunity to provide workers to an aging world. India has the youngest population in the world in the year 2000 median age of India was 23.7 years whereas incase of China, Europe and Japan the corresponding figure was 30.2, 37.7 and 41.2 years respectively. By 2025 India will have the dependency ratio (over 65 years of 12.1 for every hundred people. In case of China, Europe and Japan the dependency ration will be 19.2, 33.2 and 49.5 respectively. It appears that for the first time demographics are working is India's favour and the country are rich demographic dividend which can be harnessed through effective skills development initiatives.

In order to promote inclusive growth there is an urgent need to address the issue of skilled development and employed 'ability for which National Skills Development Counsel with the able leadership of Prime Minister Dr. Manmohan Singh should create a movement like National Literacy Mission to engage the country in skills development and employment.

Inclusive Growth Through Rural India

"The benefits of rapid economic growth, unleashed through the reforms of the last two decades, need to flow to all sections of society, particularly to rural India. Even now, almost three-fourth of our population resides in rural areas and almost the same proportion is still dependent on agriculture for sustenance. If we have to ensure inclusive and equitable growth, we need to knit and integrate our rural areas into the modern economic processes that are rapidly transforming our country. We cannot allow India to be divided into two distinct zones, one a modern, competitive, prosperous one and the other a stagnant, backward one," said Dr. Manmohan Singh Prime Minister of India.

"If we can take opportunities to rural India, there's no reason why rural India would wish to come like lemmings to urban India", said Mani Shankar Aiyar, Minister of Panchayati Raj and Youth Affairs and Sports of India.

It is no secret that India needs to make its tremendous economic growth more equitable, to spread it more fairly among society—not just wealth, but infrastructure and educational opportunities. Roughly one quarter of Indians live below the poverty line, and almost 70% of Indians live in rural areas, where desperate farmers too often find solace in suicide.

The rising discontent of these have-nots has already produced a political backlash. A radical Maoist insurrection, Naxalism, has spread through some states while, across the country, regional political parties are growing in strength, upsetting the dominance of national parties and forcing them to cobble together coalition governments—like the one now in power in New Delhi (see Figure 1).

While these new political parties offer an important voice for those disenfranchised or displaced by economic development, they often base their appeal on caste and the personality of their leader, making them divisive and raising concerns about corruption. "They can muster big crowds but they are perceived to be not very honourable", said Arun Jaitley, Leader of Opposition, Rajya Sabha.

Inclusive Economic Growth

The proliferation of coalition governments that rely on consensus decision-making could also have a diminished ability to formulate and implement effective policies. "Coalition government has its own compulsions and its own limitations", said Vilasrao Deshmukh, Chief Minister of Maharashtra, India. "It can delay decisions".

To achieve a broader mandate and regain political momentum,

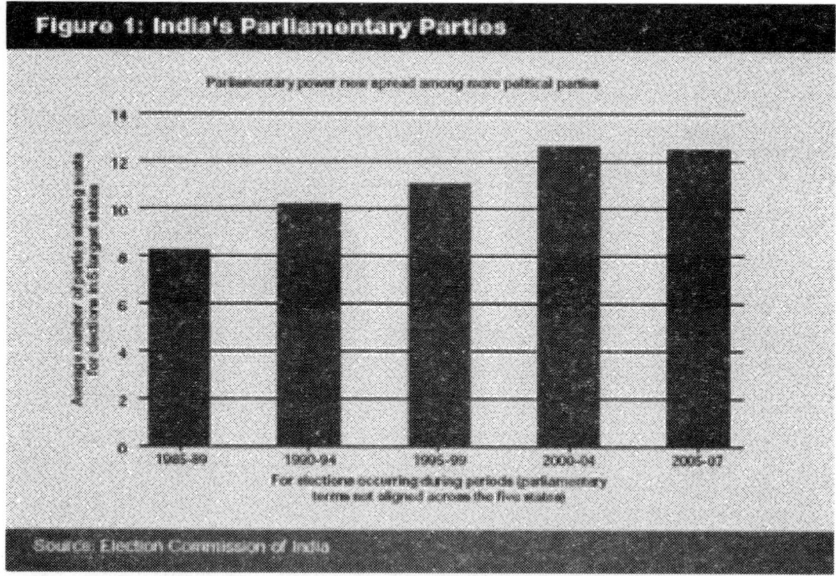

Figure 1: India's Parliamentary Parties

Source: Election Commission of India

national parties need to boost regional chapters to embrace local interests; likewise, regional parties need to develop more robust national agendas.

Achieving inclusive economic growth is a priority for India's current government. Its latest budget includes a 31% increase in spending on rural infrastructure—15% of public infrastructure funds are expected to be allocated to rural irrigation (see Figure 2)—and broadens access by farmers to credit. In doing so, it is helping to plug a gaping hole in funding for connecting rural Indians to the mainstream economy.

The private sector is also making great strides through microfinance, providing rural development capital while freeing many rural people from the grip of moneylenders. Instead, microfinance offers the rural poor a way to leverage their own industry and thrift by popularizing not only debt but also savings accounts. "The bank account has become a status symbol in the villages", said M.R. Rao, Chief Operating Officer, SKS Microfinance, India.

To realize the potential microfinance has tapped, however, India needs greater deregulation. Existing rules, for example, prevent bankers from tying up with telecommunications companies to use established cellular customer networks to distribute financial services.

Sustainable City Development and Inclusive Urban Growth

Business leaders observe that far reaching changes are imperative order for India's cities to achieve sustainable development and provide inclusive growth for its citizens.

Accountability, coordination and resources were identified as the three core areas in need of transformation. They underline the success of the Delhi Metro development as a widely recognized example of the

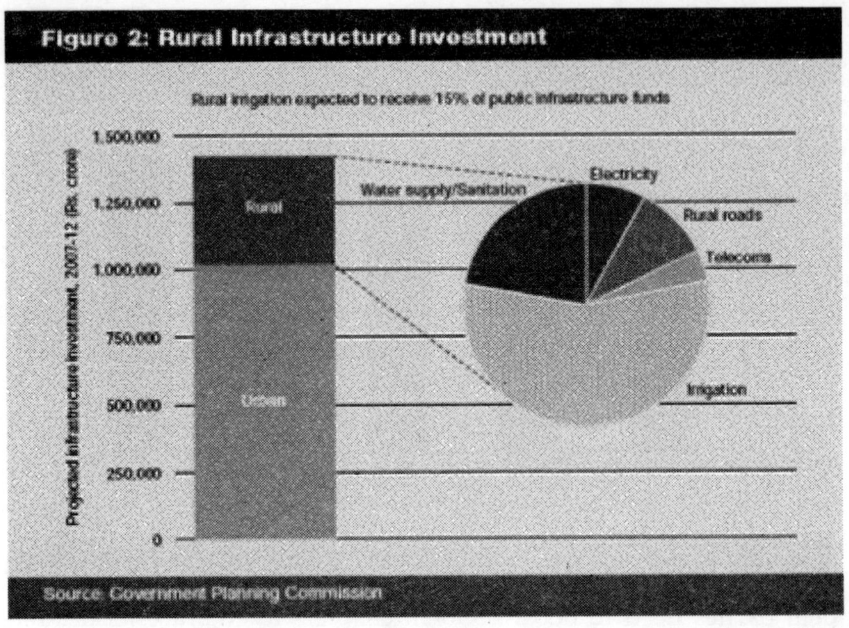

Figure 2: Rural Infrastructure Investment

Source: Government Planning Commission

overwhelming advantages of clear accountability in city governance and transparent, coordinated public sector project management. It is a fact that India possesses world-class resources, but its economic and inclusive growth can only continue if leaders from the public and private sectors rise to the challenge of putting these resources in the hands of those who need them.

India should take initiative in a global partnership of leading city mayors and private sector board executives, supported by the World Bank, the International Energy Agency, UH-Habitat and ICLEI. The initiative provides a risk-free, dynamic, multistakeholder environment within which cities and the private sector can pursue the development of energy and resource efficiency in cities.

Bankers concede, however, that their industry is also guilty of holding back. Microfinance typically charges relatively high interest rates, yet default rates among micro-borrowers remain near zero, indicating what bankers say is excessive caution on the part of micro-lenders. Part of that caution, they say, stems from the fact that there is no credit bureau to keep track of rural borrowers, nor a reliable way—such as driving licenses or birth certificates—to even identify them. Some have called for the government to issue national voter registration cards.

Bankers also have an important role to play in filling the rural education gap, by teaching rural Indians the basics of finance. To be sure, education often serves as a politically correct panacea in debates about poverty relief, but this year's Summit broke from the platitudes by outlining practical areas where education can have an immediate impact. Improved vocational training was singled out as 'a critical necessity for India that would address its growing shortage of skilled trades workers while recognizing that a higher degree may not be a realistic aspiration for the bulk of the country's youth. Vocational training is an area, moreover, where companies can get more immediate returns on their investment, either by conducting their own training, financing vocational programmes or helping to develop curricula.

The good news for India is that its economy is largely driven by domestic demand as opposed to exports. The rural population, therefore, represents a critical source of new labour for India's services-led growth.

But solving the riddle of how to raise income levels in the countryside without accelerating the rush to the cities requires new thinking on what urbanization means. In short, convincing rural Indians not to move to big cities will require moving the city closer to them. "If we can take opportunities to rural India, there's no reason why rural India would wish to come like lemmings to urban India", said Mani Shankar Aiyar, Minister of Panchayati Raj and Youth Affairs and Sports of India.

Industries that rely on rural inputs—food processing, biofuel production and handicrafts—should move closer to their production centres. Doing so will encourage the creation of new urban centres, turning villages into towns, and towns into small cities. Technology can also be used to turn rural India into a service centre for urban India in the same way that India has become a service centre for the world. "The war for talent is such that we have hundreds of millions of people who cannot monetize their skills today because we haven't connected them", said Ben J. Verwaayen, Chief Executive Officer, BT, United Kingdom.

Ultimately, it may take a more concerted push by government to make this shift out of the cities happen. Regulations and incentives may be needed to encourage companies to "ruralize". But it is clear that India can no longer afford to let investment and commerce remain confined within the city limits. "Rural and urban are not separate; both are connected, said Aiyar. "Until we see that, India will become prosperous and Indians will remain poor."

> "What do migrants want? They want diversity of income, sanitation, drinking water, power, roads. But even when they get those, they will still want the life they see on their televisions. Human beings like to live in cities; they have done so for thousands of years".
>
> "The war for talent is such that we have hundreds of millions of people who cannot monetize their skills today because we haven't connected them. It's in everyone's interest that we unleash that capability and that talent".

India's recent growth rate has been impressive, with real GDP rising by over 8 per cent a year since 2004. The country is also becoming a top global innovator for high-tech products and services. Still, India is underperforming relative to its innovation potential. Even a dynamic young population—more than half of whom are under 25 years of age—is constrained when skills training and higher education are insufficient. To sustain competitiveness, economic growth, and rising living standards over the long-term, India needs to aggressively harness its innovation potential. The term innovation is broadly defined in this book to include both the creation and commercialization of new knowledge and the diffusion and absorption of existing knowledge in new contexts. A unique feature is the book's focus on inclusive innovation, that is, knowledge creation and absorption activities most relevant to the needs of the poor. Concrete recommendations are made for increasing productivity and welfare through the disciplining role of competition, including training and education, information infrastructure, and public and private finance as support mechanisms for broad-based innovation. Unleashing India's Innovation: Toward Sustainable and Inclusive Growth provides national and local policy-makers, private sector enterprises, academic and research institutions, international organizations, and civil society with a better understanding of the power of innovation to fuel economic growth and poverty reduction.

Sustainable and Inclusive Growth in Asia

The present international economic crisis poses both challenges and opportunities in terms of realising the potential for sustainable and inclusive growth in Asia. What experiences and instruments are available for this?

The BMZ has commissioned GTZ to organize the regional conference. On the Indian side, this event is supported by the Government of India's Planning Commission.

The conference will bring together experts from Asia and Europe with the aim to facilitate an exchange on their country's specific experiences and approaches, and to stimulate dialogue and cooperation between European (particularly Germany) and Asian countries. The participants—political decision-makers, representatives from entrepreneurial associations and corporate partners, and civil society—will discuss the quality components of growth.

GTZ Joint Efforts for Inclusive Growth

India has been a partner country of German development cooperation for the last 50 years. For almost all of this time, GTZ—Deutsche Gesellschaft fuer Technische Zusammenarbeit (GTZ) GmbH—has been active in India on behalf of the German Federal Ministry for Economic Cooperation and Development (BMZ).

GTZ was established by the German government as a federal enterprise for sustainable development with worldwide operations in 1975 and works on a public-benefit basis. Its principal client is the BMZ but it also operates on behalf of other German ministries, partner-country governments and international clients, such as the European Commission, the United Nations and the World Bank. GTZ also works for private enterprises, combining the respective strengths of public and private partners to help achieve development policy goals. It provides viable, forward-looking solutions for political, economic, ecological and social development in a globalised world.

To address India's development priority of sustainable and inclusive growth, GTZ's joint efforts with the partners in India currently focus on three priority sectors: energy, sustainable economic development and environmental policy, conservation and sustainable use of natural resources. Additionally, the GTZ also supports India's public health priorities within the framework of the National Rural Health Mission. Germany and India celebrated 50 successful years of Indo-German Development Cooperation in 2008.

Indo-German Technical Cooperation began in 1958 with Germany supporting the establishment of the Indian Institute of Technology (IIT) in Chennai and skills development and training for the Rourkela Power Plant. The success of the Indo-German Watershed Development Programme led to the creation of a national programme—Watershed Development Fund (approximately €100 million in 2006) at the NABARD to implement the Indo-German programme's methodology and results across 100 poorest rain-fed districts in the country.

GTZ also supported the EcoCity programme of the Central Pollution Control Board in Kottayam, Ujjain, Vrindavan, Puri and Tirupati, leading to the improvement of various environmental parameters related to solid waste, liquid waste and air quality management. Together with the Bureau of Energy Efficiency, Ministry of Power, GTZ developed the star-rating system for electrical appliances which has been adopted across the country. Appliances like ACs, refrigerators, etc. are rated according to their energy efficiency.

Correcting the Current Course

The global financial and economic crisis poses enormous economic and social challenges for a large share of the population in many countries, for most governments, and for many entrepreneurs. This becomes manifest in rising unemployment and increasing indebtedness and budget deficits, growing impoverishment and vulnerability, as well as lack of credit and firm closures; all of which can prompt a huge loss of social capital in many countries.

Just as importantly, however, the crisis also provides an opportunity for achieving higher "quality" growth, as opposed to the merely quantitative results that have been the focus of many in the past.

During the last ten years, Asian countries have experienced admirable economic growth in quantitative terms. However, inequality has also risen due to the inappropriate distribution of growth. Another downside of this development has been the insufficient attention to the rising ecological costs of the high growth, and the inefficiencies in the consumption of energy and other non-renewable resources.

Competitiveness has served as an argument for keeping labour costs low and for concentrating productive power. High growth rates have been achieved, in great part, by export-oriented industries targeting mainly the US and European markets at the expense of further regional integration and domestic markets. In the finance sector, short-term profit orientation has often prevailed. Small- and medium-sized enterprises, lacking technological advice and good access to credit, have rarely been able to modernise production, thus limiting the growth of domestic markets.

These factors, the weakening of traditional safety nets and insufficient social protection, have made it very difficult for the broader population to benefit from increased growth. Meanwhile, additional structural deficits have arisen due to insufficient infrastructure, poor professional training opportunities and inadequate access to social services like health and education.

Neo-liberal tendencies, whereby the state retreats from the surveillance of systemic markets, could and should now be reviewed. Government, while still cautious to get involved in managing the economy, should be much more aware of its responsibility for promoting innovation and socially acceptable structural change, taking care of social justice and protection, as well as for regionally balanced growth, of promoting ecologically more sustainable modes of production and consumption, and of regulating relevant markets such as those linked to finance, energy and the environment.

Promoting regional integration, further developing domestic markets, investment in infrastructure and human capital, as well as responsible competitiveness, based on a more long-term orientation on the part of entrepreneurs and the consideration of the ecological and the social bottom-line, seem to be the order of the day. Such measures could lead to more sustainable and "inclusive" development, and the abandonment of the unevenly distributed growth path.

People still Prefer Piracy to Paying for World

We have been increasingly witnessing a tendency among business as if it exists for itself. It is part of the society and therefore it must care for society. Those who manage business seem to believe that there is no tomorrow as there is no long-term without short-term and seem to be concerned mainly about short-term. The deification of shareholder value created the impression that business and business managers must care for shareholders and not shareholders. The warnings of the Club of Rome concerning Limits to Growth are neglected to an extent whereby business is becoming unsustainable, as Robert Reich remarked in his book, "The Work of Nations", successive generations leaving behind a much poorer, inferior world than what they inherited.

The problem with many of those in business, specially the so-called professional managers who work for footloose capital, is that they are increasingly unable to decide when it is enough and how much is enough. From Enron to Satyam and GE to AIG whether it is retirement gifts or bonuses for executives in failed businesses from out of bailout money, victims of their own greed are putting even the systems and processes to shame and disuse. As Mahatma Gandhi said, society can provide for man's need, not for his greed.

Given this scenario there is a need, as Soros observed, to save capital from capitalists and the society from business. For business to be sustainable, it should care for the triple bottom line, not just profits, but also people and profits. Business should resist the temptation to cut a few thousand jobs to make a few more bucks. Instead, in the present time of slowdown and downturn, it should demonstrate social responsibility by foregoing a few thousand dollars in the interest of saving a few hundred jobs.

In 2005 July, Fortune's cover story featured the 50 most important decisions of the 20th century and listed Henry Ford's decision to increase his workers' pay as one among them. For, he believed that his business would grow when he produces cars for the masses than just the classes and when every worker who makes the Ford car is also able to buy one. 100 years ago, 80% of the Americans had agriculture as their source of livelihood. Today it is less than 3%. A futurology institute noted that the tractor has driven the animal out of the farm and . . . now the computer (technologies) are driving the human beings out of the factory. Global production chains are causing the shift in manufacturing from high labour cost economies to low labour cost areas (from 6$ an hour in US to 6$ a day in Philippines to 2$ a day in Indonesia to 1$ a day in Bangladesh to 80 cents a day in China to 65 cents a day in Vietnam and at some future day to no wage at all in some other part of the world where people are willing to work just for food like animals!). We now have a situation where 20% of the world's population consume 80% of world's resources. If only 2-4% of the people produce the wage goods for the world's population and millions and billions are without a job and hence livelihood and no consumption power, the world's markets will surely shrink and so will business.

CONCLUSION

In other words, for business to work and survive in the 21st century, it should believe in long-term, focus on all stakeholders than just the shareholders and care for people and planet also in addition to profits. Business can sustain itself and develop if it believes in practices that are geared to sustainable development with societal responsibility. This is the idea that business should pursue as its religion with missionary zeal.

References

Aiyar, Mani Shankar (2008) Minister of Panchayati Raj and Youth Affairs and Sports of India; Anand G. Mahindra, Vice-Chairman spoke at the India Economic Summit, CII.

Ajit Gulabchand, (2008) Chairman and Managing Director, Hindustan Construction Company, India, spoke at the SlimCity private session.

Anand G. Mahindra, (2008) Vice-Chairman and Managing Director, Mahindra and Mahindra, India; spoke at the India Economic Summit, CII.

Ben J. Verwaayen, (2008) Chief Executive Officer, BT, United Kingdom; spoke at the India Economic Summit on Sustainable Development.

Garima Pant (2009) "People still prefer piracy to paying for world", the *Financial Express*, June 14.

Palaniappan Chidambaram, (2008) Minister of Finance of India and Sunil Bharti Mittal, Chairman and Group Chief Executive Officer, Bharti Enterprises; President, spoke at the Confederation of Indian Industry (CII), India on "Inclusive Growth and Sustainable Development".

The regional conference, (2009) Organised by Germany's Federal Ministry for Economic Cooperation and Development (BMZ), together with the Deutsche Gesellschaft für Technische Zusammenarbeit (GTZ) on Asia "Quality of Growth: Approaches to inclusive development in Asian Societies", July 22.

CHAPTER

6

GREEN: THE EMERGING PRIMARY COLOUR

SHEENU JAIN

Green is everywhere...in magazines, newspapers and is one of the hottest topics among the Fortune 500 companies. The environment is the issue. There's a reason so many people are learning green these days. After all who doesn't want healthier environment, keep energy cost and greenhouse emission in check and doesn't squander other natural resources. This paper deals with the green colour philosophy and highlights some of exciting green examples from corporate India and narrate emerging green trends, and does not fail to emphasize on green washing.

Green Colour, Environment, Eco- friendly company, Green Practices

Green, which is Nature's colour, is restful, soothing, cheerful, and health-giving.

—*Paul Brunton*

ABSTRACT

Green makes feel different to different people in different situations. Green is considered to be the cool and soothing colour that symbolizes the nature and natural world. Colour green is considered to be representative of good luck, health, jealousy and tranquility and helps in healing and relieving from stress.

Today consumer interest is tipping and triggering point for many companies to go green. In a close competition, people are today willing to go with green company.

From planting trees, to using solar energy, to constructing smart buildings and even collecting litter, corporate India is going all green. These days, greener pastures are looking more like battlefields for some companies trying to position themselves as environmentally friendly.

GE's Ecomagination campaign, launched in May 2005, spans a number of hot topics for a company with a desultory green record. It promises to improve emissions and efficiency in its operations, to work with green organizations and to issue annual progress reports.

Green in India got its first green building in 2003—CII Godrej Business Centre, which is the greenest building in the world till date. Today there is no end to the green building undercurrent; everyone is turning green from ONGC to ITC to Airports to small eco-friendly home. Registration at Indian Green Building Council of real estate is now approximately 110 million sq. ft. India is already acknowledged as environmental friendly construction leader in the world.

In the brave new world of Wal-Mart, in which the company has recently pledged to green up its stores, its trucks, and some of its products, it could. Pantaloons Retail Fresh green stores or Reliance Fresh outlets all are working on the same lines. Consequently, individuals now have the ability to demand and subsequently purchase 'green power'. Together, environmental concern and electricity industry restructuring are enabling the development of new green power products and the emergence of a green power industry.

Green is in fashion and fashion become fad in some time. Companies want to show everything green to consumers, but the reality may be different. "If too many people start marketing themselves as green without proof points, it can appear disingenuous."

Green washing is the term to define this scenario. As consumers become more sensitive to environmental issues, green is becoming a bestseller. The long list of companies trying to sell their themselves and their products on green plank included companies such as BP, Ford Motor Company (Ford), General Electrics Company, and Wal-Mart.

It isn't that easy being green, but today there are more environment friendly small and large options available than ever before. In today's scenario green can truly be accepted as new business colour.

THE COLOUR PSYCHOLOGY OF GREEN

Green makes feel different to different people in different situations. We have heard the big terms from *Green Revolution* to *Green Marketing* today. Green is considered to be the cool and soothing colour that symbolizes the nature and natural world. Colour green is considered to be representative of good luck, health, jealousy, and tranquility.

Researchers have also done some interesting studies in this regard. It has been observed that colour green is very helpful for students for reading speed and comprehension and improves their reading ability. Interestingly in the 15th century colour green was the preferred choice for wedding gowns and it is also considered for symbol of fertility. Colour green helps in healing and relieving from stress. Naturopathy and Aloe

Vera all are associated with green colour. Greener work environment makes everyone or anyone for that matter refreshed. For calming effects, we often hear people go for relaxation in Green room.

Go Green World

From corporate boardrooms to SME's; from products to packaging; from company websites to communication colour, many companies are touting environmentally safe practices and products to gain the competitive edge. What used to be offered at few big stores is now common everywhere in an attempt to show their true colour: *Green.*

While the notion of being a "tree hugger" or "eco-friendly" once may have elicited eye-rolling and warnings about rabid environmentalism by both the general population and business community, there's been an about-face as consumers and business alike have increased their interest in all things green.

In a recent EL column, John Rooks, president of The Soap Group, a company that focuses on sustainability communications, wrote that "colours don't work well for movements." Adam Werbach, CEO, Satchi and Satchi.

I disagree.

In fact colours have played an exceptional role throughout the history. Orange revolution, corporate pink, blue are the charming colours of corporate houses.

The colour "green" lacks as an expression of sustainability is because it narrows the conversation to ecology or environment *per se.* While ecological issues touch every part of life, there are other issues (poverty, the price of a loaf of bread, the rights of women, and the cost of heating bills) that are frequently deprioritized by "green" debates. Integrated view of sustainability includes the four components of Social, Economic, Environmental and Cultural and asks that the rights of a mother trying to afford her child enough protein to thrive can be kept in balance with the desire to ensure that milk is organic.

There was a time when green movement was in its ascendancy and those who were thinking about it was attacked by some who said they were over-reacting by preparing a more mainstream movement for people living paycheck-to-paycheck. Today, most people are tightening their belts, and the only social change they can afford is change that will help them live healthier, happier lives for less than they were spending last year. Sustainability offers beautiful solutions for them, but only if we go far beyond green.

People today are making values decisions right in the aisles of the supermarket, so that's where we need to reach them. The good news is that companies who do this well will find themselves with lower operating costs, happier employees, high quality merchandise and permanently infatuated consumers.

Rooks conclude with a beautiful turn of phrase, "Sustainability is transparent, void of obscuring colour. It is clear, open, and visible. Sustainability is naked."

Altruism tells part of the story, but the real drivers behind the rising tide in green technology products are customer demand and energy cost. Nearly every form of commerce, no matter how smartly practiced, creates unwanted by-products.

Growing Trend

In the past environment responsibility was really wasn't part of the process, and today it is a boardroom discussion topic of many organizations, and integrated into the system. Today even transport companies, fuel companies to real estates; everyone is founding their own way to put themselves in green category. This is a kind of trend in the market, though it has been picked up in last 10 years. Indian market has seen many new players entering the green saga in last five years. As a marketing strategy "green" really become a lead selling point and point of differentiation today and it is slowly-slowly gaining its momentum in the market.

Recycling, Global warming, Waste management, and Renewable energy have seeped their way into the public conscious through pop culture in films like The Inconvenient Truth, companies are more likely to tap into the heightened consumer sensitivity to these causes. All these environmental initiatives for companies are generated through client demand.

Money Savings

Companies are adopting environmental-friendly practices and are looking the ways to cut cost; simply by saying this is the right thing to do. It surely means company is moving to Green.

In the past neither the company nor its employees were so concerned about efficiency and effectiveness. But today, they look for efficiency options everywhere. They started using recycled paper, energy efficient bulbs, car pooling, to switching-off computers in night. Those little things make a difference and make it greener. Even the current line of thinking includes whom they choose to do business with as well.

Consumer Interest

Today consumer interest is tipping and triggering point for many companies to go green. In a close competition, people are today willing to go with green company. Companies also agrees with the fact that, consumer's increased love for green cause them to go for large investment, but they know that in long-run, it will be beneficial for them only. On other hand, some companies do not want to follow it, as they feel it's an extra cost to organization.

However, one issue that remains to be addressed is just exactly what it means to be "green." While some industries have government regulations by which they must operate and the construction industry is monitored by a LEED certificate program that sets standards for green buildings, most other industries are not tracked as to how they use the term "green."

From planting trees, to using solar energy, to constructing smart buildings and even collecting litter, corporate India is going all green. These days, greener pastures are looking more like battlefields for some companies trying to position themselves as environmentally-friendly. Today, corporate wants to be eco-friendly in some way or the other. Take the case of Johnson and Johnson Ltd's plant in Mulund, Mumbai, where biodegradable waste is recycled or the Leela Kempinski in Mumbai that has invested in maintaining massive gardens in and around the premises of the hotel to encourage greenery and environment friendly ambience. The hotel also uses natural gas as boiler fuel that almost nullifies the air pollution compared to oil fired ones.

Environmental sustainability in business is the art of profiting from the customers' needs without harming the world around us. Today the same Green crayon has become the equipment/weapon for every organization to paint their ladder of success and move on.

Green they go..........

HCL: The call of the hour is for green focused companies. At HCL, people are highly committed and responsible towards the environment and sustainable development. They are not only Company is constantly involved in green corporate initiatives, and also make special efforts to ensure carbon neutral events, leaving no adverse ecological footprint behind. This priority, logically, is presented with the colour green.

Bharat Petroleum Corporation Ltd. (BPCL), for instance, has taken various initiatives to prevent air pollution. It launched an environment-friendly petrol pump in Delhi. With vapour recovery system, the petrol pump prevents unburned petroleum vapour from entering the atmosphere by converting it into less harmful compounds.

Bharat Heavy Electricals Ltd. (BHEL) shares the growing concern on issues related to environment and occupational health and safety. The organization has launched a host of products like wind electric generators, solar heating systems, solar photovoltaic systems, solar lanterns and battery powered road vehicles in a bid to conserve the environment.

LG Electronics have introduced environment-friendly initiatives such as rainwater-harvesting, solar water heaters for canteen applications and converting effluent, treatment plant (ETP) sludge into bricks. LG products come with energy certification and eco-friendly technology.

Punjab National Bank has initiated various environmental drives that include van mahotsav, tree plantation camps, pollution check-up camps, environment awareness camps, maintaining parks, etc. The list is exhaustive. Almost everybody is in the race. And to assist the competitors to take part in the race, there are likes of CoRE, CII's Environmental Management Division (EMD) and Concept Hospitality Ltd, amongst others.

Ford thought it had a better idea when it reoutfitted a factory with the world's largest living roof—essentially replacing a tar sheath with a carpet of plants. The proud automaker even touted its achievement by placing ads in publications such as National Geographic. But Ford is now the target of an aggressive campaign by a national coalition of environmentalist groups accusing the company of trying to advertise its way to a greener image. Ford's latest Green marketing effort—a "Fuel-Economy School" to teach motorists the art of efficient driving—yielded derisive laughter from the same environmentalists. *(CMO, 2005).*

British Petroleum had its own idea of a green makeover: The oil giant changed its logo to a Helios and began billing itself "Beyond Petroleum." Greenpeace honored the company with an Earth Day Oscar: Best Impression of an Environmentalist. And Wal-Mart promised to spend millions in the next decade to preserve an acre of wildlife habitat for every acre its buildings gobble up in India.

GE's Ecomagination campaign, launched in May 2005, spans a number of hot topics for a company with a desultory green record. It promises to improve emissions and efficiency in its operations, to work with green organizations and to issue annual progress reports. But the thrust of the initiative—and the focus of the advertising—are on GE's commitment to improving its technologies, which will help businesses meet environmental standards now and in the near future. Currently, GE is marketing 17 products, from aircraft engines to water treatment technologies, as part of its Ecomagination line.

McDonald's now publishes a "Corporate Responsibility Report" on its website detailing its environmental efforts. Bob Langert, director of environmental affairs (India), feels that kind of quiet marketing is the best strategy for McDonald's right now.

Philips India—Philips India's Pimpri unit was one of the first to discontinue use of Chloroflouro Carbons (cfc), in 1985. That was then. For the past six years, Philips has been focusing on a concept which it calls EcoDesign.

Tata Steel—We also make green steel, says the tagline. The 1.5-million trees that were planted over the past three years, as a run up to the company's millennium celebration, are beginning to bring the greenery back, and the closure of 2.2-million tones of old and environmentally unfriendly steel capacity in the past decade has made Tata Steel one of the greenest steelmakers in India. In fact, 10 per cent of the Rs. 7,000-crore spent on modernization have gone into environment-related equipment.

Toyota—Toyota's Prius may be the first major consumer product that fits nearly all of the criteria for success in the green-consumer marketplace: It comes from a trusted company and can be bought wherever the company's products are sold; it looks and feels like a "conventional" product and doesn't require consumers to change their habits to use; it is (almost) comparably priced to purchase and can save consumers money to operate; and it has added benefits—it both saves money and it's stylishly cool.

Current Green Trends

Green is the buzz of today. From magazines to newspapers to Television channels to blog everyone is today talking about environment. Researcher has tried to peep into the latest trends and exemplified some of them below:

Green Buildings

Green is in. The fate of real estate industry in the India is turned to be eco-friendly. India got its first green building in 2003—CII Godrej Business Centre, which is the greenest building in the world till date. Today there is no end to the green building undercurrent; everyone is turning green from ONGC to ITC to Airports to small eco-friendly home. A LEED certification for buildings in this direction is also catching up at fast pace. Registration at Indian Green Building Council of real estate is now approximately 110 million sq. ft. India is already acknowledge as environmental friendly construction leader in the world

Retail

If each customer who visited Wal-Mart in a week bought one long-lasting compact fluorescent light bulb, the company estimates, that would reduce electric bills by $3 billion, conserve 50 billion tons of coal, and keep one billion incandescent light bulbs out of landfills over the life of the bulb. (Company with 1.8 million employees)

Will that happen? In the brave new world of Wal-Mart, in which the company has recently pledged to green up its stores, its trucks, and some of its products, it could. And that could make Wal-Mart a force for good, or at least better, in the eyes of at least some of its critics. *(Fortune Magazine).* Pantaloons Retail Fresh green stores or Reliance Fresh outlets all are working on the same lines. Retail stores in India are turning quickly into an eco-friendly store and giving tough time to each other.

Electric Car/Two Wheeler

REVA is a battery electric vehicle designed for low speed, congested, urban conditions. REVA is designed to be unique and stands out on the road as a genuine city car with a mature expression. The advanced technologies used, make it highly differentiated and superior to other makes. It has all the inherent benefits of an Electric Car and is indeed a revelation in city mobility.

E Scooters and E Bikes are coming in India now. The study revealed that Indians are quite keen on accepting the electric vehicle concept. The E-Bike got an overall positive reaction from 62 per cent respondents, while 88 per cent wanted to go for the E-Bike Plus, 65 per cent for E-Scooters and 79 per cent for high speed E-Scooters. Acceptance of the E-Bike concept received encouraging response from teenagers, commuting adults and women, the survey pointed out.

As for purchase intention, around 30 per cent were willing to purchase an E-Bike among the teenagers as well as the commuting adults. For E-Bike Plus, women gave the maximum positive response, with over 80 per cent indicating their interest in the product and 25 per cent intending to buy the product.

Green Power

It is becoming big business. While electricity systems around the world continue to be dominated by large stations powered by either fossil-fuel, uranium (nuclear) or water (hydro), consumers are nevertheless buying more and more electricity that has been generated by alternative means. Interest in such 'green power' — which often uses renewable resources like the sun, the wind, running water or biomass to generate electricity—has been encouraged by two recent developments. The first is increasing public uneasiness about the environmental impacts of these conventional methods of generating electricity. In particular, there has been growing public concern about the atmospheric consequences of operating coal-fired power stations specifically, worsening local smog problems and accelerated global warming. Air quality issues are thus helping to stimulate peoples' interest in less polluting means of generating electricity.

The second development is the restructuring of the electricity supply industry in many jurisdictions around the world. With the introduction of competition, systems traditionally characterized by public and/or private monopolies generating, transmitting and distributing electricity are being radically transformed. With this comes increased consumer choice in electricity provision. For the residential customer, it is no longer simply a question of 'how much electricity to use?', but also 'how do I want that electricity generated?' Consequently, individuals now have the ability to demand and subsequently purchase 'green power'. Together, environmental concern and electricity industry restructuring are enabling the development of new green power products and the emergence of a green power industry.

Ecotourism

For the past 20 years or so, the reality of ecotourism has largely failed tò meet its promise. The notion that tourism could not only have a lighter footprint but also promote social and environmental good seems to have been lost amid the vast hodgepodge of what passes as "ecotourism" these days: five-star spas, jeep safaris, posh eco-lodges, "sustainable development tours," and all the rest. From different parts of India are calling to see how they can get in on the action—how to grow their lifestyle without destroying it.

Space sharing/Car Pooling

Space Share builds carpooling and other green logistics tools for festivals and conferences, underwritten by sponsors. They'll be helping make events green across the country. Sponsoring the carpool system at an event is an opportunity for green companies to put their values and products in front of tens of thousands of consumers. It's an example of the new economy they aim to create: environmental services funded by environmental marketing, the festival are greener at very little cost and the sponsor gets a more than fair ROI for their advertising dollar, no charity anywhere in the loop.

CONCLUSION

Today big names were not discussing information technology or shareholder value. They were there for meeting and conference to discuss a subject that has raced up the corporate agenda: *Green.*

In today's hypercompetitive markets, companies struggle to establish and maintain a competitive advantage. Given that consumer expectations are evolving, many of these companies are turning to green to differentiate their offerings by being greener than their competitors. As the basis of competition shifts to the green space, companies seem to be continually upping the ante by trying to outdo each other for being the greenest company in the category. Industry leaders such as Wal-Mart and Tesco, and Dell and HP—already engaged in intense battles for consumer hearts, minds and share of wallet—are playing tit for tat when it comes to green.

Green is in fashion and fashion become fad in some time. Companies want to show everything green to consumers, but the reality may be different. This trend can soon become a slipper slope. "If too many people start marketing themselves as green without proof points, it can appear disingenuous."

Green washing is the term to define this scenario. As consumers become more sensitive to environmental issues, green is becoming a bestseller. Many companies started taking advantage of the same. Companies like ITC selling eco-friendly paper while cutting trees, and telling world we are growing 10 saplings, but irony is it will take 10 years to grow. Coca-Cola in India is clearly attempting to create its green image, which is, clearly not, as their practice shows it. The long list of companies trying to sell their themselves and their products on green plank included companies such as BP, Ford Motor Company (Ford), General Electrics Company, and Wal-Mart. .

With ever increasing scientific understanding of how the Earth works, a general movement toward safer, less polluting and more environmentally sustainable practices is inevitable. Marketers that take the time now to court the deepest green consumers with truly innovative solutions to environmental concerns will be the ones who reap the biggest future opportunities.

It isn't that easy being green, but today there are more environment friendly small and large options available than ever before. In today's scenario green can truly be accepted as new business colour. This is not a fad, this is not a gimmick. This is here to stay.

There is a belief that going green is expensive; to begin with, maybe so. However, with time and thought, it has been found to be 'profitable' since it calls for waste elimination and optimum resource utilization. Apart from the supply, focus on demand side management for reducing consumption is essential. Three simple words can guide the thinking and actions of India Inc's journey towards sustainable development—Reduce, Reuse, Recycle.

Researcher see, not so far in the future, a new chapter in the business world, where increasing competitive pressures will compel it to change its ways from being a producer to also being a protector; and seek a dynamic balance between what it takes and what it gives back to the ecology. Profit will not only be a set of figures but of values with social responsibility. Researcher is aware the journey won't be a cake walk with easy decisions, but we owe this much to our future generations.

References

Aaker, D.A. (1996), Building Strong Brands, The Free Press, New York, NY.

Anderson, T. Jr and Cunningham, W.H. (1972), "The socially conscious consumer", *Journal of Marketing,* Vol. 36, No. 7, pp. 22-31.

Balderjahn, I. (1988), "Personality variables and environmental attitudes as predictors of ecologically responsible consumption patterns", *Journal of Business Research,* Vol. 17, pp. 51-6.

Belz, F.M. (1999), "Eco-Marketing 2005: Performance Sales Instead of Product Sales," in *Greener Marketing: A Global Perspective on Greening Marketing Practice,* Charter, M. and M.J. Polonsky, Eds. 2nd ed. Sheffield: Greenleaf Publishing.

Bennett, M., and James, P., (1992), ed. *"The Green Bottom line",* Sheffield: Greenleaf Publishing Ltd.

Bettman, J.R. and M.F. Luce (1998), "Constructive Consumer Choice Processes," *Journal of Consumer Research,* 25 (3), 187-217.

Gifford, B. (1991), "The Greening of the Golden Arches- McDonald's Teams with Environmental Group to Cut Waste," *San Diego lhiorz,* August 19, p. Cl.

Carter, C.R., Kale, R. and Grimn, C.M. (2000), "Environmental purchasing and firm performance: an empirical investigation", *Transportation Research,* Part E, Vol. 36, pp. 219-88.

Chase, D., and Smith, T. (1992), "Consumer's keen on green but marketers don't deliver", *Advertising Age,* Vol. 63 (June 29), pp. 2-4.

Hartman, C.L. and E.R. Stafford, (1997), "Green Alliances: Building New Business with Environmental Groups," *Long Range Planning,* April, pp. 184-96.

CMO, "The thin Green Line," December, 2005.

Coddington, W. (1993), *Environmental Marketing,* McGraw-Hill, New York, NY.

Connolly, J., McDonagh, P., Polonsky, M. and Porthero, A (2004). " Green Marketing and Green Consumers: Exploring the Myth's in D. Annandale, Marinova (eds.) *International Handbook on Environmental Technology Management,* Edward Elgar, Cheltenham, UK.

Crane, (2000), "Facing the Backlash: Green Marketing and Strategic Reorientation in the 1990's," *Journal of Strategic Marketing,* September, pp. 227-96.

Dagnoli, J. (1991), "Consciously green", *Advertising Age,* September, p. 14.

Cottam, D. (1994), "A Green Policy Committed to Print: Kyocerd's Cartridge-Free Laser Printer." *Greener Management International,* January, pp. 61-66.

Ellen, P.S. (1994), "Do We Know What We Need to Know? Objective and Subjective

Knowledge Effects on Pro-Ecological Behaviors," *Journal of Business Research*, 30, 43-52.

E.R. Stafford and C.L. Hartman, (1996), "Green Alliances: Strategic Relations between Businesses and Environmental Groups," *Business Horizons*, March-April, pp. 50-59.

Fitzgerald, Kate (1993), "It's Green, It's Friendly, It's Wal-Mart", "Eco-Store", *Advertising Age*, Vol. 1, (June 7), p. 44.

Gabor, A. and C.W.J. Granger (1961), "On the Price Consciousness of Consumers," in *Applied Statistics* Vol. 10.

"Green Cleaners." *CHOICE*, September 1990. pp. 10-14.

Hermann, S. (1992), "Pricing Opportunities—and How to Exploit Them," *Sloan Management Review*, 33 (2), 55-.

Davis, J.J. (1994), "Consumer Responses to Corporate Environmental Advertising", *Journal of Consumer Marketing, 17, 2* (1994): 25-37.

Lawrence, J. "Mobil. (1991)," *Advertising Age*. January 29, pp. 12-13.

Kapelianis, D. and S. Strachan (1996), "The Price Premium of an Environmentally Friendly Product," *South African Journal of Business Management*, 27 (4), 89-96.

Kassarjian, H.H. (1971), "Incorporating ecology into marketing strategy: the case of air pollution", *Journal of Marketing*, Vol. 35, July, pp. 61-5.

Kinnear, T.C., Taylor, J.R. and Ahmed, S.A. (1974), "Ecologically concerned consumers: who are they?" *Journal of Marketing*, Vol. 38, April, pp. 20-4.

Peattie, K. (1999a), "*Rethinking Marketing: Shifting to a Greener Paradigm*," in M. Charter and M.J. Polonsky (eds.).

Laroche, M., Bergeron, J. and Barbaro-Forleo, G. (2001), "Targeting consumers who are willing to pay more for environmentally friendly products", *Journal of Consumer Marketing*, Vol. 18, No. 6, pp. 503-20.

Carlson, L. S.J. Grove, R.N. Laczniak, and N. Kangun, (1996), "Does Environmental Advertising Reflect Integrated Marketing Communications? An Empirical Investigation," *Journal of Busine.ss Research*. November, pp. 225-32.

Segall, L. (1995), "Marketing Compost as a Pest Control Product," *Biocycle, 36, 51: 65-67.*

Marketing Research Report, (2005) "Green Consumerism," JWT, India

Drumwright, M.E. (1994), "Socially Responsible Organizational Buying: Environmental Concern as a Noneconomic Buying Criterion", *Journal of Marketing*, July, pp. 1-19.

Schuhwerk, M.E. and R. Lefkoff-Hagius, (1995), "Green or Non-Green? Does Type of Appeal Matter When Advertising a Green Product?" *Journal of Advertising*, Summer, pp. 45-54.

Murthi, B.P.S. and K. Srinivasan (1999), "Consumers' Extent of Evaluation in Brand Choice," *Journal of Business*, 72 (2), 229-56.

Osterhus, T.L. (1997), "Pro-Social Consumer Influence Strategies: When and How Do They Work?," *Journal of Marketing*, 61 (4), 16-29.

Ottman, J.A. (1992), "Sometimes Consumers Will Pay More to Go Green," in *Marketing News*, Vol. 26.

—— (1993), *Green Marketing: Challenges and Opportunities for the New Marketing Age*. Lincolnwood, IL: NTC Business Press.

Tom, P.A. (1999) "From Dirt to Dollars," *Waste Age*, August , pp. 54-62.

Peattie, K., (1992), *Green Marketing*, The M and E Handbook Series, Longman, London, 1992.

Peattie, K. (1995), *Environmental Marketing Management: Meeting the Green Challenge*. London: Pitman.

Porter, (1995b), "Toward a New Conception of the Environment-Competitiveness Relationship," *Journal of Economic Perspectives*, 9 (4), 97-118.

Reinhardt, F.L. (1998), "Environmental Product Differentiation: Implications for Corporate Strategy," *California Management Review*, 40 (4), 43-73.

Roozen, I.T.M. and P. De Pelsmacker (1998), "Attributes of Environmentally-Friendly Consumer Behavior," *Journal of International Consumer Marketing*, 10 (3), 21-41.

Roy, (1991), "Designing and Marketing Greener Products," in M. Charter and M.J. Polonsky (eds.), *Greener Marketing: A Global Perspective to Greening Marketing Practice*, 2nd ed., Sheffield, UK: Greenleaf Publishing, pp. 126-42.

Scerbinski, J (1991), "Consumers and the Environment: A focus on five products", *The Journal of Business Strategy* (September/October), pp. 44-47.

Simon, F.L. (1992), "Marketing Green Products in the Triad," *The Columbia Journal of World Business*, 27 (3-4), 268-85.

Simon, H. and R.J. Dolan (1998), "Price Customization," *Marketing Management*, 7 (3), 10-17.

Straughan, R.D. and Roberts, J.A. (1999), "Environmental segmentation alternatives: a look at green consumer behavior in the new millennium", *Journal of Consumer Marketing*, Vol. 16, No. 6, pp. 558-75

Willenborg, J.F. and R.E. Pitts (1977), "Perceived Situational Effects on Price Sensitivity," *Journal of Business Research*, 5 (1), 27.

Kilburne, W. (1998), "Green Marketing: A Theoretical Perspective", *Journal of Marketing Management*, 14, 6 (1998): 657-677.

Zaklad, A., McKnight, R., Kosansky, A. and Piermarini, J. (2004), "The social side of the supply chain: align three factors, and hitting the jackpot is a sure bet", *Industrial Engineer*, Vol. 36 No. 2, pp. 40-4.

B. Zhang, 1996, "Green Barriers—A New Trend of International Trade Protectionism", *World Economy*, 12:21 (in Chinese with English abstract).

CHAPTER

7

SUSTAINABLE MANAGEMENT OF NATURAL RESOURCES FOR FASTER AND MORE INCLUSIVE GROWTH

S.P. VASUDEVA

ABSTRACT

One of the prerequisites for moving towards sustainable mode of development leading to healthy environment is the management and conservation of natural resources. Conservation is defined as management of human use of the natural resources in the biosphere so that they may yield the greatest sustainable benefits to the present generation while maintaining the potential to meet the needs and aspirations of the future generations.

Sustainable Development is a multi-dimentional concept with three interacting angles for natural resource management—ecological security, economic efficiency and social equity. Sustainable development does not end with the sustainability of just the environmental and resource system but also requires the sustainability of economic and social system. Economic growth can be attained if poverty, which is the major cause of natural resource degradation, is addressed.

While conservation of natural resources figure as top priority on the agenda of the environmentalists, ways of building upon the economic potential linked to infrastructural development, introduction of advanced technology and increased cash flow through market economy with the sustainable use of natural resources is the primary concern of the Government which has to satisfy the needs and aspirations of the people it governs.

Air and Water are renewable while Flora, Fauna and Land are the non-renewable resources. The management of the later resources accordingly, requires greater caution, although all the five resources are required to be integrated for their sustainable use.

The need of the day accordingly is to integrate the management and development of Natural Resources towards sustainability. The potential of the animal resource has also to be utilised. The improvement in living conditions of the people and the general socio-economic environment is the other requirement, along with transport, storage, marketing and processing of natural resources products.

The approach of Integrated Management of these natural resources has to see that water available in the watershed can fulfil the human needs of drinking water, irrigation, and industrial (consumptive uses); generation of hydro-electricity and running of small mills (non-consumptive use).

In adopting this approach of Integrated Management of Natural Resources at the Watershed level it can be seen that conservation creates congenial, edaphic, hydrological and environmental conditions to enhance biological activity comprising vegetative and zoological production systems—Bio-diversity.

Strategically, efficient management of production systems require carefully planned input supply system largely based on locally available resources and technology. In watershed areas, with improved status of resources, better investments and better management practices could be possible. With these developments community may prefer to invest in resources with better quality inputs and improved breed of animals with high production potential changing ecological and economic status, and also gradually changing their attitude and capacity for investments in production.

Sustainable Management is effected by the involvement and participation of the stakeholders with the public managers shifting their role from control of management of these natural resources to facilitation through the participation of the local people. The overall impact will be sustainability of natural resources, their products leading to their conservation and equitable social and economic returns.

INTRODUCTION

Earth is the only place in the universe to be known to sustain life, however the human activities are progressively reducing its life support capacity. Over the past few decades, indiscriminate deforestation, mineral exploitation, industrialisation and urbanisation, all modes of development based on natural resources has led to unsustainable and unhealthy environment. One of the prerequisites for moving towards sustainable mode of development leading to healthy environment is the management and conservation of natural resources. ***Conservation is defined as management of human use of the natural resources in the biosphere so that they may yield the greatest sustainable benefits to the present generation while maintaining the potential to meet the needs and aspirations of the future generations*** (World Conservation Strategy, 1980).

There are five basic natural resources on earth—**Air, Water, Land, Flora and Fauna** (the rest of the natural resources have their origin from these basic resources). These resources are inter-related, inter-connected and inter-dependent with disturbance in the use and management of any one affects the other four resources. **Solar energy** another natural resource plays important synergistic and other roles but comes from a source outside the Earth—**Sun**. There is another part of the environment, made up of **metererological factors**, such as rainfall, temperature, humidity and wind speed. These meteorological factors also have varied roles to play on these natural resources.

Human beings, animals and plants were living in perfect balance and harmony in the past with each other along with their dependence on land, water and air. However, this balance began to deteriorate with the increasing population, urbanisation and man's greed for comforts at the expense of nature. As the global economy expands, local ecosystems are collapsing at an accelerating pace. With this several well established trends are shaping the future of civilisation like population growth, polluting rivers, falling water tables, shrinking cropland, collapsing fisheries, shrinking forests and loss of biodiversity all leading to decrease in per unit consumption of these resources. This has lead to raising temperature due to increase in level of carbon-di-oxide in the atmosphere causing the much alarming process of **climate change**. History is full of examples indicating as to how mismanagement and subsequent deterioration of the natural resource base has led to **poverty, conflict and hunger**. Although, it is quite late but realisation has come that the use of natural resources should be such so as not to disturb the ecological balance and to sustain their use not only for the present but for future generations as well. Such an approach brings into play the concept of sustainable management of natural resources.

Sustainable Development is a multi-dimensional concept with three interacting angles for natural resource management—**ecological security, economic efficiency** and **social equity**. Sustainable development does not end with the sustainability of just the environmental and resource system but also requires the sustainability of economic and social system. Economic growth can be attained if poverty, which is the major cause of natural resource degradation, is addressed. But distribution of growth must undergo a change and it must become less wasteful of natural resources not only between the rich and the poor countries but also between rich and poor in the same country. Sustainable development further is the result of political order in which a society is so structured that it learns fast from its mistake in the use of natural resources and rapidly rectifies its human nature relationship in accordance with the knowledge it has gained. The growth obtained through such an approach can be termed as "Inclusive" as envisaged in the 11th Plan document of the Planning Commission of India and needs to be adopted for achievements of the objectives and targets indicated therein. In 1992, United Nations Conference on Environment and Development (UNCED) popularly known as Earth Summit took place at Rio-di-jenario in which 178 countries including India participated. An important outcome of this conference was Agenda 21 a programme of action for moving towards sustainable development and management of natural resources. Agenda 21 also contemplate that without economics, ethics and equity, environment and ecology will be causality.

THE PROBLEM

The population of India was about 400 million in 1950, which has crossed 1 billion mark in 2001 and at present is around 1.20 billion. The quantity of water and air is same, however their quality has deteriorated because of mismanagement, inappropriate development and increase in pressure on them. The amount of flora and fauna has decreased to an appreciable extent, due to their exploitation for human use and pleasure. The land has been disintegrated into small-holdings, leading to decrease in its productive potential. The land is also being put to use it is not meant for as per its capability, eroded due to least preferred technologies, ultimately reducing its capacity to give appropriate returns. On the whole the total environment has been degraded and made qualitatively and quantitatively poor for the present and future generations. This is against the concept of Conservation of Natural Resources as defined by the World Conservation Strategy 1980.

While conservation of natural resources figure as top priority on the agenda of the environmentalists, ways of building upon the economic potential linked to infrastructural development, introduction of advanced technology and increased cash flow through market economy with the sustainable use of natural resources is the primary concern of the government which has to satisfy the needs and aspirations of the people it governs. Sometimes conflicts have also arisen on the question of use of Natural Resources between the people and the government. How the people-government conflicts could be turned to people government complementary or joint efforts to achieve wider and intangible ecological goals of development without hampering the immediate, localised and tangible economic needs and aspiration of rural masses is a question that needs immediate attention. Resolving this question necessitates inclusion of human and economic resources in the ambit of natural resource management and a shift in emphasis from sector-oriented administration to Integrated Management of these resources leading to their sustainable development and utilisation.

However, to achieve such a long-term sustainability, efforts are required to build up **collective strength**, **appropriate leadership** and **motivation of stakeholders** to redeem health of natural resources as this will result into equitable and sustainable resource use. Fortunately, India is not poor resource-wise. It still has a rich and productive natural resource base proper management of which can remove the abysmal poverty. The need of the hour is to ensure equity issues in programme intervention along with benefit and economic distribution of natural resource management.

The programme intervention ensures **equitable growth** opportunities through **spatial distribution**, local management and prioritising the poor. The benefit distribution considers **leadership roles**, **gender issues** and **people's involvement** and **motivation** in the programme formulation and implementation. The economic issues focus on **increased cash flow** leading to **improved sustainable income** to all the stakeholders.

Air and **Water** are ***renewable*** while **Flora, Fauna** and **Land** are the ***non-renewable*** resources. The management of the later resources accordingly, requires greater caution, although all the five resources are required to be integrated for their sustainable use. The integrated management and development of these natural resources at the level of a watershed or river basin is required in the absence of any statute for integrated conservation and preservation of these natural resources in India. This will lead to a healthy life of all living beings, sustaining cash flow and employment generation, so essential for faster and Inclusive Growth of India.

STRATEGY FOR INTEGRATED AND SUSTAINABLE MANAGEMENT OF NATURAL RESOURCES

India is a rural centred country with 70% of the population concentrated in the rural areas. About 50% of this rural population is engulfed with the menace of poverty. Lack of gainful employment, low land productivity, social inequality and inefficient use of available Natural Resources are the factors contributing to this rural poverty. The potential of Natural Resources in India is such that if used appropriately, optimally, scientifically and sustainably, it can be one of the strongest economies of the world. However, the ever-increasing human and cattle population has been exerting pressure on natural resources for the requirement of food, fibre, fuel, fodder, timber and other industrial products. In the process improper use and over-exploitation of these resources has led to disappearance of forests at many places, degradation of pastures and arable land, spread of deserts, soil erosion and has also led to dwindling water resources and growth of population on the fragile ecological zones. This has consequently affected air and water quality.

The need of the day accordingly is to integrate the management and development of Natural Resources towards sustainability. This can be achieved if the plan of action takes into account all lands along with their potential capabilities for development and reclamation, their possible contribution to food, fuel, fodder, timber production and non-timber forest produce (NTFP). It also has to encompass hydrology, drinking water needs, irrigation water supply, susceptibility to floods, drought and other natural hazards such as erosion and siltation. The potential of the animal resource has also to be utilised. The improvement in living conditions of the people and the general socio-economic environment is the other requirement, along with transport, storage, marketing and processing of natural resources products. Most of these factors are related to nature of the drainage basin or a watershed and the extent to which improvement activities are coordinated within its boundaries meaning thereby that this watershed approach has to be multi-disciplinary. ***Watershed has been accepted as a scientific unit of area development the world over. It is based on the three-fold objective of productivity, sustainability and equity. It may also be emphasised here that the proposition of watershed development is not aimed exclusively at benefiting the people or human beings, it is rather an approach to set an agreeable and sustainable relationship between man and nature.*** The methodology of Integrated Natural Resource Management is that of systems science, a system that embraces the interaction of humans, individually and institutionally with their natural resources. *The long-term strategy of the model of watershed management is oriented to increasing or maintaining the adaptive capacity of natural resources to produce material goods such as food, fibre, fuel wood, timber, fish, etc. including their value addition wherever required and services such as clean air and fresh water not only for the present generation but for future generations also* (Figure 1).

Watershed management in India in the past has mostly encompassed on soil and water conservation and less on development potential of land as a whole, including flora and fauna through the optimal utilisation of water. The impact of development of these four Natural Resources on air quality has almost been ignored. Therefore, there is need for shift in watershed development towards technologies for optimal and integrated management and development of land, water, and plant and animal resources in such a way so as to keep healthier air quality. ***This integrated management of Natural Resources based on watershed model will not only be able to meet the social, economic and cultural needs of the people but through appropriate management can lead to paradigm shift from the existing vicious cycle of scarcity to virtuous cycle of sustainability.***

Sustainable development is a process in which the exploitation of the resources, the direction of investment, the orientation of technological development, the institutional changes are all made consistent with future as well as present needs. The premises of sustainable development are that symbiotic relationship between consumer human race and producer natural systems along with compatibility between ecology and economy. The present day environmental problems are not so much due to the lack of government thrust as to the direction of its efforts resulting in legalistic, sectoral, media-specific, repair-oriented environmental planning and management that overlook the interactive nature of our common environmental and developmental concerns. The agenda for change therefore relates to the restructuring of economy based on ecological principles.

Sustainable development accompanied by environmental conservation is the only effective remedy for halting the growing hordes of environmental refuge. However, much of the development these days is not sustainable. It is based on the squandering of our biological capital viz. soil, forests, animals, plant species and air. The problem is quite complex and there is no single solution. If our environment is to be saved from further degradation there is an urgent need to remove the lacunae in the implementation of environmental protection laws, otherwise the vast majority of people both in the urban and rural areas will continue to pay the price for the misdeeds of a recalcitrant few.

FIGURE I

Integrated Natural Resource Management Model of a Watershed.

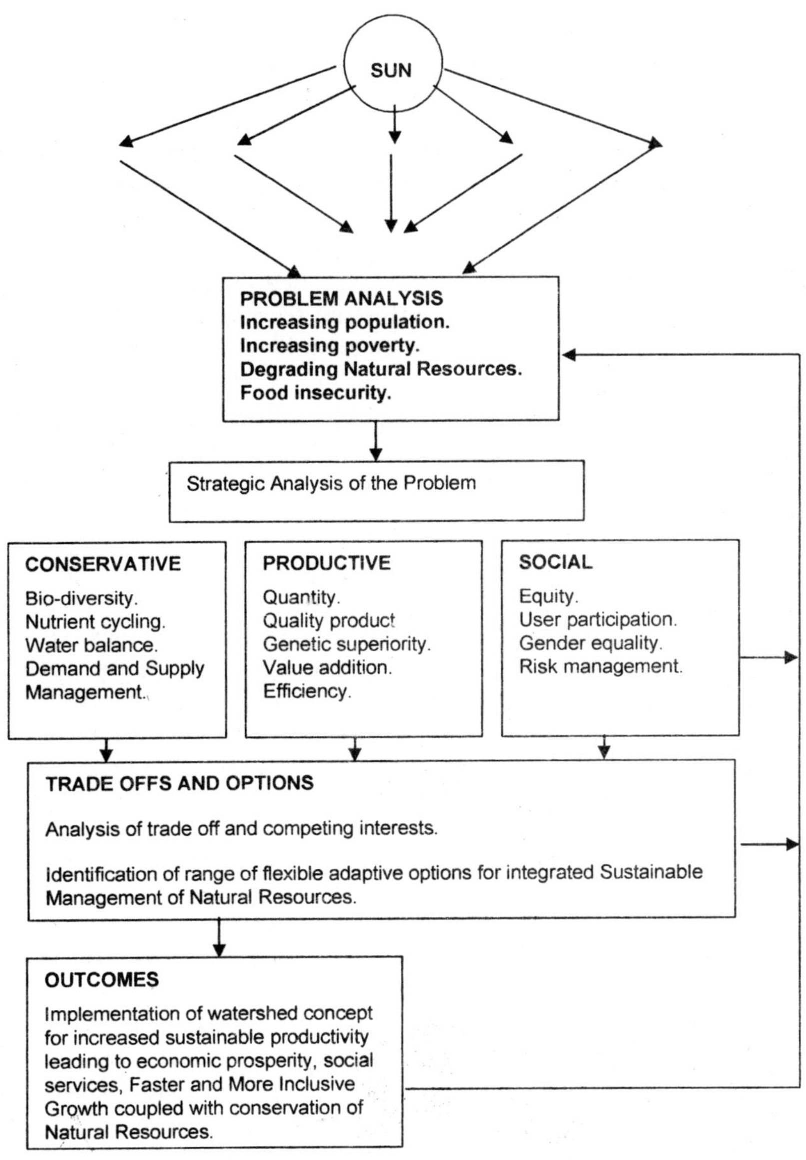

Accordingly, Sustainable Development is generally taken to mean improving the quality of human life within the carrying capacity of supporting eco-systems. Sustainable development is based on maintaining the fragile balance between productivity function and conservation practices through monitoring and identifying the status of natural resources. Agenda-21 of the Rio summit is an action programme aimed at making development socially, economically and environmentally sustainable. The Agenda suggests programmes to achieve a sustainable balance between consumption, people and life sustaining capacity of Earth. Agenda-21 model of development contemplates integration of economic development based on social justice leading to environmental conservation. ***The watershed management approach easily fits into this model which can make the growth of this country faster and more inclusive.***

PARADIGM SHIFT TO INTEGRATED AND SUSTAINABLE MANAGEMENT OF NATURAL RESOURCES

The approach of Integrated Management of these natural resources has to see that **water** available in the watershed can fulfil the human needs of drinking water, irrigation, and industrial (consumptive uses); generation of hydro-electricity and running of small mills (non-consumptive use). If water is in short supply in the watershed then the essential needs of drinking water and then irrigation has to be fulfilled first with other uses resorted only when water can be made available on sustainable basis by conservation efforts or from some other outside source. This means that industries requiring water may only be set-up if they can be supplied with ensured supply of water after meeting the drinking and irrigation water needs. Similarly, irrigation resorted to only when the primary needs of drinking water can be fulfilled. However, generation of hydro-electricity can be resorted to whenever and wherever, possible and feasible, as it is dependent on non-consumptive use of water, which can be put to any other use after generation of electricity Accordingly, utilisation of water for drinking, irrigation and industrial needs must be kept as a part of any hydro-electric project. The ways and means should also be developed by ensuring that water disposed after utilisation does not contain pollutants and if it does it should be treated before discharge. This way water can be utilised for human and animal health, clean environment, increasing land productivity, and capital and cash flow through generation of electricity and setting up of industries based on electricity.

The capability of **land** available in the watershed should be assessed and it be put to use that will give the most productive returns. If the land cannot be irrigated through any means then the best possible varieties of food crops that can give highest productive returns in the rainfed conditions cultivated. Where the land can be irrigated cash crops in addition to high production varieties of food crops raised. The slopes of hillocks may be seen before taking up cultivation on it. If the slope of land is more than 45° agro-forestry or horticulture or both practised along with grasses and legumes for best economic returns and preventing soil erosion which will be a resultant factor if agriculture is practised on such steep slopes. If the land is suitable for pastures and grasslands best possible grass cultivation practised rather than these lands put to any other landuse which in many instances had negative impact on the environment. Social and farm forestry for cultivating appropriate trees with agriculture will help in not only supplementing the income of the land owner but also ensuring the protection of land from various types of erosion. Consolidation of land-holdings also must be carried out, so that a minimum appropriate land is cultivated as a unit to give best productive returns. Landuse Policy is drafted and implemented based on these principles it will give long-term sustainable returns to the people who own these land resources.

Forest as a resource, gives tangible and non-tangible benefits. Non-tangible in the form of fresh air, pure water and mitigating the climate change and tangible in the form of timber, fuel wood, fodder, etc. This brings into play the management of both the types of benefits in a sustainable way so that it gives both social and economic returns. Government of India has banned the felling of trees above 1000 meters for any commercial purpose and has decided to use this resource for environmental stability only, which is non-tangible. If this resource is silviculturally and scientifically exploited (when the tree have attained the age and girth of exploitation) and by felling of these trees minimum amount or no silt is generated, followed by artificial or natural regeneration when the forest area felled can again perform its functions, and the trees felled able to generate capital required for the development. However, felling may not be resorted to in areas where the slope is more than 45° or which is difficult to be regenerated after felling. Such forest areas can be kept in the protection working circle (where felling of trees will not be resorted to) so that they perform ecological and environmental functions only. This way of treatment of the forest area will generate employment, raise capital for the state and so also perform its social and environmental functions. Forestry is a science, which is based on sustainability, and hence this cycle of utilisation of forest resources can be repeated again and again for the benefit of people at large but with this assurance that fresh air and water is generated in the watershed, land protected from erosion and other disasters along with improvement in land productivity. It also has to be ensured that forest area may be kept to such a level that they can absorb CO_2 produced, to prevent the green house effect at the local and global level and with that producing oxygen for the human/animal population. Forests should also be preserved to the level that they give refuge to wild animals and plants—Bio-diversity, so as to conserve the gene pool required in our future breeding programmes and to preserve the environmental balance through the food chain management. Some of the forest resources such as NTFP including medicinal plants and mushrooms have got potential as raw material for giving employment to the local people and generating cash by setting up small-scale industries. However, it has to be ensured that economic benefits from the forests through value addition or selling raw products are made good of only after the social functions of supplying fresh water, clean air, environmental stability and needs of the local people are taken care of. The application of such a role of management of forests can be ensured through preparation of working plans along with the management plans for Forest Management based on these principles.

Animal or faunal resource includes wildlife, fish and domestic animals. Wildlife also generates both tangible and non-tangible benefits. Non-tangible benefits in the maintenance of the food chain by keeping the ecological balance and tangible benefits in the form of generating capital through eco-tourism and recreational activity. However, it has to be seen that the number of wild animals are kept within the carrying capacity of the watershed lest it creates problems such as animal human conflict if this balance is disturbed. Domestic animals are also a resource, which helps, in generating cash through sale of meat, milk, wool and other products. However, the population of stray cattle which are non-productive is increasing and have to be kept under control within the carrying capacity of the pastures and grasslands or total fodder produced in the watershed so that they may not degrade the Natural Resources and their productive potential. However, the production potential of domestic and wild animals is dependent on the sustainable production of fodder in the pastures, grasslands and the maintance of forest eco-systems along with the availability of water, through their integrated management, which has to be ensured. Fish cultivation has high potential in the Watershed due to availability of water and by erection of small dams at different places. The rivers and stream in the watershed also abunded with fish. The feasibility of blue revolution in the watershed can help in employment generation, through selling of raw fish locally and exporting it to the plains besides by setting up small-scale industries on fish-based products such as fish food and pickle. Management of fish in this way will also ensure the cleanliness of water resources, due to local people being involved in this venture.

In adopting this approach of Integrated Management of Natural Resources at the Watershed level it can be seen that conservation creates congenial, edaphic, hydrological and environmental conditions to enhance biological activity comprising vegetative and zoological production systems—Bio-diversity. Agriculture being a prime production system has a complementary relationship with livestock and forestry including horticulture. The production potential of these resources depend on the land capability and availability of water. A careful study of the extent and quality of relationship between these resources before and after conservation of each of these would be helpful in fostering complementarily between them and reduction in costs of production. Besides, several other small-scale complementary production systems such as sericulture, apiculture, pisiculture, mushroom, meat, milk and NTFP having a complementary relationship with the major production systems can also be

FIGURE 2

Integration of Conservation with Production Inputs, Natural Resource-based Enterprise and Marketing

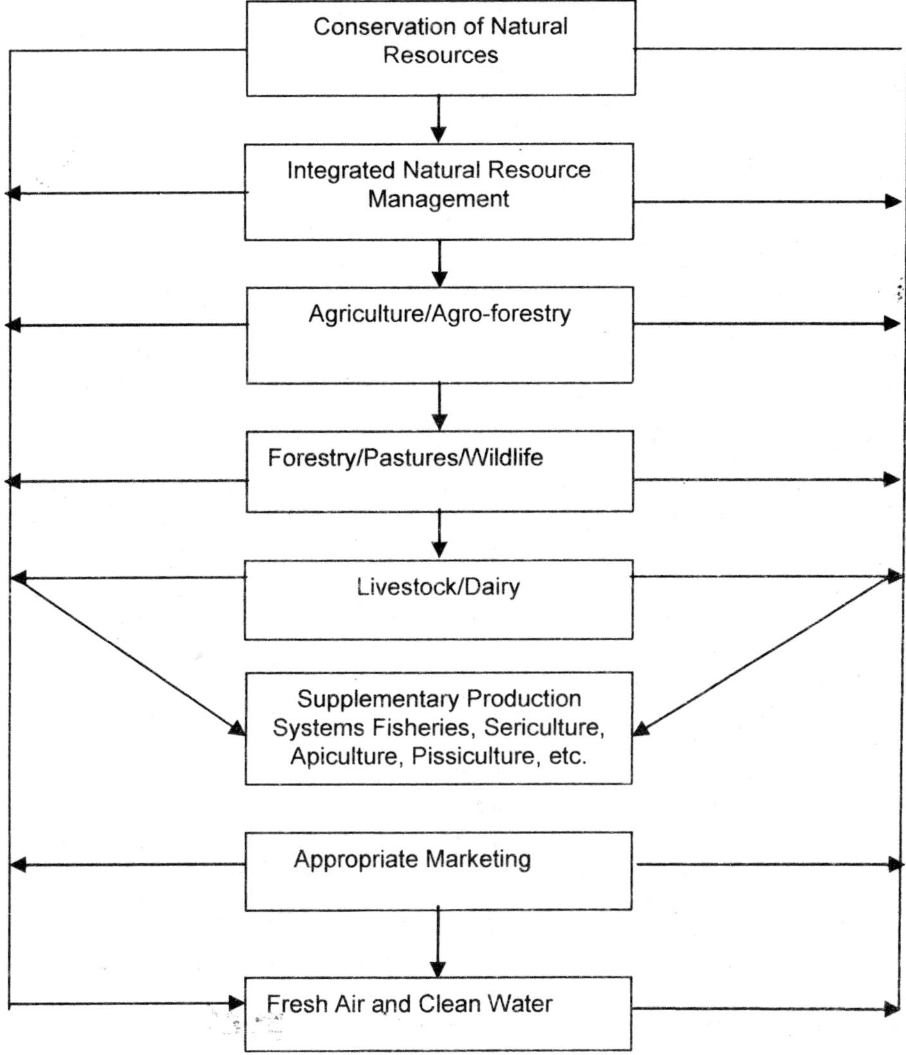

developed for generating required cash flow through marketing of these products and creating employment potential (Figure 2). The Integrated Development and Management of these Natural Resources can also improve their output and techno-economics significantly by covering the vast majority of the country's population in the rural areas thus taking the country on the path of Faster and Inclusive Growth.

DISCUSSION AND CONCLUSION

Strategically-efficient management of production systems require carefully planned input supply system largely based on locally available resources and technology. In watershed areas, with improved status of resources, better investments and better management practices could be possible. With these developments community may prefer to invest in resources with better quality inputs and improved breed of animals with high production potential changing ecological and economic status, and also gradually changing their attitude and capacity for investments in production. Use of better fuels such as LPG and electricity coupled with fuel saving devices such as solar cookers, solar heating systems, fuel efficient chullahs, etc. will help in the reduction of pressure on the Natural Resources on the one hand and improving the environmental management on the other halting the process of climate change. This will result in generation of better air and water quality. These changes justify an integrated input supply system in a phased manner and managed by organisations of resource users with their efforts being facilitated by the government. In order to encourage investments in conservation and production, producers in watershed areas must be provided with reliable credit facility wherever required. These credit facilities should not only be provided for improved production capacity of the resources but also for their value addition and marketing.

Regeneration of resources, alongwith strategies for implementation of production systems and availability of credit in area, which has been plagued with low productivity and poverty, could prove to be sterile unless attitude and capacity of the people who deal with new ecological and economic environment is developed in dealing with Integrated Management of Natural Resources. Training people to add value to a variety of raw materials being produced under different production systems from resources of different categories of ownership is important for the development of community in the watershed. However, scales of operation, quality control and resource users organisation capable of dealing with a large range of products of different shelf life and utility are not an easy task. It requires infrastructure, funds and support of professionals to increase demand of the products in the market which has to be provided. The training programmes will have to be structured and conducted in an integrated manner by an organisation sensitive to their needs. In the present age of information technology, multimedia system and internet can be extremely helpful for training and building upon the capacity of the people of both sexes and varying level of education in various aspects of conservation, production, value addition, etc. ***Empowering resource poor and resource less with useful information is extremely important for including sidetracked people into the main socio-economic stream, which is so necessarily required for achieving Faster and More Inclusive Growth in country like India.***

This Paradigm shift consisting of short, mid and long-term strategies will lead to change from the vicious cycle consisting of inappropriate governance without strategic focus, dealt with by Managers lacking skills leading to mis-management of Natural Resources to the virtuous cycle where the Management of Natural Resources is integrated and sustained through their inter-dependence and inter-relatedness to each other and to the overall production system followed by monitoring for improvement jointly by the community and Public sector managers. The Management and Development of these resources in the virtuous cycle will also lead to their sustainable utilisation through their marketing in raw form and or by setting up of small-scale industries. The virtuous cycle, besides leading to environmental stability will also result into improved cash flow and generation of employment leading to overall social and economic upliftment of the people. Sustainable Management is effected by the involvement and participation of the stakeholders with the public managers shifting their role from control of management of these natural resources to facilitation through the participation of the local people. The overall impact will be sustainability of natural resources, their products leading to their conservation and equitable social and economic returns. The problem of climate change which has arisen due to mis-management of these natural resources will also be tackled through such a mechanism of operation. Such an approach of social equity, economic efficiency and ecological security leading to flow of benefits to the people at large will take us towards 'Faster and More Inclusive Growth' as envisaged by the 11th Plan approach of the Planning Commission of India.

References

AGENDA 21 (1992). United Nations Conference on Environment and Development (UNCED) Rio-de-Junerio, Brazil.

Towards Faster and More Inclusive Growth. Approach to 11th Five Year Plan. Planning Commission of India. Yojna Bhawan. New Delhi.

Vasudeva, S.P. 2001. Strategic Approaches to Integrated Management of Natural Resource. MBA Thesis. School of Business Studies. University of Hull. Hull. U.K.

World Conservation Strategy, 1980. Living Resource Conservation for Sustainable Development. International Union for Conservation of Nature and Natural Resources.

GLOBALISATION, DISTORTIONS, ASYMMETRIES IN GLOBAL TRADING ORDER: IMPLICATIONS FOR DEVELOPING AREAS—AGENDA FOR THE NEW MILLENNIUM

M.R. Aggarwal

ABSTRACT

Globalisation may be defined as a process of increasing economic integration and growing economic inter-dependence between countries in the world economy.

The World Trade Organisation (WTO) being the pillar of Globalisation, however, denied market access, domestic support and export subsidies to the developing countries in agriculture which has been the main bone of contention between developed and developing countries.

In most of the developing countries agriculture still contributes significantly to their overall GDP consumption level and employs a large proportion of their work force but only 8% in high income countries. Several commodities like wheat, coarse grains, oil seeds, vegetable oils, dairy products, fruits and vegetables which are having a great significance for food security in under developed countries, have been subjected to high level of subsidies and tariffs by the advanced countries depress the international prices. India is one of the developing countries where food security is of immense importance.

Later on, the NAFTA, comprising of USA, Canada and Maxico and APEC (1989) a loose grouping of 18 Pacific Rim countries including USA, Japan and China, came into existence for having free trade among themselves. In 1994, the APEC members committed themselves to form FTA by 2010 for the higher income countries and by 2020 for lower income countries.

The success of WTO and the policies of market oriented reforms, from the point of view India and south's overall economic and social growth, will to a large extent depend upon increasing degree of intra-industry and intra-firm trade among the advanced countries. The advanced countries need to provide free market access, reduce non-tariff barriers and all form of export subsidies on agriculture.

Globalisation may be defined as a process of increasing economic integration and growing economic inter-dependence between countries in the world economy. It is associated not only with an increasing cross-border movement of goods, services, capital, technology, information and people, but also with an organization of economic activities which straddles national boundaries. In general, this process is mainly driven by the forces of "competition" and "efficiency" of the market mechanism.

The Globalisation of the world economic and social structure in terms of increased volumes of capital, trade and immigration is certainly one of the key characteristics of the present times, describing how the relationships among countries have changed since Second World War II. This may be labeled as the second Globalisation era. GATT (1947) and now WTO (Jan. 1995) which is wider in scope as compared to GATT and other Bretton Woods Institutions, i.e. IMF and the World Bank and its Associates are now promoting the process of Globalisation through the liberalization of trade, capital and advancement of technology around the world and Infact are its main pillars. The quick availability of the information and its rapid increase, falling transactions cost have further speeded up this process. Infact at present the world is growing smaller and smaller due to the interdependence of the markets. Licensing capital goods imports turnkey plants foreign direct investment joint ventures strategic alliances are the main channels through which technology from abroad can be acquired. This process is not new as the first era of Globalisation remained on the international scene with gold as the medium of exchange during the period 1870-1914. During the Inter-War period, thereafter the notion of "free trade in principle" and hence this process lost much of its charm, mainly because of the excessive trade and payments restrictions used by one country against another. Apart from tariffs, a large armoury of restrictive devices such as quotas, licenses, customs controls and multiple exchange restrictions appeared on the international scene. But it again got momentum immediately after the Second World War. This was based on the wisdom of the conventional pure theory of International trade which establishes the superiority of free trade over trade with restrictions, i.e. of competition, the invisible hand, over Interference Indeed; the theory fundamentally is an extension of the theory of optimization. Given that the price system works ideally equating commodity prices everywhere (abstracting from cost of transport) to marginal cost, resources are optimally allocated and the greatest possible amount of satisfaction achieved. Free trade in principle is the main prescription of the pure theory for achieving optimality in resource allocation and acceleration in economic welfare, more so at the global level. But during the Post-War II years the movement towards the formation of regional groupings, primarily in the form of customs unions or free trade areas, both in the developed and developing countries, got momentum, with the belief that a customs union or a free trade area is a step towards free trade in a number of contiguous countries.

Established on 1st January, 1995, the World Trade Organisation (WTO) a successor of GATT (1947), a pillar of the Globalisation—is the embodiment of the results of Uruguay Round (UR) held during 1986-93. An attempt infact has been, made for the first time to regulate virtually all aspects of trading relations between nations. The developing countries in this Round no doubt played a major role in the negotiations, as compared to earlier Rounds. The various agreements reached in the important sectors and the commitments made by the members, now 147 reflect clearly a keen desire on their part to establish and strengthen overtime a multilateral trading system at the global level, based on 'rules rather on power' which is equitable free, fair and non-discriminatory.[1] The working of the GATT, founded by 23 countries in 1947 was amazingly successful during the Post-War II period despite its inherent weaknesses as far as the reductions/ eliminations in the rates of tariffs were concerned among the countries of the world, thus advanced the basic objectives of free market and competition through the process of trade and capital liberalization. This is the sole reason that the different regions of the world are integrating with the global economy.[2] (Table 1). However, there have emerged serious "distortions" and "asymmetries" in the functioning of world trading order due to variety of causes since 1956, and more so after 1995, which if not corrected, will jeopardize its smooth running and have serious repercussions for the prosperity and sustainable development of both the North and South.

No serious attempt has been made till to date by the industrialized countries to minimize these "inequities" which in fact have shown an upward trend. Increasing trend towards the denial of market access by the advanced countries to the exports of third world in one pretext or the other, advent of increased use of new-protectionism, regionalism and bilateralism (grey area measures) increasing degree of intra-industry trade, among rich countries and frequent flouting of multilateral agreed rules and "discipline" imposed by the international institutions are some of the factors responsible for creating these serious distortions. The Southern countries, at the various meetings of IMF, UNCTAD, and also at 1996, 1998, 1999, 2001 and 2003. Ministerial Conferences, of the WTO, held at Singapore, Geneva, Seattle, Doha and Cancun respectively expressed their strong resentment and anguish about them and pleaded for their complete removal at the earliest*. The last three meetings ended inconclusively largely because of strong disagreement on farm reforms and trade environment and competition policies[3].

TABLE I

Integration with the Global Economy (1990-02)

Country/Region	*Trade in goods*				*Ratio of commercial service exports to merchandise exports*		*Gross private capital flows*		*Gross foreign direct investment*	
	% of GDP		*% of goods GDP*		*%*		*% of GDP*		*% of GDP*	
	1990	*2002*	*1990*	*2002*	*1990*	*2002*	*1990*	*2002*	*1990*	*2002*
World	32.5	40.3w	80.2w	116.0w	21.5	23.1w	10.1w	20.8w	2.7w	6.0w
Low income	26.9	37.3	..	..	14.6	19.4	3.0	4.4	0.5	1.7
Middle income	35.2	54.9	74.6	116.8	16.5	15.6	6.8	12.4	1.0	3.7
Lower middle income	30.6	49.2	63.2	98.0	18.7	16.8	4.1	11.0	0.8	3.6
Upper middle income	45.0	66.2	86.4	146.8	13.7	13.9	12.2	15.1	1.5	3.9
Low and Middle income	33.4	51.8	74.5	115.0	16.2	16.1	6.0	11.1	0.9	3.3
East Asia and Pacific	47.0	63.4	78.5	104.6	14.1	13.6	5.0	10.2	1.7	4.1
Europe and Central Asia	28.8	64.3	53.3	132.1	29.6	21.7	..	13.9	..	3.7
Latin America and Caribbean.	23.1	41.2	66.4	132.0	17.5	13.4	7.9	13.7	0.9	4.0
Middle East and N. Africa	46.6	50.5	84.0	90.9	116	12.2	6.0	10.3	0.8	0.9
South Asia	16.5	24.2	..	..	24.6	39.5	1.4	3.2	0.1	0.7
Sub-Saharan Africa	40.8	55.3	77.1	119.7	13.9	10.1	4.9	9.6	1.0	2.2
High income	32.3	37.6	80.9	117.2	23.2	25.5	10.9	22.9	3.0	6.6
Europe EMU	44.9	56.3	112.6	141.9	24.4	23.7	14.1	49.3	2.9	14.8

Source: The World Bank World Development Indicators, 2004.

Asymmetries and Distortions at the Global Trading Order

Non-tariff barriers (NTBs) are basically non-tax measures imposed by a member to discriminate against foreign producers and in favour of the domestic ones. While tariffs generate revenues, these can be seen as generating costs. These barriers undermine seriously the functioning of the "market" by distorting the level of prices and the forces of competition, reduce flexibility in "production" and "consumption" decisions and encourage wasteful rent-seeking behaviour. NTBs which are difficult to quantify owing to lack of transparency and the problem of identification which include quantitative restrictions (QR), orderly marketing arrangements (OMA), voluntary export restraints, (VER), non-automatic licensing, quotas and prohibitions and price controls, i.e. dumping, rules of origin, anti-dumping, export subsidies and countervailing duties, public procurement policies, administrative procedures and technical and health standards. These are more severe and biting in nature as compared to tariffs. These barriers though under the UR have been committed to be reduced progressively but still are highest in USA, and Canada in the case of semi and finished manufactured goods as compared to raw materials, agriculture, forestry and fishing. There is practically little or no change in the case of some of the countries even after the signing of "WTO agreement". Even the rates of tariffs except in the case of EU, are still the highest on the finished and semi-finished products as compared to other categories (Tables 2 and 3). And these barriers tend to reduce significantly the export opportunities of South and India by raising prices to the consumer and thereby restricting total demand.

The "low wage argument" generally advanced by the North in favour of such barriers, seems to be totally unconvincing because (a) wages are only one element in total costs, (b) the competitive advantage in the different sectors of industries depend as much on such other determinants of costs as the state of their technological advance, capital stock, gains of economies of scale and the price of raw inputs, and (c) the relative advantages resulting from the low wage paid are in general more than offset by the low level of productivity of labour so that labour and capital cost per unit of output may in fact be higher as compared to rich countries. It is true that the developing countries are also using NTBs but their intensity is falling except in Singapore, Turkey and Brazil (Table 4). Besides this, there has been a rising trend of anti-dumping and "countervailing" measures and voluntary export restraints arrangements particularly after 1995. For example, USA out of the total 1011 anti-dumping measures used the maximum followed by European Union Mexico and Canada. USA is also the highest user of the countervailing duties, followed by Mexico in 1998.[4] In the case of VERs, EU takes the lead, followed by USA in 1994. These arrangements are the highest in textiles, agriculture, steel and footwear sectors in which the developing countries enjoy comparative advantage. The members notified 360 initiation of anti-dumping investigations in 1999 to WTO, which is more that 42% over 1998. At the mid 2000, an estimated 1119 final anti-dumping measures were in place of which the USA, had the most 28%, followed by the European Union (18%) South Africa (9%) Canada (8%)2. Lastly, even all the UR tariff concessions are fully implemented by all the advanced countries, significant trade barriers in the form of high tariff peaks, exceeding 12% but in some cases exceeding 300% and tariff escalation will continue to affect seriously the exports from the developing and the least developed countries.[5]

Agreement on Textile and Clothing (ATC)

The "textile and clothing" sector—relatively a labour intensive sector remained the glaring example of the existence of NTB's by Dec, 2004. This

TABLE 2

Quantum of Tariffs and Non-Tariff Barriers in Quad (Before and after the Uruguay Round, 1988-1995)

Sector	*USA*			*EU*			*JAPAN*			*CANADA*		
	1989	*93*	*UR*	*88*	*93*	*UR*	*88*	*93*	*UR*	*88*	*93*	*UR*
Raw materials	6.0	4.8	3.1	16.4	19.8	7.7	8.9	7.6	4.9	5.2	3.7	1.6
Agri. forestry and fishing	5.4	3.85	2.7	18.0	21.1	9.5	11.1	10.4	7.0	6.4	4.4	2.3
Mining and quarring	2.3	2.3	2.3	0.0.	2.7	4.2	3.5	0.4	0.4	0.4	0.7	0.7
Manu.	8.3	6.7	.3.7	16.8	20.3	9.2	11.9	6.9	6.9	6.5	2.1	0.2
Semi-finished manu. goods	35.3	32.2	11.1	34.0	29.4	3.1	27.6	27.1	26.7	15.3	13.1	0.8
Finished manu. goods	22.0	21.8	9.7	25.7	24.2	4.2	5.3	3.7	2.3	8.7	8.9.	2.0
All products	24.1	23.6	8.5	25.9	25.2	4.3	13.7	12.6	11.1	10.3	9.5	1.6

Source : Michael Daly and Hirocki Kuwharan, The Impact of the Uruguay Round of Tariffs and Non-Tarrif barriers to Trade in Quad, The World Economy, Vol. III, No. 2,1998. Quad means USA, EU, Canada and Japan.

sector is the major foreign exchange earners for the newly industrialized countries of Asia, Latin America and India in particular. The clause of "market disruption" into the original GATT rules was incorporated by the USA, for the justification of imposing such quantitative restrictions on their imports. Since 1960 however various arrangements which were negotiated among the major exporters and importers of cotton textiles at world level practically excluded this sector from the purview of GATT negotiations. Contrary to GATT rules unilateral import restrictions were imposed by developed countries to practically every fibre which henceforth grew progressively more restrictive. Admittedly under WTO agreement there would be reintegration of this sector completely into WTO but within ten years, i.e. by January 2005 and that too in four stages. The phasing out of quotas however during the transitional period, i.e. stage I, II and III remained only 49% of the total quota and did not yield substantial results*. The estimated cost of Multi Fibre agreement in terms of income and export loss both in the developed, developing and the global level is the maximum (Table 5). It is clear from the Tables 6 and 7 that the republic of Korea has achieved impressive rates of productivity growth in these sectors. Admittedly the other major exporters viz. India, Indonesia, Malaysia, Pakistan, Philippines, Taiwan, Turkey and Chile except Mexico have also improved their productivity growth significantly but India relatively has been lagging far behind in this direction. Therefore, India will have to double its efforts to further increase its labour productivity and cut-down unit labour costs to compete and capture the export markets in the

TABLE 3

Pervasiveness of Non-tariff barriers in Quad (1996)

Product	*Production-Weighted frequency ratio*			
	USA	*EU*	*Japan*	*Canada*
Agriculture, forestry, fishing	2.8	7.2	7.0	2.1
Mining and quarrying	0.4	6.7	0.4	4.3
Coal mining	0.0	42.9	na	0.0
Crude petroleum	0.0	0.0	na	9.1
Metal ore mining.	4.0	4.4	na	0.0
Other mining	2.3	3.6	na	0.0
Manufacturing	8.1	5.4	2.5	3.9
Food, beverages, and tobacco	1.2	11.1	8.6	1.5
Textile and apparel	68.3	75.4	28.7	45.8
Wood and wood products	0.8	0.0	0.0	3.7
Paper and paper products	1.3	1.9	0.0	0.2
Chemical, petroleum products	3.2	1.6	1.4	1.3
Non-metallic mineral products	6.1	0.0	0.0	0.0
Basic metal industries	30.4	0.6	2.6	1.7
Fabricated metal products	6.1	0.0	0.0	1.4
Other manufacturing	1.7	0.0	0.0	0.8
Total all products	7.2	5.6	2.8	3.8

Source: T. Oatley, International Political Economy, 2004.

TABLE 4

Non Tariff barriers in Developing Countries (as a % of all industry categories)

Country	*Year (1989-94)*	*Year (1995-98)*
Hong Kong (China)	2.1	2.1
Indonesia	53.6	31.3
Korea	50.0	25.0
Malaysia	56.3	19.6
Singapore	1.0	2.1
Thailand	36.5	17.5
India	99.0	93.8
Nigeria	14.4	11.5
South Africa	36.5	8.3
Morocco	58.3	13.4
Turkey	5.2	19.8
Argentina	3.1	2.1
Brazil	16.5	21.6
Chile	5.2	5.2
Columbia	55.2	10.3
Mexico	27.8	13.4
Uruguay	38.3	0.0

Source: Same as that of Table 3.

advanced and developing areas (Tables 6 and 7) in the near future. This concern was shared by the WTOs collective membership which states that the integration programmes of the major importing members during the first stage, and as announced for the second and third stage included only a small number of products which had actually been under quota restrictions, therefore, leaving a large number of products for which quota restrictions would need to be eliminated during the remainder of the transition period.[6] The developing countries besides this have also been facing unexpected obstacle to their exports of the cotton textiles through the frequent misuse of the transitional protectionists safeguard, including anti-dumping, rules of origin, measures under ATC due to strong pressure put by the domestic industry. At the very outset, the USA acting under strong domestic pressure initiated as many as 24 safeguard actions on textiles/clothing item, which were in addition to the 1000 quotas which was already in place in 1994. In 1995 the US imposed restrictions on imports from India of women's and girls woollen coats and women shirts under the 'safeguard clause' and despite various representation made to Dispute and Settlement Body (DSB) and Textiles Monitoring Body (TMB) having a quasi judicial role, by India, and others but could not succeed.

TABLE 5

Costs of MFA Quotas and Tariffs on Textiles and Clothing (Income and export revenue losses)

(billion US dollars)

	Developed countries			*Developing countries*	*World*
	Quotas and tariffs	*MFA Quotas*	*Tariffs*	*Tariffs*	
Income loss					
Developing countries	23.8	1.7	22.2	28.0	51.8
Developed countries	10.9	13.9	-3.0	3.2	14.0
World	34.7	15.5	19.1	31.1	65.8
Export revenue loss					
Developing countries	39.8	22.3	17.5	41.5	81.2
Developed countries	46.3	10.3	35.9	9.0	55.4
World	86.0	32.6	53.4	50.5	136.6

Source: IMF Staff simulations with the GTAP model.

In addition there is a urgent need for addressing seriously in the next Round, the unfinished business of UR *inter-alia*—tariff peaks and 'tariff escalation' in textiles, clothing, footwear and leather industries, the postponement until 2005 of economically meaningful removal of restrictions of developing countries exports of textile and clothing, embryonic liberalization of trade in agriculture, abuse of anti-dumping measures and procedures, the problems of rules of origin, reduction of "technical standards" and "environmental barriers", and provision of "market access" so that the poor, the weak, and vulnerable sectors of the society should be able to partake of the benefits the global trade.

Agricultural Sector

It was recognised since 1950 by the industrialized countries that the long-term solution for reforming the "agricultural sector" does not lie in having administered prices, trade restrictions, supply controls and the use of export subsidies but rather on non-distorted free markets. No substantial progress however, was made in this direction upto the mid-1980s. The UR Agreement on Agriculture (AOA), was an important step towards applying multilateral rules and disciplines to global agricultural trade. The production and export of this sector has been protected by the advanced countries through tariffs, NTBs and export subsidies since 1960.

TABLE 6

Labour Productivity in Textile and Clothing Sector in Selected Exporting Countries (1980-2000) (1990 = 100)

Country	*Textiles (ISIC 321)*			*Clothing (ISIC 322)*		
	1980	*1995*	*2000*	*1980*	*1995*	*2000*
China	79.8	79.9	121.7	98.8	123.9	184.8
India	69.9	67.7	107.4	43.3	52.1	107.5
Indonesia	45.8	67.4	158.1	39.0	73.8	147.8
Malaysia	60.2	61.5	208.6	62.8	73.9	161.2
Mexico	111.7	115.9	82.3	--	118.0	85.2
Pakistan	41.2	61.0	108.1	61.0	67.0	133.8
Philippines	88.7	49.7	140.2	77.1	50.6	146.3
Republic of Korea	61.0	78.5	233.1	58.8	62.4	196.5
Taiwan	51.3	66.7	127.4	70.1	78.3	92.2
Thailand	--	--	--	--	--	--
United States	84.1	89.4	118.0	82.7	93.0	144.1

Source: UNCTAD, Geneva: Trade and Development Report, 2003.

The agreement establishes new multilateral rules governing enhanced market access, export subsidies, and domestic support for agriculture, adoption of health and safety regulations and strengthening of intellectual property protection. The 'market access provisions' contained in the AOA has basically three elements viz. (i) removal of the quantitative restrictions on imports, (ii) tariffication of non-tariff barriers into equivalent tariff rates, and (iii) establishment of tariff rate quotas. The agreement requires all members to convert "NTBs" to "tariffs" and to reduce them gradually by a simple average of 36 per cent over six years (with a minimum tariff reduction per tariff line of 15 per cent), and strictly prohibits the introduction of new NTBs to trade. Where NTBs restrict imports, the

TABLE 7

Unit Labour Costs in Textile and Clothing Sector in Selected Exporting Countries (1980-2000) (Ratios to the US Level)

Economy	*Textile*		*Clothing*	
	1980	*2000*	*1980*	*2000*
China	0.25	--	0.08	--
India	1.25	1.57	0.96	0.47
Indonesia	0.61	0.42	0.95	0.45
Malaysia	0.75	0.59	0.82	0.84
Mexico	0.85	0.88	0.69	0.54
Pakistan	--	---	---	--
Philippines	0.60	0.67	0.80	0.59
Republic of Korea	0.74	0.63	0.71	0.62
Taiwan	1.09	1.45	0.44	0.80
Thailand	0.46	0.87	0.67	1.07

Source: UNCTAD, Geneva: Trade and Development Report, 2003

agreement requires that importing countries offer minimum access of usually 3 per cent of domestic consumption raising it to 5 per cent over the six-year implementation period. In case of the use of export subsidies, the agreement stipulates that these subsidies be reduced by 21 per cent in terms of quantities and by 36 per cent in terms of "budgetary outlays" within the six years as compared with the 1986-90 level by the members except the least developed countries. However, the members may continue to use their existing export subsidies within the limits agreed, but may not in any case introduce new export subsidies. Besides this, the agreement includes rules and commitments for domestic support subsidies which are to be reduced by 20 per cent from average levels of support aggregated across all commodities for the base period 1986-88. Commitments are also being made within the six-year on the basis of this "aggregate measure of support" (AMS). The "rules" established for domestic support policies are more important as compared to required reduction commitments as the agreement defines which domestic policies are permitted (green box policies), such as income support provided to farmers independently of participation in production-limiting programs, advisory services, or domestic food assistance and the policies that are not eligible for the "green box" are automatically prohibited ("amber box" policies).

Sanitary and Phyto-sanitary Standards (SPS) and Technical Barriers to Trade (TBT)

It is the right of members to adopt and enforce measures that they deem appropriate to protect their human, plant life and health as long as such measures are not applied in an "arbitrary and unjustified" manner, in the case of application of SPS. However, such measures may not be used

TABLE 8

Domestic Support and Export Subsidies in Selected Country Groups (1995-98)

	Domestic Support				Export Subsidies			
	All WTO Members (90) $ Mn	Quad (4) Share %	Other OECD (5) Share %	Developing Countries (81) Share %	All WTO Members (24) $ Mn	Quad (3) Share %	Other OECD (5) Share %	Developing Countries (16) Share %
All the listed agricultural products	119,172	84	4	12	17897	79	4	17
Domestic Support in Green Box	1080,52	81	5	15	-	-	-	-

Source: B. Hoekman, F. Ng and M. Olarrega, *The World Bank Economic Review*, 2004, Vol. 18, 2004, No. 2.

as "disguised barriers" to trade and be based on international recognized standards where the provision exists. The members could even impose higher standards than those derived from these sources, if based on "scientific justification" and or on "risk assessment" to ensure food safety and to prevent diseases among pests and animals. The panel on dispute settlement should seek advice, if required from relevant international organizations when scientific or technical matters are at stake. New and strengthened dispute settlement procedures agreed to as part of the UR also apply to disputes that may arise under the SPS Agreement. In sum, the agreement clearly is based on the pillars of 'harmonization', 'equivalence', 'transparency', 'scientific judgment' and risk assessment. However, the serious distortions have occurred in their application by the advanced countries on the imports from developing countries.

Agriculture sector still occupies a special place in the developing countries including India, particularly in terms of GDP, employment, and for feeding and clothing the people. The members were allowed by the GATT, on the initiation of major players to provide subsidies to the export sector and use import and other restrictions which have been causing serious distortions on the free flow of trade. USA and EU have frequently used in the past huge subsidies to stabilize farm income, increase exports sales and infact shielded their farmers from foreign fair competition and are continuing with the same even after 1995. An Agreement on Agriculture (AOA) under WTO has been reached for the deep reduction or elimination of all these "subsidies" which are trade distorting" and "import restrictions" within 6 years. Surprisingly too many market access barriers continue to impede trade of food, food products and other related products. These barriers deny efficient producer the opportunity to compete in other

TABLE 9

Costs of Protectionist Policies in Agriculture (1997)

(billion U.S. dollars)

	World	*OECD*	*Non-OECD*
Agriculture policies			
World	128.2	97.8	30.4
OECD	101.4	92.7	8.7
Non-OECD	26.8	5.1	21.7
Loss of export revenue			
World	378.0	255.8	122.2
OECD	257.7	234.9	22.8
Non-OECD	120.3	20.9	99.4

Source: IMF staff simulations with the GTAP model.

markets. It is most surprising whereas most of the developing countries, including India have been phasing out gradually these subsidies but USA, EU and Japan have done little in this regard which is clearly an act of denying to developing countries market access to their markets. The Quad group accounts for 84% of the domestic support and 79% of the export subsidies at the global level. In some of the cases viz. edible vegetables and roots, edible fruit and nuts, milling products and malt, starches, animal/ vegetable fats and oils and products, prep. of vegetables, fruits and nut products, beverages, spirits and vinegar, tobacco and manufactured tobacco products, silk, cotton, vegetable, textile fibers, it exceeds more than 90% and 90% in cereals in case of export subsidies (Table 7 and Table 8) .

There exists a provision which is aimed to reduce trade conflicts and complaints (Article 13 of the Agreement) popularly known as the "Peace Clause" in which disputes cannot be brought by a member against other, within 6 years, particularly in the case of "green box policies". It is rightly felt that by removing the subsidized exports, the level of prices at the global level would increase, and the farmers in EU, Japan, USA will not be artificially encouraged to overproduce products in which they cannot compete at the global level. On the other hand, eliminating trade barriers and reducing unfair competition will also help the farmers in the less developed areas to increase production and exports by diversification change in cropping patterns and better allocation of resources. The cost of agricultural protectionist policy is very high in terms of income and export revenue loss (Table 9). Besides this the data compiled by the world bank in its document Sept. 2003, suggests that the farm subsidies are not reachable to the small households for which they are meant. On the other hand the large farmers and big corporations receive most of these government payments which are non-transparent.

The EU is still continuing Common Agricultural Policy (CAP) has notified WTO, by 2000, about $ 500,000 million in support to European

TABLE 10

Agricultural Subsidies and Producer Subsidy Equivalent in Industrial Countries, 1997 and 1998

	Billions U.S. ($)		*Subsidy per centage of Agricultural output*	
Country	*1997*	*1998*	*1997*	*1998*
United States	30.6	47.0	14	22
European Union	96.7	116.1	38	45
Japan	52.6	49.1	61	63
Australia	1.4	1.2	7	7
Canada	3.0	3.2	14	16
New Zealand	1.1	0.4	2	1
Norway	2.7	2.7	65	70
Switzerland	5.0	5.4	68	73
All industrial countries	193.1	225.1	32	37

Source : OECD, Agricultural Polices in OECD, 1999.

agriculture annually about half of which is trade distorting. Its latest policies of achieving self sufficiency in primary goods have a direct negative impart on the exports of developing countries. The subsidization of agricultural output in the North not only shuts at the imports from developing world but also leads to "unfair" competition in their own markets. The annual cost of support for agriculture in the industrial countries in 1996-98 was double the level of agriculture exports from developing countries during three years. Although EU produces half of production among the world highest cost producers of dairy products they have a 50% share of the world market.[7]

Table 10 clearly shows that the subsidy as a per centage of agricultural output not only increased from 32% to 37% (1997-98) which is clearly on the higher side in the industrialized country but is the highest in Switzerland followed by Norway, Japan, European Union and USA in 1998. These are the largest single example of distortions of agricultural trade in the world. These subsidies are incompatible with the spirit of WTO and must be frozen and reduced gradually. According to UN, FAO, when the European union cut export subsidies, on beef sales to West Africa six years ago, the result was an immediate and substantial increase in beef production across some of the world poorest countries including Mali and Niger. It is thus surprising that while the majority of the developing countries are prohibited from providing export subsidies the countries which have been distorting to a large scale the market in the past are maintaining huge subsidy regime till todate while others are prohibited from using such measures in the future. Table 11 which gives the tariff barriers on primary products and manufactured products , shows that USA, on the basis on simple mean, has increased the barriers from 2.5% to 2.7%

between 1989-2002. And on the other hand, the prices of primary commodities except that of petroleum and fertilizers have shown a declining trend hurting the export interest of developing countries, (Table 12). On the other hand, the technical barriers to trade (TBT) could be used by any member due to climatic, geographical and technological reasons, but these are used by North for unspecified reasons as (NTB's) and best known to them to ban the exports of developing countries. Lastly, the commodity price index during 1970-2003 shows that the price index of all the commodities except that of fertilizers and petroleum have shown a declining trend. On the other hand, the value of the index MUV has gone up. This is quite depressing for the developing countries that are making strenuous efforts to diversify their production and export structure. Hence, the provision of market access to their products becomes more important. If this is not done in the near future than the least developing countries and many of the under developed countries will be marginalized under the present waves of Globalisation.

TABLE 11

The Tariff Barriers on Primary Products and Manufactured Products (1988-2002) (%)

		All products		*Primary products*		*Manufactured products*	
		SM	*WM*	*SM*	*WM*	*SM*	*WM*
EU	1988	2.6	3.0	5.8	2.7	2.6	4.3
	2002	3.1	2.4	3.4	1.5	2.9	2.9
USA	1989	5.9	5.2	2.5	2.0	5.5	4.1
	2002	4.1	2.6	2.7	1.1	3.8	2.0
Canada	1989	10.8	6.4	4.3	2.6	10.5	6.6
	2001	5.1	1.1	1.9	0.5	4.7	1.0
Japan	1989	4.0	3.4	8.3	4.4	3.5	2.7
	2002	2.9	2.2	5.2	2.5	2.4	1.7

Source: World Bank: World Development Indicators—2004:
SM—Simple mean, WM—Weighted mean

Food Security

The Doha and Cancun Ministerial Conferences focussed mainly on developmental dimension of the agriculture sector by putting forward the broad issues of food security and rural and agricultural development, particularly of food importing countries. There have been clear tendencies on the part of developed countries either not to implement or implemented in the past, in such a way as the fruits of liberalization in this sector be not available to them. It could be defined as the physical and economic access on a continuing bases for all people at all times to enough food for an active and healthy life. In most of the developing countries agriculture still contributes significantly to their overall GDP consumption level and

TABLE 12

Trends in Major Primary Commodity Prices (Commodity Price Index) (1990 = 100) (1970-2003)

Sector	*1970*	*1980*	*1990*	*1995*	*1997*	*1998*	*1999*	*2000*	*2001*	*2002*	*2003*
Non-energy commodities	156	159	100	104	114	99	89	89	84	89	91
Agriculture	163	175	100	112	124	108	93	90	85	93	95
Beverages	203	230	100	129	165	141	108	91	76	91	87
Food	166	177	100	100	112	105	88	87	91	97	96
Raw Materials	130	133	100	116	110	88	89	94	82	89	98
Fertilizers	108	164	100	87	116	123	115	109	105	108	106
Metals and minerals	144	120	100	87	87	76	74	85	80	78	82
Petroleum	19	204	100	64	81	57	80	127	113	117	126
Steel products	111	100	100	91	86	75	69	79	71	73	79
MUV/G-5 index	28	79	100	117	104	100	99	97	94	93	100

The MUV G-5 index is a composite index of prices for manufactured exports from the five major industrial countries—France, Germany, Japan, the United Kingdom, and the United States to low-and middle income economies, valued in U.S. dollars.

Source: The World Bank : World Development Indicators—2004 (Various Issues).

FIGURE 1

Trends in Major Primary Commodity Prices (Commodity Price Index) (1990=100) (1970-2003)

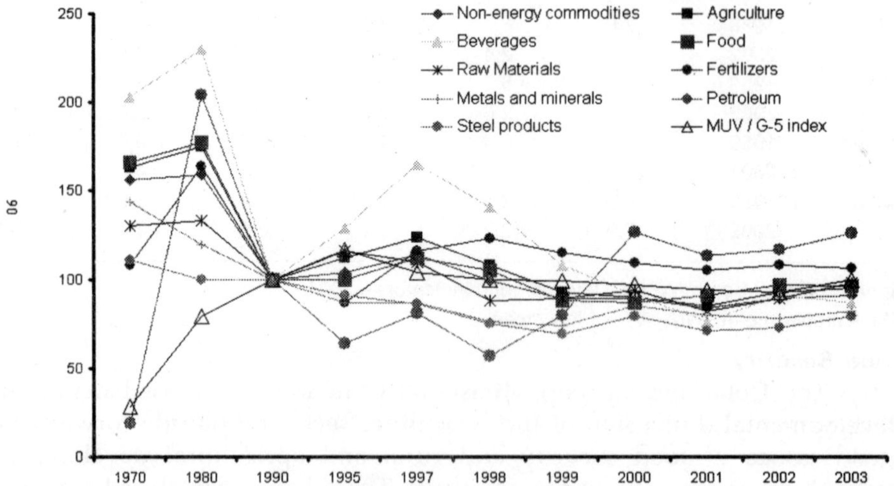

employs a large proportion of their work force and only 4% in high income countries in 2004. The "food needs" and the "supply gaps" in under developed countries are developmental problems; hence most of their efforts are directed towards increasing production and productivity. But small changes in agricultural employment opportunities or the level of global prices can have major socio-economic effects in their economies. Several

FIGURE 2

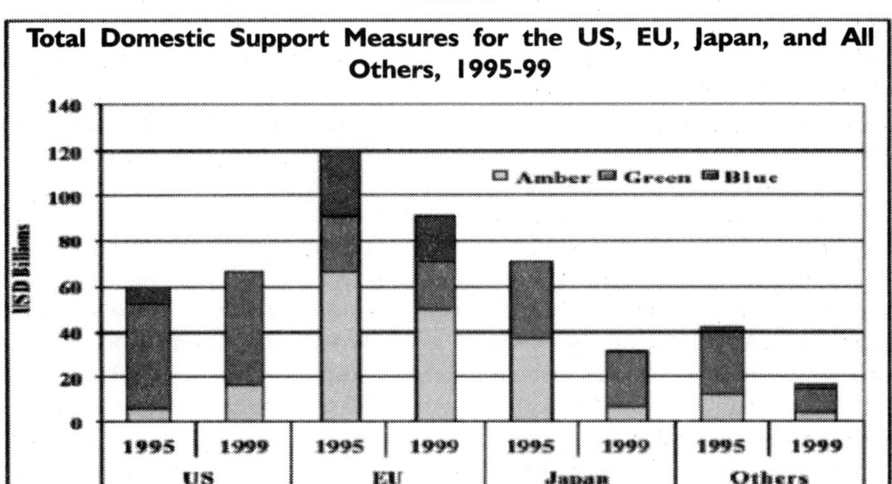

Total Domestic Support Measures for the US, EU, Japan, and All Others, 1995-99

commodities like wheat, coarse grains, oil seeds, vegetable oils, dairy products, fruits and vegetables which are having a great significance for food security in under developed countries, have been subjected to high level of subsidies and tariffs by the advanced countries which artificially as we have already noted, depress the international prices. And for a large agricultural country India, the problem of food security therefore, assumes greater importance. Flexibility in the provision of providing subsidies to key farm inputs, exemption to provide any minimum market access, measures taken by them in the past for poverty alleviation, rural development programmes and employment, denial of the application of SPS measures by the developed countries for protectionist measures are some of the steps which needs to be addressed in the immediate future negotiations. It is more so as India has been one of the major producers and exporter at the global level of coffee and its substitutes, fish (fresh, frozen and shell), rice, fruits, nuts (fresh and dried), vegetables (fresh and preserved), feeding stuff for animals and vegetable oils, taking around 2.59, 5.0, 3.0, 2.0, 0.71, 2.20, 2.0% respectively of the world total exports, in 1998-99. And the impact of the WTO regime on India's agricultural sector will begin to be felt, once all the quantitative restrictions by the industrialized countries are phased out at the earliest.

Regional Arrangements: Custom Unions and Free Trade Areas and Regional Trade Agreements

One of the most pervasive and characteristic features of the 1980's has been the remarkable renaissance of "regionalism", through the formation of trade blocs in Europe, North America Canada Latin America, Africa and South and South East Asia. (Second Wave) The first wave towards regionalism was launched with the creation of "Union of Six" and

"Union of Seven", i.e. EEC and EFTA in the late 1950's. The USA, upto to 1980 did not oppose much their formation in the different parts of the world but its trade policies were certainly marked by strong trade laws and sanctions. In 1980's there resulted a second "wave of regionalism" in which active negotiations for forming a Canada-USA free trade agreement were initiated in 1983 and the process was completed in 1988. Later on, the NAFTA, comprising of USA, Canada and Maxico and APEC (1989) a loose grouping of 18 Pacific Rim countries including USA, Japan and China, came into existence for having free trade among themselves. In 1994, the APEC members committed themselves to form FTA by 2010 for the higher income countries and by 2020 for lower income countries. USA also aimed to form a FTA embracing 34 democracies in the Western hemisphere except Cuba by 2005. The EC was enlarged from 9 members to 12 in 1986 and 15 in 1994 having now a common currency "Euro". If the Euro encourages further trade integration within Europe it would create further the intensity of trade diversion at the expense of developing countries. A common market consisting of Brazil, Argentina, Uruguay and Paraguay in Latin America came into force in 1995 (Mercosur). Within Asia, Malaysia announced in 1990 the formation of East Asian Economic Groupings. The recent agreement between Chile and Canada, the enlargment of EU from 15 to include Hungry, Poland and the efforts of EU is to have a membership with Mercosur. Vietnam joined the ASEAN in 1995, Chile and Bolivia became associate members of Mercosur in 1996 are some of the examples of the third wave in this direction. A number of smaller arrangements including the ASEAN free trade are AFTA and SAPTA also came into existence. If the number and extensions of these agreements to the MFN clause reaches a sufficiently significant level, the exception could become the rule and the multilateral system would be substantially changed. The world is witnessing a "paradoxical situation", as the pace of globalisation is gaining momentum, the urge among the countries all over the world to club together is catching speed at the regional level. According to WTO report it has been notified of almost 180 regional trade arrangements. It would be very difficult for the developing areas under these circumstances to have the benefits of increased market access" in the expanding markets of G-3 despite all their efforts to integrate with the world trading order. Though the GATT has sanctioned the formation of such regional groups under Article XXIV, with the condition that these groups should facilitate trade between the members and not to raise barriers to the trade of other contracting parties, but the formation of trade blocs not only violated the central principle of MFN clause, but also trade intra-regionally which shows that both of this and infact cannot go certainly hand in hand with the spirit of internationalization of trade and finance but also accompanied by other barriers. Besides this the EU and NAFTA contributed jointly 47% of total world exports and had 61% and 57% individually as a % of total block exports in 2002 whereas in the Latin American and African groups all have very little or negligible share in worlds exports and also as % of block exports (Table 13). In sum, the world economy has been marked by apparently two divergent trends since the 1980s one is globalisation through FDI, the other has been the regionalization of the world economy through the apparent increase in the importance of regional trade arrangements. These two "processes" whether co-exist happily or not this is a big question. But the WTO could not take any action in this regard despite strong protests till to date by the developing world as the major powers think that these arrangements in fact supplement the spirit of multilaterlism.[8]

FIGURE 3

Percentage Share of Regions to World Exports

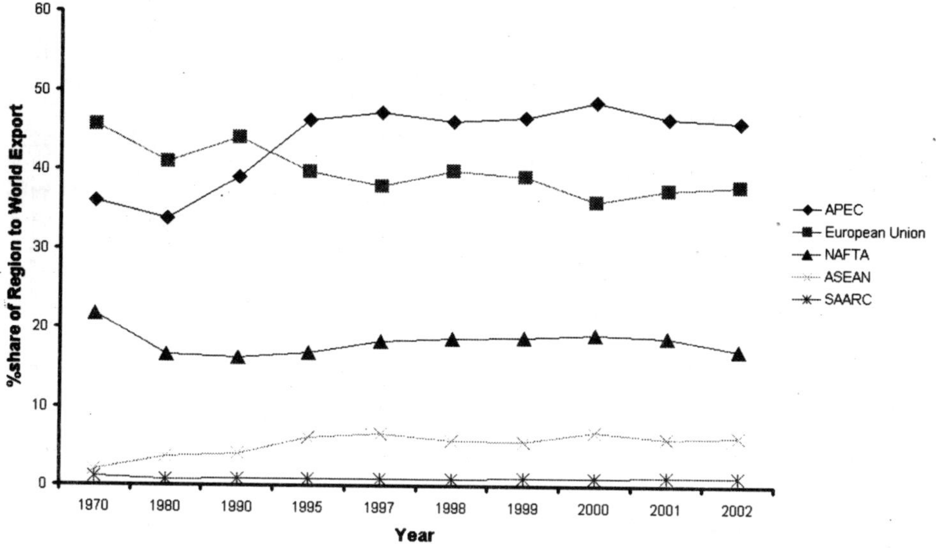

TRIPS

The Agreement on (TRIPS) including trade in counterfeit goods has been a source of maximum contention among the members of WTO. Prior to WTO, WIPO (World Intellectual Prosperity Organization) was mainly dealing with the intellectual property and these rights were not addressed by GATT—the predessor of WTO. A principal argument advanced by developed countries for the protection and enforcement of IPR is that this will lead to greater international trade, the benefits of which will be shared by all. This protection clearly increase their exports by keeping pirated products out of their markets. IT is further argued that the country which does not protect IP, will tend to be flooded with inferior illigitimate products, which in term hurt the long-term economic interests of the developing countries. Lastly, emphasis is placed not only on enacting

TABLE 13

Regional Trade Blocs (1970-02)

Region	*% of world exports*			*% of total bloc exports*		
	1970	*1995*	*2002*	*1970*	*1995*	*2002*
High-income and low and middle-income economies						
APECa	36.0	46.3	46.0	57.8	71.8	73.3
CEFTA	3.2	1.6	2.4	12,9	14.6	12.2
European Union	45.6	39.7	37.9	59.5	62.4	60.6
NAFTA	21.7	16.8	17.2	36.0	46.2	56.7
Latin America and the Caribbean						
ACS	2.8	2.6	3.7	9.6	8.5	7.1
Andean Group	1.9	0.8	0.8	1.8	12.0	9.5
CACM	0.4	0.1	0.4	26.1	21.8	11.1
CARICOM	0.4	0.1	0.2	4.2	12.1	12.5
Central America Group of Four	0.3	0.1	0.2	20.1	22.2	12.8
Group of Three	1.8	2.1	3.1	1.1	3.2	1.8
LAIA	4.5	4.1	5.0	9.9	17.1	11.1
MERCOSUR	1.7	1.4	1.4	9.4	20.3	11.6
OECS	-	0.0	0.0	..	12.6	3.8
Africa						
CEMAC	0.2	0.1	0.1	4.8	2.1	1.5
CEPGL	0.3	0.0	0.0	0.4	0.5	0.7
COMESA	1.6	0.4	0.4	8.7	7.0	6.4
Cross-Border Initiative	0.8	0.2	0.2	9.3	11.9	10.2
ECCAS	0.6	0.2	0.3	9.6	1.5	1.3
ECOWAS	1.1	0.4	0.4	2.9	9.0	10.6
Indian Ocean Commission	0.1	0.0	0.0	8.4	6.0	5.3
MRU	0.1	0.0	0.0	0.2	0.1	0.2
SADC	2.2	0.8	0.7	8.0	8.7	9.3
COMESA				4.9	2.1	1.5
UDEAC	0.2	0.1	0.1	4.9	2.1	1.5
UEMOA	0.3	0.1	0.1	6.5	10.3	12.3
Middle East and Asia						
Arab Common Market	1.6	0.4	0.6	2.2	6.7	4.8
ASEAN	2.0	6.1	6.3	22.9	25.4	23.7
Bangkok Agreement	1.6	4.6	5.1	2.7	5.0	5.6
EAEC	11.3	26.1	25.2	28.9	47.9	48.2
ECO	1.5	1.2	1.3	1.5	7.9	5.9
GCC	1.9	2.0	2.3	2.9	6.8	4.6
SAARC	1.1	0.9	1.1	3.2	4.4	4.2
UMA	1.5	0.6	0.7	1.4	3.8	2.7

Source: The World Bank World Development Indicators, 2004.

intellectual property laws, but also on marking certain those laws are enforced. The protection of IPR goods, is a monopoly right temporarily provided by the state to the owner of a new product having a market value to exclude others for using it commercially. TRIPS is an attempt to harmonise the national property rights rules at the global level. The major provisions of TRIPS, which cover patents; copyright and related rights, trade marks including service marks and geographical indications, including applications of origin layout designs of integrated circuits, industrial designs and protection of undisclosed information, i.e. trade secrets, and takes into account the provisions of WIPO, the Benre Convention, on copy rights, the Paris Convention, the Washington Treaty on Intellectual Properties. The members will have to comply with the provisions of 1967 Paris Convention on IPR. The objective of TRIPS to bring into the ambit of the WTO is to contribute to the promotion of technological innovation and transfer and dissemination of the knowledge to the mutual advantage of producers and users in a way as to create a fair social and economic global order.[9] But what actually has happened is contrary to the expectations. There is, in recent years a drastic shift in the pattern of world trade from 'high volume products' to 'high value products', i.e. knowledge-based or high tech-intensive goods due to rapid growth of technology in the advanced countries and its imitation by the under-developed countries. Within three decade of post II World War, the production and trade structures nearly was complementary between North and South but in recent years it is becoming more or less similar and is likely to become more so due to the accelerated process of globalisation.

Each of the firm in the industry tries to keep its foothold in the world market share and leadership by new innovations and the introduction of the new products by spending huge sums of money on R and D so that they may be able to reap "monopoly profits" or rent. And this monopoly advantage cannot be sustained for long without adequate protection of IPR. Incident of IPR violations which are very frequent in developing economies partly due to state sanctioned piracy, which not only discourages further investment in R and D and hence competition but also places on them high costs of adjustment both in terms of money and time and partly due to strong belief in catching up strategy based on 'imitation'. The economic cost, of adjustment at macro level however, was small, quick and easy, when the trading relations were complimentary in 1960s and 1970s due to absence of imperfections in the goods and factor markets; but become quite high, seen in terms of dynamic trade theory. Inclusion of TRIPS in WTO is a devise by which the firms mostly MNCs may be able to recover a part of the costs "incurred" on R/D.

Regional Integration Agreements Notified to GATT and WTO and inforce as of January, 1995

A. Reciprocal Regional Integration Agreements

Europe

Central European Free Trade Area, Czech Republic and Slovak Republic Customs Union, Czech Republic and Slovenia Free Trade Agreement, EFTA Free Trade Agreements with Bulgaria, Czech Republic, Hungary, Israel, Poland, Romania, Slovak Reublic, Turkey.

European Community

European Community Association Agreements with Bulgaria; Cyprus, Czech Republic, Hungary, Malta, Poland, Romania, Slovak Republic, Turkey.

European Community Free Trade Agreements with Estonia, Iceland, Israel, Latvia, Liechtenstein, Lithuania, Norway, Switzerland.

European Free Trade Association

Norway Free Trade Agreements with Estonia, Latvia, Lithuania, Slovak Republic and Slovenia Free Trade Agreement, Switzerland Free Trade Agreements with Estonia, Latvia, Lithunia.

North America

Canada—United States Free Trade Agreement, North American Free Trade Agreement

Latin America and the Caribbean

Andean Pact, Caribbean Community and Common Market (CARICOM)

Central American Common Market, Latin American Integration Association

Southern Common Market (Mercosur).

Middle East

Economic Cooperation Organization, Gulf Cooperation Council.

Asia

Australia-New Zealand Closer Economic Relations Trade Agreement,

Bangkok Agreement, Common Effective Preferential Scheme for the Association for South East Asian Nations.

Free Trade Area

Lao People's Democratic Republic and Thailand Trade Agreement,

Israel-United States Free Trade Agreement.

B. Non-reciprocal Regional Integration Agreements

Europe

Africa, Caribbean, and Pacific (ACP)—European Economic Community Fourth Lome Convention, European Economic Community Association of Certain Non-European countries and Territories, European Economic Community Cooperative Agreements with Algeria, Egypt, Jordan, Lebanon, Morocco, Syria, Tunisia.

Asia

Australia-Papua New Guinea Agreement, South Pacific Regional Trade Cooperation Agreement

Source: Raquel Fermandez and Jonathan Portes, Return to Regionalism: An Analysis of Non-traditional gains from Regional Trade Agreements, *The World Bank Economic Review*, May 1998.

Admittedly it accelerates competition among the Northern countries but it stifles competition between North and South hinders the upgradation of technologies base which is already, narrow and small in the developing areas and in fact represents a new form of "protectionism". These tendencies have been further intensified if we examine the average share of intra-industry trade in manufactured goods during 1970-2000. It is clear from the (Table 14) that the size of the intra-industry trade has gone by 13.8% to 38.4% at a global level during this period. For the developed countries, the average level of intra industry trade increased by 26.9% over the same time frame. The same is also true in the case of developing countries as a whole but it is concentrated only in some firms of a few countries. The North admittedly will be able to reap the benefits of monopoly price but this agreement should not be used as a protectionist device that may enable technology owners to reap supernormal profits while hindering or preventing the right type of transfer of technology. It is clear that the real debate should not be whether the South should go for TRIPS or not, but the choosing of right type of TRIPS, in the different sectors and sub-sectors beneficial both to Centre and Periphery.

Singapore Issues

The advanced countries, at the first WTO Ministerial Conference held in Singapore in Dec. 1996, have tried to put forward "new issues" (Singapore Issues) viz. trade and investment, trade and competition policy, transparency in government procurment policies, trade facilitation, and other social clauses (labour and enviornmetnal standards) into the WTO for negotiations. However all the developing including least developed countries opposed and resisted these attempts at the various meetings held thereafter on the ground that these be studied/examined thoroughly before any firm decision to include all of them in the WTO agenda be taken. Besides, this the developing countries have argued that loading the WTO agenda with newer and newer issues would result in the diversion of the core issues, agreed at UR. It is gratifying to note that even in the advanced countries there is not complete unanimity, on these issues regarding their implementation.

Table 14

Size of the Intra-Industry Trade in Developed and Developing Countries (1970-2000)

Economic Group/Country	*1970*	*2000*	*% Change (1970-2000)*
Developed economies (22)	35.1	62.0	26.9
Six Major exporters	41.1	61.7	20.6
France	51.9	76.7	24.8
Germany	51.0	69.2	18.2
Italy	44.3	58.1	13.8
Japan	17.7	41.0	23.3
U.K.	45.3	73.6	28.3
U.S.A.	36.0	59.6	23.6
Other developed economies (16)	32.8	62.8	30.0
Developing Countries (25)	8.1	46.5	38.4
NICs (6)	13.9	51.2	37.3
Second Generation NIC (9)	3.4	40.8	37.4
Other Developing economies (10)	8.9	28.5	19.6

Source: W.C. Sawyer, R.L. Sprinkle: International Economics, 2004.

Labour, Social and Environmental Standards (Social Clause)

The Group of 24 especially USA has been repeatedly demanding since the beginning of 8th Round of GATT, the inclusion of "Social Clause" in the negotiations which may allow them to impose restrictions on the products originating from the countries which don't comply with a specified set of minimum core labour and environmental standards. The developing countries have been forcefully opposing these demands as these represent for them a new form of disguised non-tariff barriers which would be very harmful to their exports in which they possess comparative advantage due to cheaper labour costs of production. There is nothing wrong in improving the labour standards to a level approved by ILO but these must not be used by the G-3 as an excuse for imposing restrictions to protect the inefficiencies in some of the sectors. After 1995 the issue of trade and the enforcement of minimum labour standard was taken seriously by the North due to the frequent occurrence of structural crisis and the unacceptable high levels of unemployment, in their economies which have been attributed wrongly due to the unfair relative advantage enjoyed by the developing countries. The aim of this demand is to prevent social dumping and is now being pushed with great vigor by the major industrialized countries, But the WTO is not a right platform which should enforce labour standards and social laws, and secondly it is also impossible to equalize labour standards when the levels of productivity and culture differ markedly between nations and within a nation at different stages. Lastly, the labour and environmental standards are mainly a function of prevailing culture, degree of democracy and particularly the level of development. Low level of development in general is positively correlated empirically with lower labour standards. And any effort to harmonize the labour as well as environmental standards at global level, without raising the level of development will erode the competitive advantage and hence gains from trade of developing areas. The harmonization in fact will take place automatically as the developing areas cross a certain stage of development. In fact, economic progress precedes social progress. Trade policy could only be second best or even a third best policy in this regard. Admittedly growth flowing from free trade must be environmentally benign and eco-friendly, i.e. those who reap the fruits of economic development today must not make future generations worse off by excessively degrading the earth and exhaustible resources and polluting its ecology and environment.[10] There are two types of pollution viz national and international. When "pollution" affects primarily the pollution of the country where it originates, it is national in character. On the other hand, when pollution originates in our country but affect the level of pollution of others, can be labelled as international. Article XX of the GATT and the Preamble of the GATT Agreement establishing the WTO, clearly states that Environmental concerns should not be ignored by the WTO and every efforts should be made to preserve and protect the environment both at the national regional and international level.

The protection of 'environment' at the global level in fact is a serious problem and must be a part of the guiding principles of WTO. It immediately calls for a joint action at international level to minimize the negative impact, i.e. hidden social and environmental costs of excessive trends towards globalisation. There is no denying the fact that some measures, viz. The Montreal Protocol on Substances, (1987), a global accord to regulate fishing on the high seas (August 1995), negotiations of agreements between Russia and Group of 7 regarding the availability of data to the countries fighting forest fires, and USA and 94 countries making obligatory for the 27 exporters of dangerous pesticies to disclose the countries what they are receiving (March 1998), have been taken at the global level but much remains to be done as far as the compliance of the rules and regulations relating to environmental standards. This is due to the fact that under the current scenario, the unrestricted operation of the MNC's have in fact become the prime danger to the environment due to (a) green house effect, (b) their ability to locate their plants in developing countries in order to escape the strict environmental standard imposed by their own countries, (c) having control of man than 70% of traded goods and 80% of the total world land devoted to export-oriented crops, and

(d) major users of fossil fuels which release carbon dioxide in the atmosphere. Under such conditions the developing countries should not be subject to unilateral trade restrictions measures to protect and preserve environment. On the other hand, the local pollution which does not cross national boarders should not be anybody's concern but the country's where it occurs and should be dealt with it in accordance with the strict domestic laws.

Also one should differentiate between externalities that occur when products are being consumed and externalities when the products are being produced. Hence, measures aimed at consumption externalities and measures aimed at production externalities must be taken accordingly at the domestic and international level.

Agenda for the Future

The WTO is simply overloaded with a wide range of complicated trade and economic issues and it is mistake to achieve too many objectives with its formation. However all the past commitments made by the advanced countries to developing countries, i.e. on MFN rule, removal of NTB's, binding commitments on tariffs, needs to be reviewed and implemented before taking up new commitments. Secondly, a beginning could be made by taking TRIPS out of WTO, and handled by WIPO, the Committee on Trade and Environment (CTE) whose main aim is simply to examine relationship between trade measures and environmental concerns, be wound up and the issue of environment be tackled by UNEP and the question of maintaining labour standards be excluded if the outcome of the Seattle Ministerial Meeting is any guide from the purview of WTO and be handled by ILO created in 1919 by the Treaty of Versailles to promote core labour standards. Further the issue of regional arrangements could be dealt within WTO by introducing a "sunset clause" whereby preferences available to members of the regional group against the outside world be extended to all the WTO members in say 5 years.[11] The "implementation" of the various commitments reached among the members at the UR in the different sectors, remain one of the major concern of the developing world. Whereas the developing countries infact have gone-too-far particularly in terms of overall tariff reduction and in meeting the obligations related to the services sector, not much has been done by the North in removing or reducing the "distortions" till today particularly on agriculture trade which affect seriously the expert trade of the developing world. In fact, the advanced countries have forcefully put forward, various "non-trade issues" like (competition policy) only to have something to nullify huge "payables" to the producers of agricultural goods. Statistical and theoretical evidence clearly show that removal of these "distortions" at the global level, and special and differential treatment to South in the different sectors will help considerably both the parties both in the short and long-term. Export subsidies must be made illegal for the agricultural products, and the under developed countries must support for the principle of "special and differential treatment" for under developed including least developed countries. Where the incidence of hunger and poverty is quite alarming as is revealed in (Table 15). Sub Saharan Africa, the number of people the incidence of poverty has increased and 46.5% of the people still live in poverty. On the other hand, in South Asia, around 31.3% people are still in the grip of poverty, though this ratio has decreased. The same is also true about the number of people living below the poverty line in South Asia. Trade in agriculture goods must be truly liberalized within a specified framework. All these new issues could be pressed and discussed forcefully by India and South at the next Ministerial meeting of WTO, before taking up new issues.

Cancun and After

The dust after the post-Cancun now nearly seems to be settled. However, the major gain of the Cancun conference for India and South has been the emergence of a group G-21.

In which India, China and South Africa and other major exporters of primary goods joined hands to force the industrialized countries to review the issues of decision making process, market access, domestic support and export subsidies in the near future. India must continue and strengthen these efforts.

TABLE 15

Poverty Estimates (1981-2001)

	People living on less than $1 (mn) a day			*Share of people living on less than $1 a day (%)*			*People living on less than $2 a day (mn)*			*Share of people living on less than $2 a day (%)*		
Region	*1981*	*1990*	*2001*	*1981*	*1990*	*2001*	*1981*	*1990*	*2001*	*1981*	*1990*	*2001*
East Asia and Pacific	767	472	284	55.6	29.6	15.6	1,151	1,117	868	83.4	69.9	47.6
China	606	377	212	61.0	33.0	16.6	858	830	596	86.3	72.6	46.7
Europe and Central Asia	1	2	18	0.3	0.5	3.7	8	58	93	1.9	12.3	19.7
Latin America and Caribbean	36	49	50	9.7	11.3	9.5	99	125	128	26.9	28.4	24.5
Middle East and North Africa	9	6	7	5.1	2.3	2.4	52	51	70	28.9	21.4	23.2
South Asia	475	462	428	51.5	41.3	31.1	821	958	1,059	89.1	85.5	76.9
Sub-Saharan Africa	164	227	314	41.6	44.6	46.5	288	382	514	73.3	75.0	76.3
Total	1,451	1,219	1,101	39.5	27.9	21.3	2,419	2,689	2,733	65.9	61.6	52.8
Excluding China	845	841	888	31.5	26.1	22.8	1,561	1,858	2,137	58.3	57.6	54.8

Source: The World Bank, World Development Indicators, 2004.

Finally, the success of WTO and the policies of market-oriented reforms, from the point of view India and south's overall economic and social growth, will to a large extent depend, given the increasing degree of intra-industry and intra-firm trade among the advanced countries, and problem of food security and environment upon the intensity of the desire on the part of the industrialized countries to provide free market access, reduce non-tariff barriers and all form of export subsidies on agriculture, reduction of trade distorting domestic support, overcome internal structural impediments to growth by having low rates of inflation and interest, and adjust their macro-domestic policies consistent with each other in a global framework of co-operation, and not confrontation, keeping in view the larger developmental interests of the Southern World. WTO may be good or bad but it should be understood clearly that it has now become a reality. The real question is now how to manage WTO/the waves of globalisation at the international level so that its benefits could be shared widely and the resultant negative costs be kept at the minimum level. For this South must make all efforts to expand and deepen the ongoing internal reforms, increase intra-regional trade through the progressive elimination of tariffs and non-tariff barriers, avoiding inappropriate trade liberalization policies, expand complementarily cushion, and create favorable climate for good" governance", as bad governance measured in terms of 'corruption and inefficiencies' makes even good economics as bad economics.

Notes and References

1. The Legal Texts, Marrakesh Agreement, Establishing the WTO, 1995, p. 6.
2. WTO, Focus, News Letters, 2000, 1999 and 1998.
3. UNCTAD, Trade and Development Report 1999, Report by the Secretariat of the UNCTAD, also WTO, Trading Into The Future Introduction to WTO (1999).
4. WTO Document, Major Review of the Agreement on Textiles and Clothing in the Stage I of Integration Process, p. 4. Also Trade and Development Report, *Ibid.* (1999). Mar Cello Raffaelli and Tripti. Jenkins, the Drafting History of the Agreement on Textiles and Clothing (ITCB, Geneva, Nov. 95). Also GATT increases in market access resulting from Uruguay Round, News of the Uruguay Round, April 1994.
5. WTO, Trading Into Future, Feb. 1998. WTO Trade Policy Review of India: Report by the Secretariat, Document, March 1998.sss
6. The Legal Texts, GATT, Art. XXIV. WTO, The Multilateral Trading System, 30 years of Achievement, 1998. Also H. Joa Chum and Rabi. Distortions in World Trade, Recent Developments,,,Economics, Vol. 41 (ed) Institute for Scientific Co-operation, Tubinger; Also OECD, Observer—The High Cost of Protection No. 150, Feb.-March 1988.
7. The Legal Texts, Agreement on Trade Related Aspects of Intellectual Property Rights, Art. 7 and Art. 8. Also WTO, Trading into future, *Ibid.* Feb. 98. Mascus Keith, Denise Normative Concerns in the International Protection of IPR, The World Economy, 13 (1990)
8. WTO, The Report on the Committee on Trade and Environment, 1996 (Nov.) Also *The Economist*, London, Oct. 1999, Jagdish N. Bhagwati, Labour Standards Social Clause and WTO (1994), Columbia University (Mimeo). Asian Development Bank, Challenges for Asia's Trade and Environment, Economic

Staff Paper-57. T.R. Manoharn, Beena Pandey, Zafar Dad Khan, Trade and Environment Linkages, *A Review of Conceptual and Policy Issues*, (RIS-2000).

9. Panchmukhi, V.R., WTO and India Challenges and Perspectives, RIS (Discussion Papers), 2000. By the same author, Globalisation, Competition and Economic Policy—The Second D.T. Lakdawala Memorial Lecturer at All India Economic Association (1998). Also by the same author, South-South Co-operation : An Overview of Possibilities and Challenges, paper presented at South-South Co-operation on Trade, Investment and Finance, organised by the Carto Rica, January 1997.
10. Michall Finger, J., ERD Working Paper Series No. 21, Economic and Research Deptt. (ADB) The Doha Agenda and Development: A View from the Uruguay Round, Sept. 2002.

SUSTAINABLE DEVELOPMENT: GLOBAL WARMING

P.K. Vasudeva

ABSTRACT

Although under Kyoto Protocol (2008-2012) ratified by the UNFCCC, India does not have a legal or binding obligation to reduce carbon emission, United States, the biggest polluters or carbon emitter continues to state that emerging economies like China, India, Brazil and South African must also take action on reducing carbon emission.

According to an analysis of data from UNFCC by Centre for Science and Environment (CSE) carbon emissions of the rich industrialized countries have increased 14.5% during 1990-2006.

With just 15% of the world population, rich countries account for 45% of carbon dioxide emissions. Developing countries like Japan, European Union, United States have been asking for 'interim targets' for emission reduction for the developed countries (25-40% reduction by 2020 from 1990 baseline), while developed countries are non-committal on this.

With little substantive progress in establishing a consensus on global climate policy and developing countries (especially India and China) unwilling to adopt greenhouse gas restrictions that will undermine their economic development, U.S. policy-makers are faced with the possibility that companies facing higher costs under unilateral climate restrictions will find it much harder to compete with foreign competitors with lower business costs.

Punitive trade measures, direct subsidies, tax credits, government loans, and other government support programs could violate WTO rules against subsidies and countervailing duties. Trade measures that treat countries differently undermine the non-discriminatory basis for global trade that has helped promote prosperity around the world.

Climate change is being described as the most important environmental challenge before humankind today. The mitigation of climate change, by drastically reducing GHG emissions and stabilising the carbon dioxide concentration in the atmosphere has become a prerequisite to avoid a strong alteration of the climate system. In terms of GHG emissions, the trends are rising rapidly as well.

The market mechanism available to developing countries is the Clean Development Mechanism (CDM), which allows entities that have an emission reduction targets to purchase emission reduction from projects in developing countries. As a developing country, India does not have any emissions reduction target, but it is able to sell certified emission reductions (CERs) pursuant to the CDM, to large emitting countries that have emission reduction targets under the Kyoto Protocol.

The WTO/UNEP report on "Trade and Climate Change" published recently examines the intersections between trade and climate change from four perspectives: the science of climate change; economics; multilateral efforts to tackle climate change; and national climate change policies and their effect on trade.

At the recent G-8 meet in Italy, to which China and India were invited, global warming and climate change figured prominently and two Declarations of far-reaching consequence emerged.

INTRODUCTION

As India pushes for 'equitable' global sharing of carbon space while dealing with negotiations on climate change mitigation, the global attention would be focused on developed countries' initiatives towards drastic carbon emission reduction.

According to Ministry of Environment and Forest officials, India would definitely push for larger allocation toward green technology transfers from developed to developing countries which would faced with lots of opposition. "The funds for technology transfer should be well and above the Official Development Assistance committed by developed countries".

Amid Financial Turmoil, World Turns Focus on Carbon Emission

Although under Kyoto Protocol (2008-12) ratified by the UNFCCC, India does not have a legal or binding obligation to reduce carbon emission, United States, the biggest polluters or carbon emitter continue to state that emerging economies like China, India, Brazil and South African must also take action on reducing carbon emission.

Even Kyoto protocol, which asked for 5% emission cut by developed countries failed as United States walked out.

According to an analysis of data from UNFCC by Centre for Science and Environment (CSE) carbon emissions of the rich industrialized countries have increased 14.5% during 1990-2006. "In fact, carbon dioxide emissions of countries like Australia have increased as much as 40% during the period," Sunita Narain, Director, CSE said.

As per the US department of energy figure of 2007, during 1980-2005, the total emissions of the US were almost double that of China and more than seven times that of India. With just 15% of the world population, rich countries account for 45% of carbon dioxide emissions.

Developing countries like Japan, European Union, United States have been asking for 'interim targets' for emission reduction for the developed countries (25-40% reduction by 2020 from 1990 baseline), while developed countries are non-committal on this. Japan is pushing for a 2050 target without defining a baseline.

While the shared vision agreed by most of the countries stresses the need for 'a shared vision for long-term cooperative action, including a long-term global goal for emission reductions. In principle of common but differentiated responsibilities', the US has been demanding that every country has to take emission reduction targets which has been rejected by G77 countries like India, Brazil along with China.

"We may not be able to get the kind of financial resources commitments required from the developed countries towards climate change mitigation and adaptation given the acute financial crisis," Shyam Saran Prime Minister's special envoy on climate change had said recently. He said the attention given to climate change issues might be given lower priority as the whole attention is focused towards reviving the financial system in the developed countries.

Free Trade Cleaner Environment: US

Regardless of the scientific merit behind doomsday predictions of global warming, President Obama and Congress seem intent on instituting a U.S. policy regime to address the specter of climate change.

The debate on the most effective way to "green" America—cap-and-trade, carbon taxes, tough energy standards and regulations, some hybrid approach, or sticking to open markets—will be a heated one. With affordable green technologies still in development, policy-makers need to recognize that the economic cost of limiting U.S. production of greenhouse gases on U.S. consumers and companies will be high—high enough to question whether the costs are worth the equally uncertain benefits such measures would bring.

Costs and Benefits

The projected cost of a climate scheme on the U.S. economy—evidenced from Europe's problematic climate program and the Kyoto Protocol's failure to affect emissions in signatory nations—illustrate how difficult it is for governments to impose binding climate restrictions without undermining economic growth.

If Congress and the President do embark on such a potentially treacherous course, households and firms will face much higher costs for energy and energy-intensive goods, categories that include virtually every product in our economy. Hard-pressed U.S. consumers and producers will find no relief from artificially inflated prices by turning to lower-cost imports, as the climate change zealots propose to erect trade barriers to raise the costs of foreign products produced under less severe environmental policy constraints.

Some U.S. companies and policy-makers may find it fair for the government to prop up domestic businesses, whose profitability will have been destroyed by new climate change regulations, against foreign competitors whose governments have chosen to be less draconian. America's trade partners are unlikely to agree.

Many such trade restrictions could violate World Trade Organization (WTO) rules and lead to legal sanctions against the U.S. Even if some of the proposed measures hold up against legal scrutiny in the WTO, the potential for nations to retaliate against U.S. trade measures is very real. Any U.S. restrictions, whether consistent with WTO agreements or not, would undermine development in poorer countries and make it more difficult to achieve a multilateral consensus on the rules of trade that best support environmental objectives.

When all these negative effects are taken into account, it is clear that the adoption of protectionist polices as a part of a U.S. climate regime does far more harm than good and should be avoided.

Climate Legislation and Trade

With little substantive progress in establishing a consensus on global climate policy and developing countries (especially India and China) unwilling to adopt greenhouse gas restrictions that will undermine their economic development, U.S. policy-makers are faced with the possibility that companies facing higher costs under unilateral climate restrictions will find it much harder to compete with foreign competitors with lower business costs. Consequently, American firms may fail or may take their jobs and flee to countries with less costly business environments.

While such productivity-boosting moves are good for the U.S. economy in the long run, they can impose short-term costs on specific firms and individuals and are a political lightening rod. Unfortunately for those who would attempt to control global climate, such measures also undermine any impact U.S. greenhouse gas restrictions might have on reducing global levels of emissions.

For the advocates of climate change legislation, trade-related measures can potentially counteract the loss of competitiveness that such environmental regulations impose on U.S. businesses and, in theory, compel other countries to adopt similar climate regimes.

Tax credits, subsidies, government loan guarantees, and other policy mechanisms designed to compensate partially for the cost of carbon controls on U.S. firms would then work hand in hand with more explicit tariffs or quotas on imports from countries without comparable environmental restrictions.

The idea that punitive trade measures against carbon-intensive products would motivate countries to implement carbon restrictions depends on the ability to measure carbon intensity in imports and on the level of trade that would be affected by U.S. policy.

Countries may not export enough carbon-intensive products to the U.S. for trade measures to drive nations to adopt carbon restrictions. More problematic, because production processes, energy sources, and capital stock vary by country, industry, and even by product, the information needed to accurately tax imports for carbon content would be very difficult to obtain.

Therefore, the most likely result is the imposition of a more bureaucratically feasible one-size-fits-all approach to taxing carbon-intensive products at the border. Unfortunately, such an approach has the perverse effect of penalizing clean foreign producers, who may have higher costs, at the expense of dirtier ones while reducing the incentive to better internalize the cost of carbon in traded goods.

Moreover, energy standards and regulations may run up against trade rules that dictate that domestic and foreign firms should be treated identically and may create technical barriers to trade disallowed under WTO agreements. Punitive trade measures, direct subsidies, tax credits, government loans, and other government support programs could violate WTO rules against subsidies and countervailing duties. Trade measures that treat countries differently undermine the non-discriminatory basis for global trade that has helped promote prosperity around the world.

The gains from trade include economic growth and rising incomes in all countries. For developing countries—which would likely be hardest hit by trade restrictions in climate legislation—the economic stress will be particularly great. This, perversely, will likely increase the harm done to the environment: Economic growth increases the ability for developing countries to afford protecting the environment.

Historically, as a nation's prosperity increases, its desire—and more importantly, the resources available—to adopt environmental protections become stronger and result in policies that accommodate the individual needs of the country. Engaging in freer trade can better promote the evolution of good regulations by empowering countries with the economic opportunity to develop and raise living standards.

Protectionism is Against Competitiveness

Trade measures in carbon-control legislation may appear necessary for protecting U.S. competitiveness and promoting broader international participation in such schemes. However, in reality, such measures will likely create a more hostile trade environment that costs U.S. firms access to global markets.

Even if countries do not file complaints within the WTO or resort to outright retaliation against America for raising trade barriers, protectionism cannot guarantee a cleaner environment. Current efforts to find a multilateral consensus within the WTO on lowering trade and non-tariff barriers against trade in clean technologies will be more difficult as climate-related trade disputes rise. Worst of all, the general contraction in trade that protectionism would induce will only make developing countries poorer and less willing and able to address environmental concerns.

Rather than using trade policy as a weapon, America should keep markets open. Policy-makers—regardless of the shape of any final climate bill—should maintain the integrity and freedom of global markets as a means to transfer clean technologies, keep international investment flowing, and promote economic growth and prosperity in the U.S. and around the world.

If what gets measured gets managed, then a majority of the Indian companies have begun well to take on the climate change challenges. More than half (55%) of Indian companies are maintaining either complete or partial greenhouse gas (GHG) inventory, according to the trends emerging from the FE-EVI Green Business Survey. The inference is based on the responses of 200 firms.

GHGs like carbon dioxide, methane, nitrous oxide, perfluorocarbons, hydrofluorocarbons and sulphur hexafluoride cause anthropogenic or human induced global warming. Corporations use GHG inventories to track the sources of their emissions to minimise them and comply with mandatory or voluntary caps. A GHG inventory also serve as a source for baseline data for companies engaged in emission trading under Clean Development Mechanism (CDM).

While 15% Indian companies claim that they have developed a complete GHG inventory, another 40% say that they maintain a partial GHG inventory. Most of the energy intensive power companies (84%) claim to keep either partial or complete GHG inventory. The remaining 45% organisations have not made any GHG inventory. PSUs lag Indian private sector companies and MNCs in developing GHG inventories.

Tata Group Top Corporate Leader in Sustainable Development

The Tata Group has emerged as the top corporate leader in sustainable development in India. The Tatas are followed by Reliance and Infosys, according to communication solutions and services provider BT, which launched India's first sustainability index last week. Respondents also mentioned companies like ITC, Wipro, Suzlon, Airtel, Honda, ONGC, IL&FS and Satyam.

Developed in collaboration with public opinion and research company, GlobeScan, the index is meant to assess the progress of businesses on sustainable development. The index is based on the responses of 215 opinion leaders from academics, businesses, government and NGOs. Besides, 1,168 IT employees joined in an online survey. The survey focused on questions related to long-term economic growth, inclusive employment, education, employment creation, health, corporate/government collaboration, land and displacement, natural resources, climate change, corporate governance, solid waste and water.

Launching the Sustainable Development Index: An Assessment of Business Performance in India, Teri's director-general R.K. Pachauri said, "The index is important because what gets measured gets managed." He added, "Major social challenges can't be addressed by only governments and NGOs. The role of businesses is crucial. Businesses can't succeed in societies that fail."

The report reveals that Indian companies are getting proactive on sustainable development, but their performance is still disappointing. The respondents blamed it on lack of awareness in corporate as well as lack of will in the political leadership. Said Nitin Desai, a former United Nations under-secretary general, "Sustainability has to be integrated in corporate strategy. Corporate have to look beyond CSR in their own self-interest."

Saying that China, Japan and the European Union are ahead of India in addressing issues like climate change, corporate governance and water resource management, Chris Coulter of Globscan added, "It's time for India to catch up. The world needs India to become a leader in sustainability."

The index is planned as an annual event. Said BT India chairman Arun Seth, "It'll encourage companies to benchmark their sustainability initiatives." Locating the index in the current financial meltdown, Allen Ma, president BT Asia Pacific, added, "You don't look at 18 months of recession when you make decisions for the next 18 years. We don't have to be only lean and mean, but also clean now."

Green Jobs can Help Cope with Financial Meltdown

In these days of financial meltdown, green jobs, as they are labelled, ensure both job security and energy security. They are the portals to the new nature-dependent, climate-sustaining and pro-nature economic order. The fossil fuel, carbon emission and pollution-driven energy economy will have to give way to new way of power generation, consumption and maintenance. Billions of dollars are being invested on agro-forestry, fuel-feedstock cultivation, biofuels, organic agriculture, wind power generation, solar photovoltaic cell manufacturing, installation and maintenance, green buildings, recycling of metals, etc. In this process millions of men and women will find employment and advancement in sustainable way of living.

The Worldwatch Institute and Greenpeace have said that the pursuit of green jobs will be a key economic driver of the 21st century.

The current employment in renewables and supplier industries are estimated at about 2.3 million worldwide. The wind power industry employs some 3,00,000 people, the solar photovoltaics (PV) sector an estimated 1,70,000, and the solar thermal industry more than 6,00,000. More than one million jobs are found in the biofuels industry.

Climate-proofing the global economy will involve large-scale investments in new technologies, equipment, buildings and infrastructure, which will provide a major stimulus for much-needed new employment and an opportunity for retaining and transforming existing jobs.

"The potential for green jobs is immense. But much of it will not materialise without massive and sustained investment in the public and private sectors. Governments need to establish a firm framework for greening all aspects of the economy, with the help of targets and mandates, business incentives and reformed tax and subsidy policies. It will also be critical to develop innovative forms of technology transfer to spread green methods around the world at the scale and speed required to avoid full-fledged climate change. Cooperative technology development and technology-sharing programmes could help expedite the process of replicating best practices," says Michael Renner, researcher with Worldwatch Institute and author of Working for People and the Environment.

In India, wind power equipment manufacturing capacity and installation of windmills, both by Indian and foreign companies are slated for a quantum jump, offering employment in cities and remote villages for lakhs of people. More than a dozen companies, including Reliance, Videocon, Moser Baer and Emco Energy have announced setting up of facilities for producing solar power films and panels. Green building are also getting popular.

The Centre for Jatropha Promotion (CJP) is set to implement its New Biodiesel Tree Plantation. The NBTP Project, which aims to plant 5 trillion Jatropha trees in Rajasthan, Gujarat and Madhya Pradesh. The target is to produce 10 million tonne of Jatropha-biodiesel a year, and to initiate a sustainable biofuel industry in those states. The CJP is dedicated to the development of alternative fuels from non-food oilseed bearing trees. The centre aims to enhance ecologically sensitive, pro-poor investments in sustainable non-food biodiesel feedstocks in the developing world.

Construction jobs can be greened by ensuring that new buildings meet high performance standards. And retrofitting existing buildings to make them more energy-efficient has big job potential for construction workers, architects, energy auditors, engineers and others.

It is estimated that the auto-sector can create over 8 million jobs worldwide in the green auto manufacturing. Currently, only 2.5 lakh are employed in this sector.

"Modern rail and urban transit systems offer a greener alternative, but they need fresh commitment and investments to reverse the job erosion of recent decades. In a growing numbers of cities, good jobs are being generated by the emergence of bus rapid transit systems. There are also substantial green employment opportunities in retrofitting old diesel buses to reduce air pollutants and in replacing old equipment with cleaner compressed natural gas (CNG) or hybrid-electric buses. In New Delhi, the introduction of 6,100 CNG buses by 2009 is expected to create 18,000 new jobs," adds the World Watch Institute report.

The steel, aluminum, cement and paper industries are highly energy-intensive and polluting. But increasing scrap use, greater energy efficiency and reliance on alternative energy sources may at least render them a pale shade of green. Worldwide, more than 40% of steel output and one-quarter of aluminum production is based on recycled scrap, possibly employing more than a quarter million people.

Agriculture and forestry often still account for the bulk of employment and livelihoods in many developing countries. Small farms are more labour—and knowledge-intensive than agro-industrial farms. They even use fewer energy and chemical inputs. Organic farming is still limited. But because it is more labour-intensive than industrialised agriculture, it can be a source of growing green employment all over the world.

There is additional job potential in efforts to cope with climate change. Building flood barriers, terracing land and rehabilitating wetlands is labour-intensive work.

"Green jobs need to be decent jobs—offering good wages and income security, safe working conditions, dignity at work and adequate workers' rights. Sadly, this is not always the case today. Recycling work is sometimes precarious, involving serious occupational health hazards and often generating less than living wages and incomes. Growing crops at biofuels plantations in countries like Brazil, Colombia, Malaysia and Indonesia often involves excessive workloads, poor pay, exposure to pesticides and oppression of workers. These cautionary aspects highlight the need for sustainable employment to be good not only for the environment but also for the people holding the jobs. Still, an economy that reconciles human aspirations with the planet's limits is eminently possible," says the World Watch Institute report.

Poor Nations to get Funds to Fight Climate Change

Negotiators at a UN climate conference broke through red tape and freed up millions of dollars to help poor countries adapt to increasingly severe droughts, floods and other effects of global warming.

"This could be the one thing to come out of Poznan," said Kit Vaughan of WWF-Britain. The decision in the final hours of the two-week conference could begin to release some $60 million within months, according to delegates and environmentalists following the closed-door talks.

"This is an important step," said delegate Mozaharul Alam of Bangladesh. Alam said ministers and senior delegates from dozens of countries decided to give a blocked fund's governing board the authority to directly disburse money to developing countries for projects to reduce greenhouse gases. Until now, the UN-backed Adaptation Fund board could not operate as its board had no right to approve and sign those contracts.

The fund is derived from a 2% levy on offset investments that industrial nations make on green projects in the developing world. The negotiators have been discussing ways to ramp up the fund into the billions.

The agreement was one of the few concrete goals the delegates set for Poznan when the talks began on December 1. Delegations from 190 countries are negotiating a new climate change pact, to be completed next December in Copenhagen, to succeed the Kyoto Protocol when it expires in 2012.

Former US Vice-President Al Gore, who shared last year's Nobel Peace Prize for raising awareness of climate change, urged the conference to stay focused on the task of reducing global carbon emissions that have begun to change the conditions of life on Earth.

Winning cheers and ovations, Gore called on heads of state to convene several climate change summits over the next 12 months to spur on the talks ahead of the crucial meeting in Copenhagen. This challenge "affects the survival of human civilisation," Gore said. "We cannot negotiate with the facts, we cannot negotiate with the truth about our situation, we cannot negotiate with the consequences of unrestrained dumping of 70 million tons of global warming pollution.

Clouded on Climate

Temperatures are set to rise as negotiators gather to prepare for the crucial December Copenhagen climate agreement that will replace the Kyoto Protocol.

With climate negotiations reduced to a rich *versus* poor slanging match, the US will be on watch as usual, with the Obama administration making its first appearance at such a meeting. Thus far the US has opposed the Kyoto Protocol caps, unlike the European Union that plans to cut emissions by at least 20 per cent by 2020 and is ready to go up to 30 per cent if other industrialised nations agree. Though the US President, Mr Barack Obama's "we will get it done" statement on climate legislation augurs well for the Bonn negotiations, it is not clear how far domestic realities will allow Washington to go beyond the good intentions. Further, the US would want to see key co-GHG contributor China—the two account for more than 40 per cent of the world's GHG emissions—increase its commitment to emissions reduction. It would also want enforceable targets set for other major developing countries such as India and Brazil that were exempted till 2012 under the Kyoto Protocol. Though the advanced developing nations will not accept absolute cuts. This group may yet strike some common ground with the industrialised countries, but the position of the other developing countries, represented by G77, remains tentative as they are unable to arrive at a consensus on major issues, hampered by their vastly divergent interests. The negotiators will thus have to devote time to the 'Nationally Appropriate Mitigation Actions' (NAMA) and 'Reducing Emissions from Deforestation and Degradation' (REDD) that have emerged in recent times.

Countries will also need to think up improvements to existing systems, such as the Clean Development Mechanism (CDM), and the shape and place of new ones, such as for land use and forestry or the inclusion of new gases. No one expects all the answers in December but most would be happy to get some, for such issues as near-term emission cuts for industrialised and developing countries, how much funds developed nations will allocate to help poorer countries invest in clean technologies, and structures to ensure these resources are deployed efficiently and effectively. The negotiators have one more session, in Bangkok in September/October, to warm to an accord on climate change.

Carbon Finance Fund: Potential and Benefits

Climate change is being described as the most important environmental challenge before humankind today. The mitigation of climate change, by drastically reducing GHG emissions and stabilising the carbon dioxide concentration in the atmosphere has become a prerequisite to avoid a strong alteration of the climate system. With its vibrant economy and a growing population, India has become a major energy consumer. Access to reliable, affordable electricity is a prerequisite for socio-economic development. In terms of GHG emissions, the trends are rising rapidly as well. The historical share in cumulative emissions, measured over the period 1900-2005, amounted 2% for India. This pattern changes radically during the period 1900-2030, when the emissions rise to 4%. Nonetheless, per capita emissions in India still represent a fraction of those of industrialised countries.

The Kyoto Protocol, which was adopted in 1997 pursuant to the UN Framework Convention on Climate Change, represents an agreement that international efforts are required to reduce anthropogenic GHG emissions that contribute to global climate change. In accordance with the principle of 'common but differentiated responsibilities', the industrialised countries, which are responsible for the vast majority of historic GHG emissions, agreed to collectively reduce GHGs by an average of 5.2% as compared to the 1990 levels between 2008 and 2012.

The market mechanism available to developing countries is the Clean Development Mechanism (CDM), which allows entities that have an emission reduction targets to purchase emission reduction from projects in developing countries. As a developing country, India does not have any emissions reduction target, but it is able to sell certified emission reductions (CERs) pursuant to the CDM, to large emitting countries that have emission reduction targets under the Kyoto Protocol.

The number of projects from India is substantial; however, in terms of the certified emission reductions (CERs) available for trade, it is far less. In 2006, India's market share, measured in signed Emission Reduction Purchase Agreements (ERPA) was at 12%, second only to China, which supplied 61% of ERPA's. The Indian carbon market is largely driven by small and medium enterprises (SMEs), which is largely disadvantaged in the current carbon market. The proposed Carbon Finance Fund seeks to address the issue of upscaling the carbon finance operations in India. The first cycle of the Kyoto Protocol is between 2008 and 2012. While India has a relatively well-developed financial system, it seems project proponents have been unable to access carbon finance due to lack of suitable project finance instruments for this purpose and a conducive policy framework for project entities to optimise utilisation of this window.

There is a potential for the market share to go up through market-based initiatives such as developing the Carbon Finance Fund (CFF) and integrating it with the ongoing efforts. The CFF would act as a platform for financial resource management, carbon trade, information collection and dissemination, and technical support through extensive domestic and international cooperation. The CFF would introduce a holistic approach to enable project entities to explore the carbon finance window for earning resources for the project on a sustainable basis. CFF would thereby help significantly upscale new investments with carbon finance as an additional source. It will also help in replication of successful projects.

Government of India should establish the CFF as a permanent, sustainable financing mechanism which could be a unique partnership between the government of India, International Financial Institutions (IFIs), bilateral donors and public and private sector financial institutions to coordinate and implement a carbon finance programme in order to maximise the number of projects, which can be registered with CDM EB. This would complement and reinforce the ongoing efforts currently in operation.

CFF will blend resources grants and loans, both domestic and external for the purposes of determining the overall cost of its funds. CFF would potentially raise resources through a number of ways including the following: World Bank Group loan or IDA credit channeled through GoI (by way of corpus contribution); GOI budgetary contributions as loans/grants to the CFF corpus; bilateral donors; market borrowings by CFF with/without GOI guarantees; public sector institutions' contributions as corpus funds; and private sector (equity) contributions, loans, and co-financing under the public-private sector initiatives.

To conclude, India acceded to the Kyoto protocol in 2002, although it does not have GHG emissions commitments, it has taken steps to address the issue of climate change, notably by encouraging projects under the CDM. The potential under CDM is enormous and the key initiatives that India needs to focus is on a strategic overview of CDM opportunities available and the international demand for emission offsets; identification of CDM projects for key sectors; key institutional, legal, financial and regulatory prerequisites to facilitate CDM project development and implementation, implement and process CDM projects in India; human and institutional capacity building to identify, develop and capacity to exploit global opportunities. The Carbon Finance Fund seeks to address these...

Aligning Trade and Climate Change Agendas

The issue of climate change has attracted increased attention among the world community lately, particularly as it is intertwined with the consequences of higher global temperatures caused by the rapidly increased concentration of greenhouse gases (GHG).

The 4th Assessment Report of the Intergovernmental Panel on Climate Change (IPCC) said the present-day patterns of resource consumption and population growth would cause the average temperature levels to rise by more than 2 degree Celsius which is the critical point that environmental disasters can occur. The IPCC's work also showed that temperature rises of between one and two degrees would already result in issues with water availability, flood risk, rising sea levels and threats to human health.

The intensive emission of CO_2 is the direct consequence of worldwide over-consumption. United Nations Environmental Programme (UNEP) estimated that it required 1.4 globes to sustain the current use of the natural resources of mankind. When considering the issue of historical emission of greenhouse gases, we cannot deny that the developed countries, having long benefited from industrialisation and a high standard of living, have been consuming the earth's environmental assimilative capacity.

The Kyoto Protocol has created and prioritised mechanisms that put a heavier burden on developed nations under the principle of "Common But Differentiated Responsibilities (CBDR)." However, when its first period of implementation is completed in 2012, the future negotiations will cause more complications and concerns among the developing countries, especially in connection with the trade-related agenda.

Tackling climate change obviously requires collective action to mitigate greenhouse gases, but it also touches upon the issue of fairness in which each country accepts responsibilities. The major challenge in designing international structures that are responsive to environmental considerations is to create greenhouse gas mitigation systems that embody both efficiency and fairness.

In order to realise effective enforcement which most multilateral environmental agreements (MEAs) are lacking, the alignment of international trade and climate change must be strengthened. Nonetheless, international trade must be used in such a way that it can improve the binding capacity of environmental agreements while avoiding trade protectionism and exacerbating inequity situation. In order to do so, there are some issues of concerns to be addressed.

First, carbon off-shoring and leakages which is the relocation of production sites from the Annex I countries to the non-Annex I countries, as specified by the Kyoto Protocol. Part of the increase in volume of greenhouse gas emission from developing countries is from foreign direct investment. Pressure has built up to force these developing countries into mitigation commitments while they, on the other hand, argue that the main cause is the increased production to serve the demands of the developed countries.

Second is Border Carbon Adjustment (BCA) which was introduced to deal with the problems of carbon leakage. The proponents of BCA consider the concept as compatible with WTO's Article XX. However, there are still some discrepancies, for example, the argument whether BCA could create discrimination between "like" products. The final goods, locally-produced or imported, are basically identical, but the manufacturing process can generate differentiated embedded carbon levels.

Though the use of BCA is to internalise the externalities generated by the foreign producers, this applies only to the present externalities. The current application of BCA by developed countries will indirectly force developing countries which should not be held responsible for historical emission, to immediately take full responsibility for GHG mitigation. If BCA is unavoidable, the countries that use it should at least set aside the revenue gained from this tax collection to establish a technological assistance fund. However, if BCA demands that the exporting countries buy offsetting carbon credits instead of paying extra tariffs, it will not be possible to set-up such a fund.

Third is the issue of production-based versus consumption-based approach in calculating the national inventory of GHG under the Kyoto Protocol. The production-based approach is preferred for its simplicity as GHG can be calculated directly during the production process and the amount of energy used. However, this ignores the embedded carbon emission from the international transport sectors and the issue of imports and exports.

This approach, together with CBDR principle, has depleted the competitiveness of the Annex I countries while boosting that of the non-Annex I members. To rectify the loss in competitiveness, some countries consider using BCA to level the playing field.

While the production-based approach is the polluters pay principle, another approach, consumption-based, is the beneficiaries pay principle. This is calculated by subtracting the net exports to the figure obtained in the production-based approach. It can address carbon off-shoring problems by concentrating on the consumption side and shifting responsibility back to the consumers.

The current study by the Good Governance for Social Development and the Environment Institute supported by Thailand Research Fund found that Thailand's overall inventory difference as calculated between these two approaches was only 1%. But in many sectors, such as food manufacturing, rubber and plastic products, non-metallic products, and textiles, there is over 35% difference.

This existing gap implies different responsibilities and, therefore, calls for future negotiation of greenhouse gas mitigation to consider its inventory based on the consumption approach for the sake of fairness and placing the responsibility on those who should bear it.

Therefore, the most important point to be made here is that "control of demand" is a noteworthy alternative to the mitigation of climate change problems. Based on oriental wisdom, aligning economic development and climate change solutions must not only emphasise economic efficiency and green technology, but also tackle the unnecessary and wasteful consumption caused by greed. The Asia-Pacific region offers several alternative development models based on Oriental Wisdom, including the Gross National Happiness of Bhutan and the Sufficiency Economy Philosophy of the King of Thailand, both of which may need to be more frequently discussed, studied, and adopted in concrete ways.

Clean Energy Systems

Climate Change possibilities and protocols for reductions of carbon emissions and exotic chemical removal from emissions, air, water bodies and earth eco-systems, land, rivers—energy alternatives, clean air initiatives, US agreements encourage robust alternative clean energy systems and fuel alternatives.

Carbon Sequestration

Carbon sequestration is one of the most promising ways for reducing the buildup of greenhouse gases in the atmosphere. In fact, even under the most optimistic scenarios for energy efficiency gains and the greater use of low- or no-carbon fuels, sequestration will likely be essential if the world is to stabilize atmospheric concentrations of greenhouse gases at acceptable levels.

The Office of Fossil Energy (FE), through research conducted at the National Energy Technology Laboratory is transforming the fundamental science of carbon sequestration into a portfolio of practical, affordable and safe technologies and mitigation strategies that the energy industry can use to reduce emissions of greenhouse gases.

Microbes and plants play substantial roles in the global cycling of carbon through the environment. The Office of Science's Biological and Environmental Research program continues to leverage new genomic DNA sequence information on microbes important to the global carbon cycle by characterizing key biochemical pathways or genetic regulatory networks in these microbes. Research in genomics and biological and environmental research are conducted at the universities and national laboratories supported by the Office of Science.

(a) use the most recent IPCC guidelines as a basis for estimating and reporting greenhouse gas emissions and removals from the land-use sector;
(b) respect Parties' respective goals for sustainable development;
(c) while having as its ultimate goal comprehensive accounting of all sources and sinks from land use, provide the flexibility for Parties to implement a staged approach beginning with those categories appropriate to national circumstances and capacities, with incentives for including additional landuse categories commensurate with increased capacity, technologies, and methodologies;
(d) allow for the evolution of national REDD-plus action plans, including: (1) self-financed actions; (2) actions eligible for

capacity building, technical assistance and financial support; and (3) actions that result in emissions reductions or removals with sufficient integrity to become eligible for market-based approaches;

(e) provide for reference levels (taking into account historic data and other relevant factors) that adjust over time and are guided by a long-term pathway that results in a sustainable level of standing carbon stock within a reasonable time period;

(f) be consistent with overall approaches to measurement, reporting, and verification under this Agreement, recognizing the need for higher levels of MRV for market-based eligibility;

(g) provide for further consideration of the economic, environmental, and social impacts of REDD-plus, including with respect to promoting biodiversity, the interests of relevant local and indigenous communities, and other benefits and risks of REDD-plus; and

(h) encourage all Parties to find appropriate ways to relieve the pressure on forests and land that results in greenhouse gas emissions.

WTO and Climate Change

The WTO/UNEP report on "Trade and Climate Change" published recently examines the intersections between trade and climate change from four perspectives: the science of climate change; economics; multilateral efforts to tackle climate change; and national climate change policies and their effect on trade.

The WTO and UNEP are partners in the pursuit of sustainable development and this report is the outcome of collaborative research between the WTO and UNEP.

"With a challenge of this magnitude, multilateral cooperation is crucial and a successful conclusion to the ongoing climate change negotiations is the first step to achieving sustainable development for future generations," said WTO Director General Pascal Lamy and UNEP's Executive Director Achim Steiner.

Both Steiner and Lamy urge the international community to seal an equitable and decisive deal at the crucial UN climate convention meeting in Copenhagen, Denmark in December 2009. They also urge nations to conclude the Doha trade round which includes opening trade in environmental goods and services, a complementary track towards reducing greenhouse gas emissions to scientifically-defensible levels.

The scientific evidence is now clear that the Earth's climate system is warming as a result of greenhouse gas emissions which are still increasing worldwide, and will continue to increase over the coming decades unless there are significant changes to current laws, policies and actions. Although freer trade could lead to increased CO_2 emissions as a result of raising economic activity, it can also help alleviate climate change, for instance by increasing the diffusion of mitigation technologies.

The global economy is expected to be affected by climate change. Sectors such as agriculture, forestry, fisheries, tourism and transport infrastructure which are critical for developing countries are more specifically affected. These impacts will often have implications for trade.

Opening up trade and combating climate change can be mutually supportive towards realizing a low carbon economy the new report says. Contrary to some claims, trade and trade opening can have a positive impact on emissions of greenhouse gases in a variety of ways including accelerating the transfer of clean technology and the opportunity for developing economies to adapt those technologies to local circumstances. Rising incomes, linked with trade opening can also change social dynamics and aspirations with wealthier societies having the opportunity to demand higher environmental standards including ones on greenhouse gas emissions. In addition there is evidence that more open trade together with actions to combat climate change can catalyze global innovation including new products and processes that can stimulate new clean tech businesses.

National policies, from traditional regulatory instruments to economic incentives and financial measures, have been used in a number of countries to reduce greenhouse gas emissions and to increase energy efficiency. The report highlights the effects that this complex web of measures might have on international trade and the multilateral trading system. In recent years, there has been a proliferation of technical requirements (voluntary standards and labelling) related to climate-friendly goods and energy efficiency. Likewise, financial support programmes for the use of renewable energies have also increased recently.

The report also reviews extensively two particular types of pricing mechanisms that have been used to reduce greenhouse gas emissions: taxes and emissions trading systems. Incidentally, the report reflects the debate that is taking place on policies aimed at preventing carbon leakage and protecting competitiveness, including on border measures.

Overall, the report highlights that there is scope under WTO rules for addressing climate change at the national level. However, the relevance of WTO rules to climate change mitigation policies, as well as the implications for trade and the environmental effectiveness of these measures, will very much depend on how these policies are designed and the specific conditions for implementing them.

Climate Change and G-8 Countries

At the recent G-8 meet in Italy, to which China and India were invited, global warming and climate change figured prominently and two Declarations of far-reaching consequence emerged. First, leaders of the G-8 declared that they recognised the broad scientific view that the increase in global average temperature above pre-industrial levels ought not to exceed two degrees Celsius. Thus, for the first time, a direct quantitative limit to permissible warming was mentioned in any such declaration.

The G-8 leaders also agreed to the goal of reducing their GHG emissions by 80 per cent by the year 2050 as part of a worldwide goal of a 50 per cent cut by that year — meaning that all nations, including the poor, would contribute to this effort. Significantly, the base year for calculating the cuts was left uncertain. It could be 1990, as the UN Framework Convention on Climate Change envisaged, or a recent year like 2005.

Examining the Declaration

Second, leaders of the 'Major Economies Forum' on energy and climate followed suit by reiterating the two degree limit in their Declaration and proceeded to affirm that "progress towards the goal would be regularly reviewed, noting the importance of frequent, comprehensive, and accurate inventories". Speculation is rife on the scope of these developments. So is the cry in India that, by acceding to the Declaration of the Forum, the Indian delegation had committed the country to accepting quantitative reduction targets and to outsider verification of its efforts. That would mean a significant departure from the tough stand India has been taking all along.

It is pertinent to examine whether the mention of the figure of 2 degrees Celsius in the Declarations was a mere underscoring of the urgency of climate action or a ploy to tie down China and India.

We need to look at several sources to arrive at a definitive answer to this question. First, let's us look at the Stern Review (October 2006), which was commissioned by the UK government. According to Stern: "If annual emissions continued at today's levels, greenhouse gas levels would be close to double pre-industrial levels by the middle of the century. If this concentration were sustained, temperatures are projected to eventually rise by 2-5 degree Celsius or even higher." Stern was clearly batting for invoking temperature in defining climate goals in preference to the debatable GHG levels. Second, Working Group I of the Inter-governmental Panel on Climate Change (IPCC) had observed, as early as in February 2007, that: "For the next two decades a warming of about 0.2 degree Celsius per decade is projected. Even if the concentrations of all GHGs and aerosols had been kept at year 2000-levels, a further warming of about 0.1 degree Celsius per decade would be expected."

Therefore, given the temperature rise of 0.74 degree Celsius already recorded and the prognosis of the IPCC for the oncoming decades, it would be reasonable to conclude that global warming would be close to 2 degree Celsius by the end of this century.

Setting the Focus

Thus, in the context of global warming and climate change, the result of emissions, that is, temperature rise, has come to occupy attention, in the final boundary-setting, in place of the cause, namely GHG levels. No matter what the GHG levels are, the rise in temperature should not be allowed to cross 2 degree Celsius. In this overarching view, claims for carbon space on grounds of historic deprivation or raising low living standards to comparable international levels become secondary.

Having fixed a tolerable rise in temperature as the goal of climate action, the strategy of the developed countries is to erect milestones in terms of global GHG reductions. Emissions will need to peak soon, say by 2015, and start falling so that they are halved from present levels by 2050 at the latest. This would mean developed countries cutting their emissions by 80 per cent by 2050 and emerging economies such as China and India pitching in with a cutback of 65 per cent.

The G-8 has done its homework well. By introducing the limit of 2 degree Celsius in the Declarations, it obtained an endorsement, though political, from developing countries to share the burden of the common cause instead of harping on the historic responsibility of the developed members to make all the necessary sacrifices.

Mentioning Specifics

One may note that the Declaration made no mention of the extent of GHG reductions that developed countries would make or of the reductions that developing countries would be called upon to shoulder. Entitlement to carbon space has thus become a discarded argument, much to the chagrin of China and India.

Was India taken by surprise at the G-8 meet? Perhaps, yes. A pointer to the 2 degree Celsius limit being raised at the meet was available in the statement made by the British Prime Minister, Mr Gordon Brown, days before the meet. The Indian delegation must have noted this statement. But the US viewpoint on the new tack was not known at that time. It was only at the meet that the US President got around to mentioning this limit specifically in the G-8 Declaration. Having made a specific mention of the limit in one document, it was just a short hop to include it in the second.

Game Point

With the sudden departure of the Chinese President before the major economies meeting, India could not have mustered enough support to stall the mention of the limit in the major economies' Declaration, even had it wanted to. In the event, even China turned out to be one of the signatories.

That the 2 degree Celsius limit would be invoked at every turn from now on is an eventuality India must face. So is the matter of verification of India's mitigation efforts and other actions. There may be no quantitative targets fixed for India but the measures it proposes to take must be "measurable, reportable and verifiable" as agreed to under the Bali Action Plan.

The climate end game of the developed countries is now clear. By invoking a tolerable limit to global warming, they hope to shift a good part of their burden on to China and India. (See Box A).

Box A

Tool to Counter Climate Change

Brazil and Peru had in 2007 proposed to the World Trade Organization (WTO) that biofuels and organic foods be classified as "environmental goods," thereby qualifying the two countries for deep tariff cuts. This proposal prompted an outcry from the United States, the European Union and other members of the WTO, once again placing the environment at the forefront of the Doha Development Agenda. Many have now been compelled to ask: What does this development mean for the future of Doha? One of Doha's nine negotiating groups is trade and the environment, and one of its key components is the elimination of trade barriers for environment-related goods and services.

"By negotiating reduced barriers to trade in environmental goods, we are attempting to make these goods cheaper and more readily available to increase the trade in this department," said Keith Rockwell, chief spokesperson for the WTO.

However, the complexities lie in where to draw the line between environmental and non-environmental goods. "The Japanese say that their washing machines are very efficient in the use of water, so is that an environmental good?" asked Rockwell. "Qataris say that natural gas gives off fewer CO_2 emissions than petroleum, so that should be an environmental product as well."

As the debate pits Brazil and Peru against other WTO members, the question remains: Where to draw the line in determining an environmental good?

Despite the undeniable environmental benefits of ethanol and other biofuels, countries such as the US, the European Union nations and Korea posit that only industrial goods, not farm products, should be considered when assigning the favourable status of "environmental product." Brazil, on the other hand, responded to critics calling its proposal a means of reconciling the persistent divisions between the WTO members about how to integrate the mandatory component of Doha on trade barriers and environmental goods.

The paradox of reducing trade barriers, however, lies in the increased carbon emissions from the cars, boats and planes needed to ship goods internationally. Approximately one quarter of the world's energy-related output of greenhouse gases (GHGs) is attributed to the transport sector. Fresh strawberries are out of season during the winter in the US and Britain, yet transporting these fruits from a country such as Kenya would produce substantial CO_2 emissions.

Critics say that the goal should not be solely to increase access to environmentally friendly products, but to ensure that they are actually put to use. Yet some, like...

Rockwell, believe the benefits are worth it.

"Trade is the efficient allocation of resources," he explained. "If every country had to make all of the things it consumes, we would have a disastrous situation. For all the concern about food miles, this is what the whole principle of comparative advantage is about. At the end of the day, you are producing wealth while ensuring access to such things as solar panels and wind turbines that help fight climate change."

Also crucial to increasing trade in energy and environmental goods is the other main component of Doha's environmental agenda — the coordination of trade policies with environmental policies. While the prevalence of trade-distorting subsidies has left many in the developing world impoverished, with farmers unable to compete with the artificially low market prices of imported goods, subsidies have also adversely affected the environment.

"The key point in coordinating environmental and trade policies is to ensure that they really are environmental measures and not protectionist tactics," said Rockwell. "Governments will employ standards which may not necessarily be for the protection of consumers or the environment, but are merely designed to protect the welfare of domestic farmers, or whatever industry it may be."

A case in point is fishing subsidies. The World Wildlife Fund estimates that nearly 70% of the world's fishing revenues come from direct governmental support, as the global fishing supply has dramatically dwindled in the process. Governments and communities, many believe, must accept sacrifices in order to join the fight against global climate change. Critics say that international institutions such as the WTO must not solely advance the age-old paradigms of economic growth, but must also create new frameworks that prioritise environmental progress.

Though all governments have opened their eyes to the menace of increasing carbon emission levels, rapid increase in the production of waste, destruction of natural habitats and many such problems that have cropped up with growth and development, they are yet to reach a consensus on each country's share of responsibility in mitigating the issues.

As the per capita emission levels of developed countries like USA, Canada and Australia are high, they are mandated by the Kyoto Protocol to reduce emissions (based on figures in the year 1990) at higher per centages — more than 90% in all cases — which in turn became unacceptable to these countries.

Developing countries like India, while clamouring for a per capita method of calculation of emission...

levels, has already taken up initiatives in Clean Development

Mechanism on a large scale. Ensuring equity among its masses while implementing sustainable development programmes, working out ways for financing of clean technology and foreseeing and avoiding various pitfalls in the transferring and implementation of clean technology are the challenges faced by the country in the current scenario.

Source: *The Financial Express*, July 6, 2008.

Climate: Countdown to Copenhagen

Climate negotiations have so far been fairly evenly balanced between rich and poor countries. Yet, if the EU's recent draft agreement is adopted in its present form later this year at Copenhagen, the scales will tilt decisively in favour of the rich, says N.R. KRISHNAN, the former Secretary, Ministry of Environment and Forests, Government of India.

The draft agreement contains propositions that may mark the end of the sovereignty of developing economies.

In the garb of combating climate change, developed countries have been attempting to slow down the economic progress of rapidly industrialising countries such as China, India, Mexico, Brazil and South Africa. The current economic recession affecting the developed world, in particular, and doubts on how long it would last, seem to have lent a new edge to these efforts.

Added to these is the compulsion of the climate calendar to arrive at a new international agreement by December, 2009 to limit global warming to not more than 2 degrees Celsius by the year 2100.

The European Union, which spearheads global climate action, is going about this task with surgical precision.

Recognising that the observed global warming of 1degree Celsius since 1860 was the result of growing concentrations of greenhouse gases (GHGs) in the atmosphere, arising from the development strategies pursued in the developed countries, the UN Framework Convention on Climate Change (UNFCCC) urged them to reduce their emissions of these gases in a time-bound targeted manner.

As for the developing countries, the Convention, invoking the principle of "common but differentiated responsibilities", envisaged no such targets, but exhorted them to take appropriate national actions, to limit the release of global warming gases.

Climate Discipline

The experience of the developed countries so far in limiting their emissions of GHGs has not been a happy one, given that most of them would not like to see their already low rates of economic growth drop further. Alongside this has been the slow and steady shifting of its industrial base to new centres such as China and India accompanied by substantial increases in the latter's GHG emissions.

While these emerging powers have prepared their own national action plans to limit their emissions in keeping with economic and social development needs, they do not want to get weighed down by targets that they feel would greatly hamper their development. India, in particular, emits far less GHGs per person (1.1 tonnes per year) compared to the global average of 4 tonnes because of its low energy consumption *vis-a-vis* growth. In recent years, the efforts of the developed world, particularly EU countries, have been to subject the emerging economic powers to targeted climate discipline.

The Fourth Report of the Inter-governmental Panel on Climate Change, which says temperatures will rise by over 2 degrees Celsius if the present GHG concentration of 385 parts per million (ppm) in the atmosphere exceeds 450 ppm has come in handy for the developed countries to advance their case for curbs on the developing world.

The former have drawn up a new global agreement to be adopted by all countries at Copenhagen later this year, notwithstanding that in December 2007, in Bali, they accepted a workable proposal to prepare and adopt national action plans whose results would be "measurable, reportable and verifiable".

'Common but Shared Responsibilities'

The new agreement, a draft of which was prepared by the Office of the European Commission and presented to the European Council, the European Parliament and related bodies on January 28, seeks to modify the principle of "common but differentiated responsibilities" of the developed and developing countries that forms the basis of the UNFCCC. In its place, a new principle of "common and shared responsibilities" is sought to be introduced.

The purpose of the move is clear. The EU would like the developing countries—at least, the more advanced ones like China and India—to be treated at par with the developed countries in the matter of quantitative reductions in GHG emissions.

Though the developed countries are responsible for the climate predicament, the EU draft is anchored on the premise that, in the fight against climate change, "developed country leadership is...not enough: a significant contribution from developing countries is also required." This assertion prepares the ground for diluting the responsibilities of developed countries and shifting a part of the burden to others.

The next step in the EU draft is to divide the developing countries into the "poorest" and others. Needless to say China, India and a few others would not count among the poorest and, hence, would be brought under the new climate discipline.

The draft does not mince words. It is strident that the better off among the developing countries will have to "commit to adopting low carbon development strategies by the end of 2011" and these strategies would "cover all key emitting sectors, especially the power sector, transport, as well as major energy-intensive industries..."

In quantitative terms, the EU would expect these countries to reduce their GHG emissions by 15-20 per cent from a "business-as-usual" scenario by 2020. It is not difficult to imagine the hard blow such strategies would deliver to India's economic growth.

After outlining the steps to shackle the economies of China and India, the EU draft states "Ensuring a level of ambition will be (the) key." The 'ambition' thus expected to be displayed will be monitored to see whether it is sufficient or not and, if need be, would be corrected.

CONCLUSION

According to the draft: "If, by 2016, the combined mitigation efforts of the group of developing countries (read China and India) are insufficient, the UN Climate Change Conference should set national ambition levels..." Does this mean that nations would abdicate their political and economic sovereignty in favour of some international body?

And, granting that sacrifices on the lines desired by the EU would be made by the developing countries, would the rich be forthcoming to fund the switchover to low-carbon technologies?

The EU's facile reply is that domestic finances of the developing countries should take care of much of their needs and any shortfall that results after the monetised gains of climate control action are deducted from the expenditures, may possibly be met by an international funding organisation.

This goes against the hitherto accepted principle of "no mitigation without compensation". Does the EU expect anyone to consider this proposition seriously?

The EU's line of thinking seems to have received the endorsement of the UN Secretary-General. During his visit to New Delhi recently, he supported the modified principle of "common and shared responsibilities" as opposed to "common but differentiated responsibilities" to govern climate action and hoped for a new agreement to emerge at Copenhagen which would be "comprehensive and balanced and effective". He will be convening meetings soon to canvas global support for this modified principle.

In the climate negotiations so far, the balance has been maintained evenly between the rich and the poor. But that, it appears, is set to change.

In the coming months, the position may swing decisively in favour of the rich. The developing world should do its utmost to reverse this trend. Copenhagen should not mark the end of their sovereignty or their economies.

REFERENCES

Daniella Markheim (2008). Climate Policy: Free Trade Promotes a Cleaner Environment, WebMemo #2408

Joseph Vackayil (2008), "Green jobs can help cope with financial meltdown", *The Financial Express,* November 24.

Measure emissions to check climate risks (2008), feBureau, *The Financial Express,* November 24.

Poor nations to get funds to fight climate change (2008), *Associated Press,* December 14.

Rajeev Singh (2008), Carbon finance fund: potential and benefits, *Business Line,* December 31.

Sandip Das (2008), Amid financial turmoil, world turns focus on carbon emission, *The Financial Express,* December 6.

Vasudeva P.K. (2008), Tools to Counter Climate Change, *The Financial Express,* July 6.

http://www.state.gov/g/oes/rls/other/2009/124101.htm

http://www.epa.gov/superfund/

http://www.egovmonitor.com/node/25933

http://www.aft.gouv.fr/

CHAPTER

10

GROWTH AND GREENERY SHOULD GO TOGETHER

Kewal Raj Dawar

ABSTRACT

Whenever an economy is set on the path of growth, some structural changes in the production sphere are bound to emerge in response to the domestic and global market variations with further implications upon resource usage as well as the ecology of the country. With the increase in the development activity, the pace of industrialization and urbanization speeds up and ecology becomes the natural casualty. The same is happening in India. After the achievement of independence, the economy was to be rehabilitated and there was a need to feed 36 crore people. With agrarian nature of the economy and traditional modes of cultivation, the performance efficiency on the economic front was not up to the mark and the overall growth rate of GDP remained stuck to 3.5 per cent for almost two and a half decades. With some policy changes during eighties and nineties, the industrial and trade activities picked up which stimulated the growth process. The economy started experiencing higher growth rate accompanied by rising population, increasing mobility and growing consumerism. All these factors taken together, in association with external influences started causing disturbance in the ecological balance of the country. The result was continuous rise in the carbon emission. There is an intense need for reducing green house effect and convert India in to a low carbon economy which can be possible with the introduction of refined production technology, change in the living style and extension of green cover.

INTRODUCTION

The growth activity going all over the world around though indispensable is resulting in the creation and accentuation of ecological imbalances visible in the form of environmental pollution. Being a cause of serious concern, it has thus started attracting the maximum attention of the development planners and environmentalists. With the development of civilization, the human needs multiply and there takes place expansion of economic activities which if not properly monitored, results in serious adverse implications upon the ecology. The unregulated growth activity and population rise, have generated unprecedented pressure upon natural resources and upset the environmental balance. Due to the combined effect of these factors, the greenhouse grasses are accumulating all over the world. Realizing the gravity of the problem, in Rio Earth Summit held in 1992, it was agreed by the participating nations that there needs to be maintained complete environmental sustainability. But after ten years, i.e. in 2002, there have been found evidences of growing ecological unevenness, rising carbon emission and environmental pollution. In India, too these problems have equal severity. The country has become vulnerable to the climate change. In carbon emission, India, with 1.17 billion tones stands at fifth position in the world as exhibited in Table 1

TABLE I

World's Top Ten EMITTERS (2005)

Country	*Carbon Emission (in billion tonnes)*
U.S.A	5.96
China	5.32
Russia	1.70
Japan	1.23
India	1.17
Germany	0.84
Canada	0.63
Britain	0.58
South Korea	0.50

Source: Nethetlands environmental Assessment Agency.

As per International Energy Agency (2007), estimates the per capita CO_2 Emission in India is 1.05 tones where as it is 19.61 tones in USA and 3.88 tones in China (www.domain-b.com/environment/2007 1207-india-co.html-11k). Three million premature deaths are occurring annually in the world due to outdoor and indoor air pollution and the highest numbers are assessed to occur in India (iipenvis.nic.in/ncy06/jun/jun05. htm-8k). This is a cause for severe concern for the country which is already in the grip of unending problem of poverty, growing sectoral imbalances and widening regional disparities. The environmental pollution is emerging as an acute crisis within the crisis. With the pollution, having a direct linkage with the growth activity, the sustainability of the development becomes susceptible.

Going back to the history of development of independent India, it is evident that pace of economic growth remained slow up to mid-seventies and the pollution was not that serious problem. Since then, with the stepping up of growth activity, resulted in environmental disturbances and the issue started receiving serious attention from the side of the government as well as NGOs. With the enhanced production practices leading to higher growth rate during 1980s and post-liberalisation era, the imbalances in the ecology started becoming more and more distinct. At present it has taken the shape of one of the burning problems of the country and hence is being hotly debated.

OBJECTIVES AND METHODOLGY

This paper aims at identification of the causal factors responsible for the problem of pollution and estimate their respective influence. It transcends into investigating the measures to bring down the level of pollution to an acceptable norm in order to restore the ecological balance in the country with a view to sustain its development. It further ventures to assess how far the extension in the forest and tree cover can be useful in this regard. The period of study has been fixed from 1990-91 to 2006-07. The environment pollution has been measured in terms of carbon-dioxide emission with the idea that this is the most important gas among the greenhouse gases that maintains a strong link between humanity and greenery. In fact this is instrumental in establishing reciprocal relationship between the two in the sense that what ever is exhaled by one is inhaled by the other and *vice versa*. The explanatory factors such as Population and GDP have been hypothesized as the main determinants. The variable of GDP has been taken at constant prices (1999-2000) in order to avoid inflationary influence and presented in Appendix-A. Due to the existence of problem of multicollinearity, a bi-variate log linear regression analysis has been executed.

EMPIRICAL ANALYSIS

The computed results have been exhibited below for further interpretation.

$$\text{Log } CO_2 = -1.267 + 1.432 \text{ Log Pop} \quad t = 6.014 \quad \text{sign: } 000 \quad R^2 = 0.687 \qquad \text{—(1)}$$

$$\text{Log } CO_2 = 0.308 + 0.668 \text{ Log GDP} \quad t = 9.361 \quad \text{sign: } 000 \quad R^2 = 0.844 \qquad \text{—(2)}$$

With a look upon the above equations (1) and (2), it is evident that population rise and GDP generation have a significant bearing upon carbon emission in the country with their respective exponential values being 1.432 and .668 respectively. It is evident that if population grows by one million than carbon emission goes up by 1.432 million metric tones. With regard to this factor, it is not only the volume of population, but its mode of living, economic conditions, increasing mobility, shift from rural to the urban areas, lack of awareness and thoughtless use of energy are some of the factors causing carbon emission in the country. The migration to the cities has resulted in increasing number of the slums and unplanned construction. About 40.6 million populations which constituted twenty-three per cent of the urban population lived in slums (Census of India, 2001). The living conditions of slum-dwellers are absolutely unhealthy and unsanitary. The majority of the rural population too lives in almost similar type of conditions either due to poverty or lack of awareness. Out of total carbon emission in the country approximately 40 per cent is shared by the fossil fuel alone. This is how population is causing carbon emission in the country.

The impact of income generation activity expressible in terms of GDP upon carbon emission has been explained in equation no. (2). The exponential value of GDP indicates that with income rise of one thousand crore rupees,0.668 million metric tons of carbon dioxide is emitted. In the post liberalization period, the rate of GDP growth improved significantly from 5 per cent to 9 per cent. The opening of the economy further resulted in the stepping up of growth activities in all the sectors of the economy. With the increase in agricultural activity, development of industry and expansion of trade and transport, the ecological balance has been disturbed as indicated by the rising carbon emission level (see Appendix A).

In the agriculture sector, there is increasing use of chemical fertilizers, pesticides and insecticides. With the mechanization of agriculture and irregular power supply, the use of diesel has gone up considerably. Similarly in the secondary sector, the phenomenal rise in the industrial activity has not been accompanied by corresponding improvement in the industrial technology to eliminate industrial waste and to protect the wholesomeness of the air. The industries particularly linked with mining of metals are a direct cause for deforestation particularly in the states like Orissa, Bihar, M.P., Rajasthan and Goa. The activity of mining has resulted in small scale and large scale deforestation. In 1990-91, with liberalization, the mining contracts have been signed with the Multi National Companies which required a vast area and thus deforestation. The rising level of carbon emission is a direct consequence of felling of trees which absorb carbon dioxide and exude oxygen There is a direct emission of smoke by the industry also which raises CO_2 level in the economy. The problem is becoming more acute due to the lack of monitoring. Only 50 per cent of the industries are monitored properly and the monitoring programme does not include small and medium enterprises which have a huge cumulative effect upon the environment. Further despite India's best efforts to develop alternative sources of energy, coal remains the dominant fuel as it satisfies 50 per cent of the country's energy needs and in the coming twenty years the demand for coal will be three fold. The replacement of highly polluting coal fired plants with advanced technology will require decades due to higher capital cost. Consequently carbon emission will go on rising. (iipen vis. nic.in/ncy06/jun/jun05. htm-8k). In tertiary sector due to the increasing number of the vehicles as well as their thoughtless use, the carbon emission level in the country is significantly rising. In addition to the public vehicles, number of the private vehicles has gone up exponentially from 2 crores in 1991 to 10 crores in 2007, i.e. five times and it is expected to be many fold. As per the estimates of Petroleum Conservation Research Association, by 2016, India will emerge as seventh largest car manufacturer, second largest two wheeler manufacturer and the largest three wheeler and tractor manufacturer in the world. On the trading side, when the required power supply is not available to brightly lit and shining multiplexes there is no other option except using diesel contributing to the carbon emission. The findings about the impact of GDP on carbon emission in particular have been empirically endorsed (Md. Abdus Salam and Anil Kumar Thakur, 2005).

It has been observed that the problem of carbon emission has been mainly due to population and income rise. A glance upon of equations (1) and (2), makes it clear that he impact of GDP (t=9.36, R^2 =0.844) has been found to be more consistent than that of population (t=6.014, R^2 =0.687). But both these variables are essential components of societal development. In case of Indian economy, the problem of over population and its living conditions have heavily caused imbalance in the environment of the country. In addition to the control of the rising population, there is an intense need for bringing about changes in the life style of the people by creating awareness and providing better living facilities to all sections of the society with different income layers. The increase in income along with rising carbon emission is an indicator of the fact that growth activity, going on in the country is not environment-friendly. The production technology needs overhauling. Then and only then development of the country can be sustained. Economic growth which has become the national religion of modern India, should not mean effluence of the present generation at the cost of posterities. The growth sustainability needs to be accompanied by environmental sustainability. But these measures are not sufficient to cope with the situation and achieve the objective of carbon reduction in the economy. Simultaneously due emphasis is required to be laid upon the extension and maintenance of the green cover in the economy for the growth activity to attain permanence and stability.

Extension of Forest and Tree Cover

In addition to the above cited measures, extension of the forest and tree cover in the country can be effectively instrumental in maintaining the ecological balance. The area under forest has almost remained the same over sixteen years in the sense that it was 6.8 million hectares in 1990-91 and 6.9 million hectares in 2006-07. Rather per capita forest area has come down from 0.08 hectares to 0.06 hectares in the corresponding years. On the contrary the carbon emission per capita increased from 0.80 metric tones to 1.04 metric tonnes, i.e. by 30 per cent. (See Appendix A). In the world perspective also, we are relatively poor in the forest wealth, as with 16 per cent of world population and 2.4 per cent of land area, we have 1.7 per cent of world's forest wealth. We need much larger forest cover than what we have at present. If the growth activity had remained at the same level as it was in 1990, even then we need at least 8.9 million hectares of forests cover, in order to keep the rising population which is by 24.4 per cent higher than the earlier one at the same level of carbon emission per capita, i.e. 0.80 MMT. But the forest expansion could not keep pace with the population growth. In fact the forest area measuring 821 thousand hectares was diverted to non forestry proposes during 1990-2004 which has been termed as deforestation by Food and Agricultural Organisation of UN (FAO).

No doubt the problem of forest loss is not confined to India only but it is world wide and acute in South-East Asia. (http://en.wikipedia.org/wiki/Deforestation). rather in India On the positive side in India, there has been reforestation too, due to which the net forest area could go up from 6.8 million hectares to 6.9 million hectares. If we go by the criterion of Maximum Attainable level of cleanliness under the given Indian conditions, then Chandigarh standard of 35.5 per cent of the total city area under forest and tree cover can be fixed as an acceptable norm. Accordingly 11.7 million hectares should be under forest and tree cover implying the need for putting additional 3.8 million hectares under forestry and tree plantation which can bring the carbon emission to a much lower level as one hectare of forest has the capacity to absorb about 6 metric tons of carbon dioxide (www.idpem.com/newsletter/vol6htm-41k). The cultural land measuring 1.3 million hectares is laying waste in the country which can be used for this purpose. Simultaneously, in the process of urban development, the sanction to the new colonies must be given only after fixing the minimum norm of 35.5 per cent area to be kept vacant for parks and trees. In the rural sectors, particularly rural roads, most of them are without trees on both sides can be put under tree plantation. In the pursuit of forestry expansion, the corporate sector needs to be involved either by compulsion or by incentives.

The MNCs earning huge profits may be persuaded to invest a part of their profits in forestry. Without the involvement of private sector the Green Goal of even putting 33 per cent area under forest and tree cover by 2012 can not be achieved not to speak of this new norm of 35.5 per cent. Not being confined to only celebration of VANMAHOTSV, we must follow China example where every body between the ages of 11 to 60 years, was required to plant three to five trees or do the equivalent amount of work in the forest services. The result was, since 1982 one billion trees had been planted every year (http://inwikipedia.org/wiki/Deforestation). The Rural Employment Guarantee scheme too can be partially utilized for the maintenance of forestry and tree cover.

CONCLUSION

The concluding observation is that with the rise of both population and income, it is essential to introduce desired changes in the production technology as well as extend forest and tree cover with a view to make the growth process secure, stable and sustainable. Towards this end, not only the government, but the other market contestants should undertake and promote those growth activities which ensure the maintenance of welfare of future generations. Simultaneously, the people need to be made conscious about the existence of the pollution problem and its likely implications upon the posterities. We should form a joint front including the government, corporate sector and the people to fight the problem. If we want the civilization to survive and growth to sustain, we must ensure that growth and greenery go together.

REFERENCES

Lal, Ashawani Kumar (2008) "Combating Global Warming", *Yojna*, June

Salam, Abdus Md., and Thakur, Anil Kumar, (2005) "Energy Production, Consumption and Economic Growth in India", *The Indan Economic Journal*, Vol. 3, Number 2 Jul-Sept.

Leah Temper, Joan Matinez-Alier (2007) "Is India Too Poor To Be Green", *Economic and Political Weekly*, April 28-May 4, Vol. L11, No. 17.

Promod Singh (1987), (ed.) Ecology of Rural India, Ashish Publising House, New Delhi.

Ravinder Sandhu (2003), (ed.) Urbanization in India, Sage Publication, New Delhi, *The Times of India*, July 21, 2005.

Census of India, 2001.

India Development Report, 2008, Indira Gandhi Institute of Development Research, Mumbai.

(http://inwikipedia.org/wiki/Deforestation)

(www.idpem.com/newsletter/vol6htm-41k)

(www.iipenvis.nic.in/ncy06/jun/jun05.htm-8k)

www.sanctuaryasia.com/resources/quickstarts/index.php-33k

http://wikipedia.org/wiki/listof_countriesbycarbon_dioxids_emission_capita. Key World Energy Statistics, 2007, www.domain-b.com/environment/2007 1207-india-co.html-11k.

APPENDIX A

Year	Carbon emission (MMT)	GDP at FC (in thousands crores)	Population (in Million)	Forest cover (in thousands hectare)	Carbon emission (MMT)	Carbon emission Per Capita	Area under forest per capita
1990-91	666	1084	833	67805	666	.80	.080
1991-92	681	1099	852	67866	681	.80	.079
1992-93	781	1158	668	67984	781	.90	.077
1993-94	796	1224	884	68314	796	.90	.076
1994-95	810	1302	900	68603	810	.90	.075
1995-96	922	1397	922	68817	922	1.0	.074
1996-97	1030	1508	942	68750	1030	1.0	.072
1997-98	1056	1573	960	69012	1056	1.1	.071
1998-99	1076	1678	978	68980	1076	1.1	.071
1999-00	1096	1787	996	69124	1096	1.1	.069
2000-01	1116	1864	1015	69621	1116	1.1	.068
2001-02	1137	1973	1033	69511	1137	1.1	.067
2002-03	1261	2048	1051	69645	1261	1.2	.067
2003-04	1271	2223	1068	69674	1271	1.2	.064
2004-05	1303	2388	1086	69672	1303	1.2	.064
2005-06	1240*	2612	1109	69769**	1240*	1.12	.063
2006-07	1178a	2864	1122	698668**	1178a	1.04	.062

Source: (1) http://wikipedia.org/wiki/listof_countriesbycarbon_dioxids_emission_apita

(2) *Economic Survey*, 2007-08.

(a) The figure obtained from Key World Energy Statistics, 2007.

* estimated figure on the basis of average of the preceding and succeeding figure

** estimated on the basis of average rate of growth in the forest area in the preceding five years.

CHAPTER

11

RENEWABLE ENERGY: NEED OF THE HOUR

P.K. VASUDEVA

ABSTRACT

Renewable energy is energy generated from natural resources—such as sunlight, wind, rain, tides, and geothermal heat—which are renewable (naturally replenished). In 2006, about 18% of global final energy consumption came from renewables, with 13% coming from traditional biomass, such as wood-burning. Hydroelectricity was the next largest renewable source, providing 3% of global energy consumption and 15% of global electricity generation.

Some renewable energy technologies are criticized for being intermittent or unsightly, yet the renewable energy market continues to grow. Climate-change concerns, coupled with high oil prices, peak oil, and increasing government support, are driving increasing renewable energy legislation, incentives and commercialization. New government spending, regulation and policies should help the industry weather the 2009 economic crisis better than many other sectors.

From the end of 2004 to the end of 2008, solar photovoltaic (PV) capacity increased six-fold to more than 16 gigawatts (GW), wind power capacity increased 250 per cent to 121 GW, and total power capacity from new renewables increased 75 per cent to 280 GW.

Large solar thermal power stations include the 354 megawatt (mW) Solar Energy Generating Systems power plant in the USA, Nevada Solar One (USA, 64 mW), Andasol 1 (Spain, 50 mW), PS20 solar power tower (Spain, 20 mW), and the PS10 solar power tower (Spain, 11 mW).

Renewable energy projects in many developing countries have demonstrated that renewable energy can directly contribute to poverty alleviation by providing the energy needed for creating businesses and employment. Renewable energy technologies can also make indirect contributions to alleviating poverty by providing energy for cooking, space heating, and lighting. Renewable energy can also contribute to education, by providing electricity to schools.

Sustainable development and global warming groups propose a 100% Renewable Energy Source Supply, without fossil fuels and nuclear power. Scientists from the University of Kassel have suggested that Germany can power itself entirely by renewable energy.

Overall, hydroelectric power can be far less expensive than electricity generated from fossil fuels or nuclear energy, and areas with abundant hydroelectric power attract industry.

Large hydroelectric power is considered to be a renewable energy by a large number of sources, however, many groups have lobbied for it to be excluded from renewable electricity standards, any initiative to promote the use of renewable energies, and sometimes the definition of renewable itself.

Solar power is all set to light up the renewable energy industry in the country with the launch of Jawaharlal Nehru National Solar Mission on November 14. The Prime Minister's Council on Climate Change approved the Rs. 91,684-crore draft plan, which aims to install 20,000 mw of solar power in the first phase ending 2020, in principle recently.

INTRODUCTION

Renewable energy is energy generated from natural resources—such as sunlight, wind, rain, tides, and geothermal heat—which are renewable (naturally replenished). In 2006, about 18% of global final energy consumption came from renewables, with 13% coming from traditional biomass, such as wood-burning. Hydroelectricity was the next largest renewable source, providing 3% of global energy consumption and 15% of global electricity generation.

Wind power is growing at the rate of 30 per cent annually, with a worldwide installed capacity of 121,000 megawatts (mW) in 2008, and is widely used in European countries and the United States. The annual manufacturing output of the photovoltaics industry reached 6,900 mW in 2008, and photovoltaic (PV) power stations are popular in Germany and Spain. Solar thermal powerstations operate in the USA and Spain, and the largest of these is the 354 mW SEGS power plant in the Mojave Desert. The world's largest geothermal power installation is The Geysers in California, with a rated capacity of 750 mW. Brazil has one of the largest renewable energy programs in the world, involving production of ethanol fuel from sugar cane, and ethanol now provides 18 per cent of the country's automotive fuel. Ethanol fuel is also widely available in the USA. While most renewable energy projects and production is large-scale, renewable technologies are also suited to small off-grid applications, sometimes in rural and remote areas, where energy is often crucial in human development. Kenya has the world's highest household solar ownership rate with roughly 30,000 small (20-100 watt) solar power systems sold per year.

Some renewable energy technologies are criticized for being intermittent or unsightly, yet the renewable energy market continues to grow. Climate-change concerns, coupled with high oil prices, peak oil, and increasing government support, are driving increasing renewable energy legislation, incentives and commercialization. New government spending, regulation and policies should help the industry weather the 2009 economic crisis better than many other sectors.

MAIN FORMS/SOURCES OF RENEWABLE ENERGY

Three Energy Sources

The sun powers the majority of renewable energy technologies. The Earth-Atmosphere system is in equilibrium such that heat radiation into space is equal to incoming solar radiation; the resulting level of energy within the Earth-Atmosphere system can roughly be described as the Earth's "climate." The hydrosphere (water) absorbs a major fraction of the incoming radiation. Most radiation is absorbed at low latitudes around the equator, but this energy is dissipated around the globe in the form of winds and ocean currents. Wave motion may play a role in the process of transferring mechanical energy between the atmosphere and the ocean through wind stress. Solar energy is also responsible for the distribution of precipitation, which is tapped by hydroelectric projects, and for the growth of plants used to create biofuels.

Renewable energy flows involve natural phenomena such as sunlight, wind, tides, and geothermal heat, as the International Energy Agency explains:

Renewable energy is derived from natural processes that are replenished constantly. In its various forms, it derives directly from the sun, or from heat generated deep within the earth. Included in the definition is electricity and heat generated from solar, wind, ocean, hydropower, biomass, geothermal resources, and biofuels and hydrogen derived from renewable resources.

Each of these sources has unique characteristics which influence how and where they are used.

RELATIVE COST OF ELECTRICITY BY GENERATION SOURCE

When comparing renewable energy sources with each other and with conventional power sources, three main factors must be considered:

- capital costs (including, for nuclear energy, waste-disposal and decommissioning costs);
- operating and maintenance costs;
- fuel costs (for fossil-fuel and biomass sources—for wastes, these costs may actually be negative).

These costs are all brought together, using discounted cash flow, here. Inherently, renewables are on a decreasing cost curve, while non-renewables are on an increasing cost curve. In 2009, costs are comparable among wind, nuclear, coal, and natural gas, but for CSP-concentrating solar power and PV (photovoltaic) they are somewhat higher.

There are additional costs for renewables in terms of increased grid interconnection to allow for variability of weather and load, but these have been shown in the pan-European case to be quite low-overall, wind energy costs about the same as present-day power.

WIND POWER

Vestas V80 Wind Turbines

Airflows can be used to run wind turbines. Modern wind turbines range from around 600 kW to 5 mW of rated power, although turbines with rated output of 1.5-3 mW have become the most common for commercial use; the power output of a turbine is a function of the cube of the wind speed, so as wind speed increases, power output increases dramatically. Areas where winds are stronger and more constant, such as offshore and high altitude sites are preferred locations for wind farms.

Since wind speed is not constant, a wind farm's annual energy production is never as much as the sum of the generator nameplate ratings multiplied by the total hours in a year. The ratio of actual productivity in a year to this theoretical maximum is called the capacity factor. Typical capacity factors are 20-40%, with values at the upper end of the range in particularly favourable sites. For example, a 1 mW turbine with a capacity factor of 35% will only produce an average of 0.35 mW. Over a year, output would be .35x24x365 = 3,066 mWh instead of 24x365 = 8,760 mWh. Online data is available for some locations and the capacity factor can be calculated from the yearly output.

Globally, the long-term technical potential of wind energy is believed to be five times total current global energy production, or 40 times current electricity demand. This could require large amounts of land to be used for wind turbines, particularly in areas of higher wind resources. Offshore resources experience mean wind speeds of ~90% greater than that of land, so offshore resources could contribute substantially more energy. This number could also increase with higher altitude ground-based or airborne wind turbines.

Wind power is renewable and produces no greenhouse gases during operation, such as carbon dioxide and methane.

WATER POWER

Energy in water (in the form of kinetic energy, temperature differences or salinity gradients) can be harnessed and used. Since water is about 800 times denser than air, even a slow flowing stream of water, or moderate sea swell, can yield considerable amounts of energy.

One of 3 Pelamis P-750 Ocean Wave Power Machines in the Harbor of Peniche, Portugal

There are many forms of water energy:

- Hydroelectric energy is a term usually reserved for large-scale hydroelectric dams. Examples are the Grand Coulee Dam in Washington State and the Akosombo Dam in Ghana.
- Micro hydro systems are hydroelectric power installations that typically produce up to 100 kW of power. They are often used in water rich areas as a Remote Area Power Supply (RAPS). There are many of these installations around the world, including several delivering around 50 kW in the Solomon Islands.
- Damless hydro systems derive kinetic energy from rivers and oceans without using a dam.
- Ocean energy describes all the technologies to harness energy from the ocean and the sea:
  - o *Marine current power*. Similar to tidal stream power, uses the kinetic energy of marine currents.
  - o *Ocean thermal energy conversion (OTEC)* uses the temperature difference between the warmer surface of the ocean and the colder lower recesses. To this end, it employs a cyclic heat engine. OTEC has not been field-tested on a large scale.
- Tidal power captures energy from the tides. Two different principles for generating energy from the tides are used at the moment:
  - o *Tidal motion in the vertical direction*—Tides come in, raise water levels in a basin, and tides roll out. Around low tide, the water in the basin is discharged through a turbine, exploiting the stored potential energy.
  - o *Tidal motion in the horizontal direction*—Or tidal stream power. Using tidal stream generators, like wind turbines but then in a tidal stream. Due to the high density of water, about eight-hundred times the density of air, tidal currents can have a lot of kinetic energy. Several commercial prototypes have been built, and more are in development.
- Wave power uses the energy in waves. Wave power machines usually take the form of floating or neutrally buoyant structures which move relative to one another or to a fixed point. Wave power has now reached commercialization.
- Osmotic power or salinity gradient power, is the energy retrieved from the difference in the salt concentration between seawater and river water. Reverse electrodialysis (PRO) is in the research and testing phase.
- Vortex power is generated by placing obstacles in rivers in order to cause the formation of vortices which can then be tapped for energy.

- Deep lake water cooling, although not technically an energy generation method, can save a lot of energy in summer. It uses submerged pipes as a heat sink for climate control systems. Lake-bottom water is a year-round local constant of about 4°C.

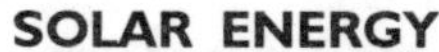

SOLAR ENERGY

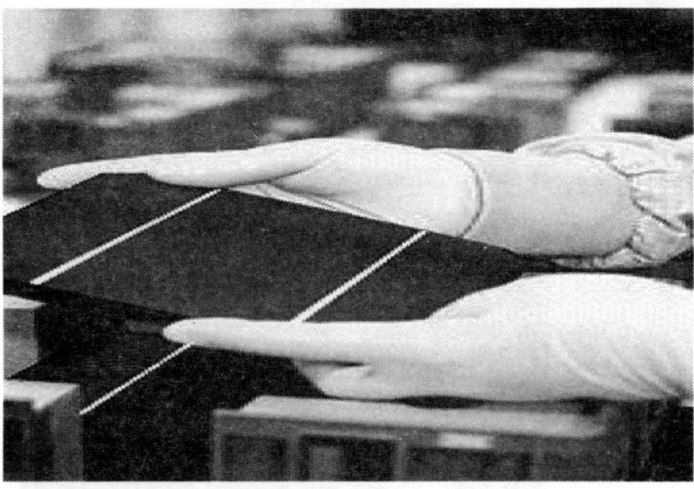

Monocrystalline Solar Cell

In this context, "solar energy" refers to energy that is collected from sunlight. Solar energy can be applied in many ways, including to:

- Generate electricity using photovoltaic solar cells.
- Generate electricity using concentrated solar power.
- Generate electricity by heating trapped air which rotates turbines in a Solar updraft tower.
- Generate hydrogen using photoelectrochemical cells.
- Heat and cool air through use of solar chimneys.
- Heat buildings, directly, through passive solar building design.
- Heat foodstuffs, through solar ovens.
- Heat water or air for domestic hot water and space heating needs using solar-thermal panels.
- Solar air conditioning

Growth of Renewables

From the end of 2004 to the end of 2008, solar photovoltaic (PV) capacity increased six-fold to more than 16 gigawatts (GW), wind power capacity increased 250 per cent to 121 GW, and total power capacity from new renewables increased 75 per cent to 280 GW. During the same period, solar heating capacity doubled to 145 gigawatts-thermal (GWth), while biodiesel production increased six-fold to 12 billion liters per year and ethanol production doubled to 67 billion liters per year.

Selected Renewable Energy Indicators

Selected global indicators	2006	2007	2008
Investment in new renewable capacity	63	104	120 $ bn
Existing renewables power capacity including large-scale hydro	1020	1070	208 $ bn
Existing renewables power capacity excluding large hydro	207	204	280 GW
Wind power capacity (Existing)	74	94	121 GW
Ethanol production (annual)	39	50	65 bn ltrs
Countries with policy targets for renewable energy use	00	66	73

New Generation of Solar Thermal Plants

Large solar thermal power stations include the 354 megawatt (mW) Solar Energy Generating Systems power plant in the USA, Nevada Solar One (USA, 64 mW), Andasol 1 (Spain, 50 mW), PS20 solar power tower (Spain, 20 mW), and the PS10 solar power tower (Spain, 11 mW).

The solar thermal power industry is growing rapidly with 1.2 GW under construction as of April 2009 and another 13.9 GW announced globally through 2014. Spain is the epicenter of solar thermal power development with 22 projects for 1,037 mW under construction, all of which are projected to come online by the end of 2010. In the United States, 5,600 mW of solar thermal power projects have been announced. In developing countries, three World Bank projects for integrated solar thermal/combined-cycle gas-turbine power plants in Egypt, Mexico, and Morocco have been approved.

World's Largest Photovoltaic Power Plants

First Solar 40 mW PV Array installed by JUWI Group in Waldpolenz, Germany

As of January 2009, the largest photovoltaic (PV) power plants in the world are the Parque Fotovoltaico Olmedilla de Alarcon (Spain, 60 mW), the Moura photovoltaic power station (Portugal, 46 mW), and the Waldpolenz Solar Park (Germany, 40 mW). Several other PV power plants were completed in Spain in 2008: Planta Solar Arnedo (30 mW), Parque Solar Merida/Don Alvaro (30 mW), Planta solar Fuente Álamo (26 mW), Planta

photovoltaica de Lucainena de las Torres (23.2 mW), Parque Photovoltaico Abertura Solar (23.1 mW), Parque Solar Hoya de Los Vincentes (23 mW), Huerta Solar Almaraz (22.1 mW), Solarpark Calveron (21 mW), and the Planta Solar La Magascona (20 mW).

Topaz Solar Farm is a proposed 550 mW solar photovoltaic power plant which is to be built northwest of California Valley in the USA at a cost of over $1 billion. Built on 9.5 square miles (25 km^2) of ranchland, the project would utilize thin-film PV panels designed and manufactured by OptiSolar in Hayward and Sacramento. The project would deliver approximately 1,100 gigawatt-hours (GW·h) annually of renewable energy. The project is expected to begin construction in 2010, begin power delivery in 2011, and be fully operational by 2013.

High Plains Ranch is a proposed 250 mW solar photovoltaic power plant which is to be built by SunPower in the Carrizo Plain, northwest of California Valley.

However, when it comes to renewable energy systems and PV, it is not just large systems that matter. Building-integrated photovoltaics or "onsite" PV systems have the advantage of being matched to end use energy needs in terms of scale. So the energy is supplied close to where it is needed.

China Serious on Solar Energy

In November 2009, Santa Clara's Applied Materials Inc. is scheduled to open a giant solar energy R&D center. The company is investing up to $300 million in the facility. It will not be situated in California, nor in the United States, but in Xian, China, because China's where the action is.

"If the U.S. does not get serious, China's going to own this industry," said Applied Materials spokesman David Miller. He points to the Manhattan Project-like push for alternative energy adopted by Chinese officials, which includes up to $60 billion annually in government investment. And here? "Here, we're way behind," said Miller. "We're still messing around with energy bills. We need to get serious, to get capital spending flowing, to get the government truly behind it, to get focused."

Miller and his company are not simply blowing smoke. In as little as two years, analysts predict, China will be the world's biggest consumer of solar energy. By 2013, its clean tech market could amount to $1 trillion annually, according to a report earlier from the China Greentech Initiative, a consortium of U.S. and Chinese companies that includes Cisco Systems and the Silicon Valley VC firm VantagePoint Venture Partners, which specializes in clean tech investments.

Neither is Applied Materials alone in its views. Numerous Bay Area executives and investors have expressed similar views with business ties to China. "They get that these are the industries of the 21st century," says VantagePoint managing partner Alan Salzman, whose Bay Area clean tech investments include Tesla Motors, BrightSource Energy and Solazyme. "The level of support for green tech there is breathtaking. It exceeds anything done here on a state or federal level."

As if any more wake-up calls were needed, two other VantagePoint Venture Partners' portfolio companies, Santa Clara's Miasolé, which produces advanced, thin-film solar panels, and Sunnyvale's Bridgelux, developer of energy-efficient LED lighting, are reluctantly considering locating their manufacturing facilities outside the United States. "From a global competitiveness perspective, we're just not there," said Salzman.

Developing Country Markets

Renewable energy can be particularly suitable for developing countries. In rural and remote areas, transmission and distribution of energy generated from fossil fuels can be difficult and expensive. Producing renewable energy locally can offer a viable alternative.

Renewable energy projects in many developing countries have demonstrated that renewable energy can directly contribute to poverty alleviation by providing the energy needed for creating businesses and employment. Renewable energy technologies can also make indirect contributions to alleviating poverty by providing energy for cooking, space heating, and lighting. Renewable energy can also contribute to education, by providing electricity to schools.

Kenya is the world leader in the number of solar power systems installed per capita (but not the number of watts added). More than 30,000 very small solar panels, each producing 12 to 30 watts, are sold in Kenya annually. For an investment of as little as $100 for the panel and wiring, the PV system can be used to charge a car battery, which can then provide power to run a fluorescent lamp or a small television for a few hours a day. More Kenyans adopt solar power every year than make connections to the country's electric grid.

Potential Future Utilization

Sustainable development and global warming groups propose a 100% Renewable Energy Source Supply, without fossil fuels and nuclear power. Scientists from the University of Kassel have suggested that Germany can power itself entirely by renewable energy.

Industry and Policy Trends

Many countries and states have implemented incentives - like government tax subsidies, partial co-payment schemes and various rebates over purchase of renewables to encourage consumers to shift to renewable energy sources. Government grants fund for research in renewable technology to make the production cheaper and generation more efficient.

Development of loan programs that stimulate renewable favoring market forces with attractive return rates, buffer initial deployment costs and entice consumers to consider and purchase renewable technology. A famous example is the solar loan program sponsored by UNEP helping 100,000 people finance solar power systems in India. Success in India's solar program has led to similar projects in other parts of developing world like Tunisia, Morocco, Indonesia and Mexico.

Imposition of fossil fuel consumption and carbon taxes, and channel the revenue earned towards renewable energy development.

Also oil peak and world petroleum crisis and inflation are helping to promote renewables.

Many think-tanks are warning that the world needs an urgency driven concerted effort to create a competitive renewable energy infrastructure and market. The developed world can make more research investments to find better cost efficient technologies, and manufacturing could be transferred to developing countries in order to use low labor costs. The renewable energy market could increase fast enough to replace and initiate the decline of fossil fuel dominance and the world could then avert the looming climate and peak oil crises.

Most importantly, renewables is gaining credence among private investors as having the potential to grow into the next big industry. Many companies and venture capitalists are investing in photovoltaic development and manufacturing. This trend is particularly visible in Silicon valley, California, Europe, Japan.

Central to the discussion over what power sources are renewable are definitions in law, which may determine whether certain projects are eligible for subsidies (or tax benefits). As a result, environmental groups and vested interests have done considerable lobbying and affected the definition of renewable or sustainable sources in legislation.

Hydroelectricity

The major advantage of hydroelectric systems is the elimination of the cost of fuel. Other advantages include longer life than fuel-fired generation, low operating costs, and the provision of facilities for water sports.

Operation of pumped-storage plants improves the daily load factor of the generation system. Overall, hydroelectric power can be far less expensive than electricity generated from fossil fuels or nuclear energy, and areas with abundant hydroelectric power attract industry.

However, there are several major disadvantages of hydroelectric systems. These include: dislocation of people living where the reservoirs are planned, release of significant amounts of carbon dioxide at construction and flooding of the reservoir, disruption of aquatic ecosystems and birdlife, adverse impacts on the river environment, potential risks of sabotage and terrorism, and in rare cases catastrophic failure of the dam wall. (See Hydroelectricity article for details.)

Large hydroelectric power is considered to be a renewable energy by a large number of sources, however, many groups have lobbied for it to be excluded from renewable electricity standards, any initiative to promote the use of renewable energies, and sometimes the definition of renewable itself. Some organizations, including US federal agencies, will specifically refer to "non-hydro renewable energy". Many laws exist that specifically label "small hydro" as renewable or sustainable and large hydro as not. Furthermore, the line between what is small or large also differs by governing body.

Hydroelectric power is now more difficult to site in developed nations because most major sites within these nations are either already being exploited or may be unavailable for other reasons such as environmental considerations.

THE INDIAN POWER SECTOR: AN OVERVIEW

Decades of economic planning in India following independence placed significant emphasis on the development of the power sector. Electricity generation capacity with utilities in India had grown from 1713 mW in December 1950 to over 124,287 mW by March 2006 (CEA, 2006a). However, per capita electricity consumption remains much lower than the world average and even lower than some of the developing Asian economies Table 1 Investment in the sector has not been able to improve access and keep pace with the country's growing demand for electricity (Singh, 2006). As on March 2005, the official statistics state that 85% of India's 587,000 villages have been electrified. However, the recent population census (2001) reveals that 44.2% of the households do not have access to electricity. Consumers, who are connected to the grid, also face severe power shortages. The energy shortage was recorded to be 7.4% (7.1%) in 2004-05 (2003-04). The peak shortage was estimated to be 10.5% (11.2%) in 2004-05 (2003-04). The last decade of the previous century witnessed some of the worst power supply situations to date. Peaking shortages reached 20.49% in 1992-93 and energy shortages reached 11.7% in 1996-97 (CEA, 2005a, 2006a). Power shortages are real and are hurting the competitiveness of the economy. Due to the lack of a reliable grid supply, industrial units are installing generators. While about 21% of Chinese firms and 17% of Brazilian firms own electricity generators, 61% of the Indian firms have generators installed to cope with power shortages. Real cost of power in India is 39% higher than that in the PRC (WB/IFC, 2004).

TABLE I

Per Capita Electricity Consumption (2003)

S. No.	*Country*	*Per Capita Electricity Consumption (Kwh)*
1.	Argentina	2185
2.	Brazil	1883
3.	PRC	1379
4.	India (2004-05)	613
5.	Japan	7818
6.	Mexico	1801
7.	Thailand	1752
8.	USA	13078
9.	World	2456

Source: World Bank (2006) and CEA (2006a)

The Sixteenth Electric Power Survey projects a capacity requirement of about 100,000 mW for the period 2002-12 (CEA, 2001). Apart from generation capacity addition and associated network strengthening, additional investment is required to extend the transmission and distribution network to meet the requirement of the unserved population. A new rural electrification scheme, Rajiv Gandhi Grameen Vidyutikaran Yojana, was introduced in April 2005. It aims to electrify all villages and provide access to all households within five years. The Indian power sector requires an investment of Rs. 9000 billion (approximately USD200 billion) at 2002-03 prices to finance generation, transmission, sub-transmission, distribution and rural electrification projects (GOI, 2005a). IEA (2003a) estimates the total investment requirement in the Indian power sector (for the period 2000-30), including generation, refurbishment, transmission and distribution, to be USD665 billion. Such requirements reflect the foreseeable economic growth in the years to come.

The poor financial status and operational efficiency of SEBs/state utilities is imposing a heavy burden on the economic resources of the respective state governments. On the financial side, the lack of expenditure prudence and skewed tariff structure has led to a deterioration of the financial health of state utilities. The gap between the average cost of supply and average tariff increased from 50 paise/kWh in 1996-97 to 110 paise/kWh in 2001-02. The number of subsidized categories, assisted by the growing network and rural electrification drive, increased. However, an increasing number of consumers, including industrial and commercial consumers have acquired captive power generation capacities that provide better economy, quality and reliability. Poor operational and technical efficiency, along with the above factors, has resulted in ballooning financial losses in the sector. The commercial losses of SEBs (before subsidy) during 2001-02 were estimated to be Rs. 331.77 billion as compared to Rs. 113.05 billion during 1996-97. After including the subsidy payable by state governments, the above figures are Rs. 248.37 billion and Rs. 46.74 billion, respectively.

The average consumer tariff for state utilities during 2004-05 (2003-04) is estimated to be 359.39 paise (361.00 paise). After including electricity departments in the Union Territories, this is estimated to be 276.54 paise (274.29 paise). The gap between average cost of supply and average tariff declined from 114.83 paise/kWh in 2000-01 to 82.85 paise/kWh in 2004-05 (RE) 86.71 (provisional). The loss on the sale of power is expected to remain over Rs. 277.29 billion (lower than the Rs. 304.27 billion registered in 2001-02).

The transmission and distribution losses remain abysmally high, being over 40% in some states. A significant proportion of this loss is of a non-technical nature, primarily due to theft of electricity. This is further worsened by the poor payment record of customers, a situation which keeps collection efficiency low in many states. This leads to cash flow problems for utilities resulting in delayed payments for purchased power, coal, and rail transportation. The SEB dues reached Rs. 25,727 Cr. in Feb. 2001 (GOI, 2001). The Ahluwalia committee recommendations led to a one-time settlement of SEB dues through their securitisation as state bonds in favour of the debtors. A tripartite agreement was signed to ensure that such a precarious situation would not develop in the future. In the case of the failure of a state's utilities to pay dues, the creditors can have recourse to the state's plan allocations and its share of central taxes.

A natural-monopoly-public-utility argument was used to justify government ownership of the sector, barring some exceptions. The sector retained a legal monopoly status leading to the development of vertically integrated state electricity boards (SEBs). Historically, however, there were islands of private licensees in a few urban regions. The lack of competition, accompanied by political influence and operational inefficiency, has steered the sector towards the abyss of financial distress. Persistent political interference, even in the era of 'independent' regulation, has reduced hopes for a speedy recovery. A lack of project management expertise and accountability has led to inordinate delays in planned investments and has exasperated misgivings regarding the sector. The task of bridging the capacity shortages through large-scale investments cannot be completely entrusted to public planning, which has often slipped over its targets. Policy-makers recognized this in the early 1990s and opened up the sector for greater private participation. Encouraged by favourable policy developments and the advent of independent regulation, greater private participation is becoming visible in the sector, though not to the extent desirable.

The existing ownership structure of the generating capacity is dominated by CPSUs and state utilities (Table 2). Only 13.4% of the generating capacity in the country is owned by the private sector. Nearly all of the inter-state transmission capacity is owned by the Central Transmission Utility (CTU), Power Grid Corporation of India Ltd. (PGCIL). All intra-state transmission capacity is owned by the respective state transmission utilities. Under a recent initiative, a joint venture between public (PGCIL) and private (a Tata group company) investor is constructing a transmission line, which is nearing completion. Other private investors such as Reliance Energy Ltd. have recently applied to the CERC for transmission licensees. Apart from the privatisation of distribution utilities in Orissa and Delhi, private distribution licensees have been operating for decades in the urban areas like Mumbai, Kolkata (Calcutta), Surat, Ahmedabad and Noida. A number of policy developments, as discussed in the next section, in the sector have emphasised the increasing role for private investors and reforms of the sector to improve its financial performance.

TABLE 2

Generation Capacity by Source and Ownership (in mW: March 2006)

Ownership	*Hydro*	*Steam*	*Gas*	*Diesel*	*Nuclear*	*Renewable*	*Total*
State	25248	38305	3500	605	0	68	67725
Central	6172	25973	4419	0	3360	0	39924
Private	906	4241	4771	597	0	6123	16639
Total	32326	68519	12690	1202	3360	6191	124287

Note: Additional Captive Generating Capacity = 19485mW.
Source: CEA (2006a).

India and Power Requirements

Power is an essential requirement for all facets of our life and has been recognized as a basic human need. It is the critical infrastructure on which the socio-economic development of the country depends. The growth of the economy and its global competitiveness hinges on the availability of reliable and quality power at competitive rates. The demand of power in India is enormous and is growing steadily. The vast Indian power market, today offers one of the highest growth opportunities for private developers.

India is endowed with a wealth of rich natural resources and sources of energy. Resources for power generation are unevenly dispersed across the country. This can be appropriately and optimally utilized to make available reliable supply of electricity to each and every household. Electricity is considered key driver for targeted 8 to 10% economic growth of India. Electricity supply at globally competitive rates would also make economic activity in the country competitive in the globalised environment.

As per the Indian Constitution, the power sector is a concurrent subject and is the joint responsibility of the State and Central Governments. The government dominates the power sector in India. The State and Central Government sectors account for 58% and 32% of the generation capacity respectively while the private sector accounts for about 10%. The bulk of the transmission and distribution functions are with State utilities. The private sector has a small but growing presence in distribution and is making an entry into transmission. Power Sector, which had been funded mainly through budgetary support and external borrowings, was opened to private sector in 1991.

Growth of Power Sector

Growth of Power Sector infrastructure in India since its Independence has been noteworthy making India the third largest producer of electricity in Asia. Generating capacity has grown manifold from 1,362 mW in 1947 to 113,506 mW (as on 30.09.2004). The over all generation in India has increased from 301 Billion Units (BUs) during 1992-93 to 558.1 BUs in 2003-04.

In its quest for increasing availability of electricity, India has adopted a blend of thermal, hydel and nuclear sources. Out of these, coal-based thermal power plants and in some regions, hydro power plants have been the mainstay of electricity generation. Oil, natural gas and nuclear power accounts for a smaller proportion. Of late, emphasis is also being laid on non-conventional energy sources, i.e. solar, wind and tidal.

All India Fuel-wise Generating Installed Capacity (as on September 30, 2004)

INSTALLED CAPACITY GROWTH (MW)

Year	*Thermal*	*Hydro*	*Nuclear*	*Total*
March 1992	48,086	19,194	1,785	69,065
March 1993	50,749	19,576	2,005	72,330
March 1994	[illegible]	20,379	2,005	76,753
March 1995	58,113	20,833	2,225	81,171
March 1996	60,083	20,986	2,225	83,294
March 1997	61,877	21,642	2,225	85,744

For detailed and updated information on the Indian Power Sector, refer to the report—'Overview of Power Sector in India, 2005—revised edition'.

Electricity Consumption

The elasticity ratio (elasticity of electricity consumption with respect to GDP) was 3.06 in the first Plan and peaked at 5.11 during third plan and declined to 1.65 in the Eighties. While consumption went up by 3.14% for every 1% growth in GDP in the first five-year plan period (1951-56), it went up by only 0.97% in the eighth plan period (1992-97).

The growth in electricity consumption over the past decade has been slower than the GDP's growth. This could be due to high growth of the services sector or it could reflect improving efficiency of electricity use. Moreover, captive generation—which isn't captured by these numbers—has also increased. However, as growth in the manufacturing sector picks up, the demand for power is also expected to increase at a faster rate. Demand will also increase along with electrification. In order to support a rate of growth of GDP of around 7% per annum, the rate of growth of power supply needs to be over 10% annually.

Per Capita Consumption of Electricity

Per capita consumption of electricity is expected to rise to over 1000 kilowatt hours per annum (kWh/annum) in next 10 years (from present level of 580 kWh). Compare this against over 10,000 kWh/annum in the developed countries!

Plant Load Factor (PLF)

The actual all India PLF of Thermal Utilities during April 03- March 04 was 72.7% as against the target of 72.0%.

16th Electric Power Survey (EPS) projections

By the year 2012, India's peak demand would be 157,107 mW with energy requirement of 975 BU.

Unbalanced Growth and Shortages

Along with this quantitative growth, the Indian electricity sector has also achieved qualitative growth. This is reflected in the advanced technological capabilities and large number of highly skilled personnel available in the country. While this must be appreciated, it must also be realized that the growth of the sector has not been balanced. The availability of power has increased but demand has consistently outstripped supply and substantial energy and peak shortages of 7.1% and 11.2% prevail in India. Coupled with this is the urban-rural dichotomy in supply—as per Census 2001, only about 56% of households have access to electricity, with the rural access being 44% and urban access about 82%. In the case of those who do have electricity, reliability and quality are matters of great concern. The annual per capita consumption, at about 580 kWh is among the lowest in the world.

These problems emanate from:

- inadequate power generation capacity
- lack of optimum utilisation of the existing generation capacity
- inadequate inter-regional transmission links
- inadequate and ageing sub-transmission and distribution network leading to power cuts and local failures/faults
- T&D losses, large scale theft and skewed tariff structure

- slow pace of rural electrification
- inefficient use of electricity by the end consumer
- lack of grid discipline

ENERGY SHORTAGE

Year	*Demand*	*Available*	*Shortfall*	*% kWh*
1990-91	267.632	246.560	21.072	7.87
1991-92	288.974	266.432	22.542	7.80
1992-93	305.266	279.824	25.442	8.33
1993-94	323.252	299.494	23.758	7.35
1994-95	352.260	327.281	24.979	7.09
1995-96	389.721	354.045	35.676	9.15
1996-97	413.490	365.900	47.590	11.51
2000-01	507.216	467.400	39.816	7.8
2003-04	559.264	519.398	39.866	7.1

PEAKING SHORTAGE (in mW)

Year	*Demand*	*Available*	*Shortfall*	*% kWh*
1990-91	44,005	37,171	6,834	15.53
1991-92	48,035	39,027	9,008	18.79
1992-93	52,805	41,984	10,821	20.49
1993-94	54,875	44,830	10,045	18.31
1994-95	57,530	48,066	9,464	16.45
1995-96	60,981	49,836	11,145	18.28
1996-97	63,853	52,376	11,477	17.97
2000-01	74,872	65,628	9,244	12.3
2003-04	84,574	75,066	9,508	11.2

India's Peak Power Shortage Stands at 10,625 mW

India faces a peak power shortage of 10,625 mw, or 12.1% of total demand, power minister PM Sayeed told the Rajya Sabha on Wednesday. Against the peak demand of 87,906 mw, only 77,281 mW electricity is generated in the country, he said.

Power: A new scheme of rural electricity infrastructure and household electrification has been approved for the attainment in the National Common Minimum Programme of completing rural household electrification in five years, Mr. Sayeed said.

GDP share: The share of the public sector in the GDP at current prices for 2003-04 stood at Rs. 5.9 lakh crore while that of private sector stood at Rs. 19.35 lakh crore, which was 76.8% of the total share in GDP, commerce and industry minister Kamal Nath said.

Exports: India's export share in world exports stood at 0.8% in 2003, according to the latest economic survey.

Solar Power

Solar power is all set to light up the renewable energy industry in the country with the launch of Jawaharlal Nehru National Solar Mission on November 14. The Prime Minister's Council on Climate Change approved the Rs. 91,684-crore draft plan, which aims to install 20,000 mw of solar power in the first phase ending 2020, in principle recently.

The proposed government expenditure includes generation-based incentives of Rs. 69, 985 crore and interest subsidy of Rs. 7,300 crore spread over 30 years. Says K Subramanian, CEO, Tata BP Solar India, "The launch of the plan will open up a big opportunity for businesses to tap the solar power market."

Rajiv Arya, CEO, Moser Baer Photo Voltaic said, "While the government should lay down an enabling framework, private sector should think innovatively to come out with energy solutions and customised products."

It's this entrepreneurial spirit that has seen India install grid interactive renewable capacity of 14,485 mw, including solar power of 2 mw. India is also the seventh largest manufacturer of solar photovoltaic cells.

The rapid scale up of solar power to 20,000 mw is expected to make the sector cost-competitive. For example, power from conventional sources, which costs Rs. 3.5/kwh, is expected to increase annually by 3% to reach Rs. 4.70/kWh by 2020. In contrast, solar specific tariff, which is Rs. 18/kWh, is expected to fall to Rs. 5.60/kWh or lower by 2017-2020. The plan aims to achieve grid tariff parity by 2020, and parity with coal-based thermal power by 2030.

The industry can promote a host of industries and generate employment for 1 lakh people by 2020. "Installation of solar thermal power plants will also promote SMEs to manufacture components like boilers and turbines, which can even be exported," adds Manoj Upadhyay, MD, Acme group, a leader in solar thermal power. The ministry of new and renewable energy offers generation-based incentives for grid-interactive power of up to Rs. 12/kwh for solar photovoltaic and Rs. 10/kWh for solar thermal.

Wind power market

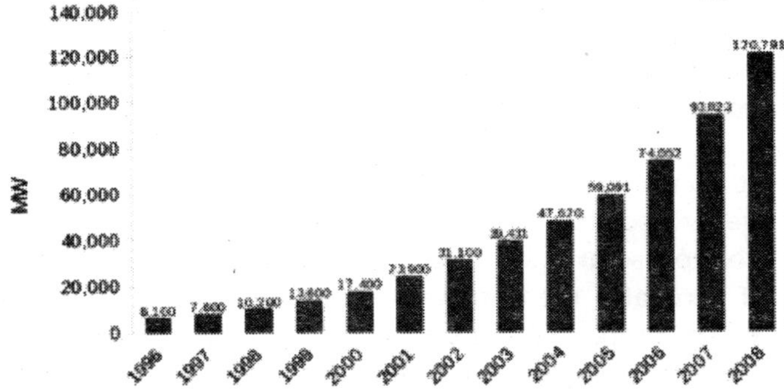

Wind power: worldwide installed capacity 1996-2008

At the end of 2008, worldwide wind farm capacity was 120,791 megawatts (mW), representing an increase of 28.8 per cent during the year, and wind power produced some 1.3% of global electricity consumption Wind power accounts for approximately 19% of electricity use in Denmark, 9% in Spain and Portugal, and 6% in Germany and the Republic of Ireland. The United States is an important growth area and installed U.S. wind power capacity reached 25,170 mW at the end of 2008.

Horse Hollow Wind Energy Center, in Texas, is the world's largest wind farm at 735.5 mW capacity. It consists of 291 GE Energy 1.5 mW wind turbines and 130 Siemens 2.3 mW wind turbines. A proposed 4,000 mW facility, called the Pampa Wind Project, is to be located near Pampa, Texas.

In the UK, a licence to build the world's largest offshore windfarm, in the Thames estuary, has been granted. The London Array windfarm, 20 km off Kent and Essex, should eventually consist of 341 turbines, occupying an area of 230 km². This is a £1.5 billion, 1,000 megawatt project, which will power one-third of London homes. The windfarm will produce an amount of energy that, if generated by conventional means, would result in 1.9 million tonnes of carbon dioxide emissions every year. It could also make up to 10% of the government's 2010 renewables target.

Wind farms

Wind power is one of the most environmentally friendly sources of

renewable energy

A wind farm, when installed on agricultural land, has one of the lowest environmental impacts of all energy sources:

- It occupies less land area per kilowatt-hour (kWh) of electricity generated than any other energy conversion system, apart from rooftop solar energy, and is compatible with grazing and crops.
- It generates the energy used in its construction in just 3 months of operation, yet its operational lifetime is 20-25 years.
- Greenhouse gas emissions and air pollution produced by its

construction are low and declining. There are no emissions or pollution produced by its operation.
- In substituting for base-load coal power, wind power produces a net decrease in greenhouse gas emissions and air pollution, and a net increase in biodiversity.
- Modern wind turbines are almost silent and rotate so slowly (in terms of revolutions per minute) that they are rarely a hazard to birds.

Studies of birds and offshore wind farms in Europe have found that there are very few bird collisions. Several offshore wind sites in Europe have been in areas heavily used by seabirds. Improvements in wind turbine design, including a much slower rate of rotation of the blades and a smooth tower base instead of perchable lattice towers, have helped reduce bird mortality at wind farms around the world. However older smaller wind turbines may be hazardous to flying birds. Birds are severely impacted by fossil fuel energy; examples include birds dying from exposure to oil spills, habitat loss from acid rain and mountaintop removal coal mining, and mercury poisoning.

Longevity issues

Though a source of renewable energy may last for billions of years, renewable energy infrastructure, like hydroelectric dams, will not last forever, and must be removed and replaced at some point. Events like the shifting of riverbeds, or changing weather patterns could potentially alter or even halt the function of hydroelectric dams, lowering the amount of time they are available to generate electricity.

Some have claimed that geothermal being a renewable energy source depends on the rate of extraction being slow enough such that depletion does not occur. If depletion does occur, the temperature can regenerate if given a long period of non-use.

The government of Iceland states: "It should be stressed that the geothermal resource is not strictly renewable in the same sense as the hydro resource." It estimates that Iceland's geothermal energy could provide 1700 mW for over 100 years, compared to the current production of 140 mW. Radioactive elements in the Earth's crust continuously decay, replenishing the heat. The International Energy Agency classifies geothermal power as renewable.

CONCLUSION

In November 2009, Santa Clara's Applied Materials Inc. is scheduled to open a giant solar energy R&D center. The company is investing up to $300 million in the facility. It will not be situated in California, nor in the United States, but in Xian, China, because China's where the action is.

"If the U.S. does not get serious, China's going to own this industry," said Applied Materials spokesman David Miller. He points to the Manhattan Project-like push for alternative energy adopted by Chinese officials, which includes up to $60 billion annually in government investment. And here? "Here, we're way behind," said Miller. "We're still messing around with energy bills. We need to get serious, to get capital spending flowing, to get the government truly behind it, to get focused."

Miller and his company are not simply blowing smoke. In as little as two years, analysts predict, China will be the world's biggest consumer of solar energy. By 2013, its clean tech market could amount to $1 trillion annually, according to a report earlier from the China Greentech Initiative, a consortium of U.S. and Chinese companies that includes Cisco Systems and the Silicon Valley VC firm Vantage Point Venture Partners, which specializes in clean tech investments.

Neither is Applied Materials alone in its views. Numerous Bay Area executives and investors have expressed similar views with business ties to China. "They get that these are the industries of the 21st century," says VantagePoint managing partner Alan Salzman, whose Bay Area clean tech investments include Tesla Motors, BrightSource Energy and Solazyme. "The level of support for green tech there is breathtaking. It exceeds anything done here on a state or federal level."

As if any more wake-up calls were needed, two other VantagePoint Venture Partners' portfolio companies, Santa Clara's Miasolé, which produces advanced, thin-film solar panels, and Sunnyvale's Bridgelux, developer of energy-efficient LED lighting, are reluctantly considering locating their manufacturing facilities outside the United States. "From a global competitiveness perspective, we're just not there," said Salzman

India should take a cue from China and draw a five-year plan for the enhancement of solar energy to overcome its power shortage keeping in view the dangers of global warming.

References

Rajiv Tikoo (2009), "Solar energy mission from Nov. 14, eyes 20k mw by 2020", *The Financial Express*, 17 August.

Vasudeva P.K. (2008), "WTO and Climate Change", *The Financial Express*.

www.wikipedia.org

SUSTAINABLE FINANCE—FACILITATING INCLUSIVELY SUSTAINABLE DEVELOPMENT

SOMAK GHOSH AND NEHA KAPOOR

ABSTRACT

While there are many pieces to the sustainability puzzle, and each of them significant in their own right, this paper will dwell on the role of financial institutions, particularly banks, in mainstreaming sustainability.

On the face of it, it would seem that being part of the tertiary sector, banks do not have a significant ecological foot print. A closer look, however, reveals the indirect impact that the financial industry has over development given its position of influence over a score of economic actors whose activities have a wide ranging and direct impact on sustainability—environmental and social.

In exploring the role of banks in enabling sustainable development, paper will argue that banks can work at both a reactive—weighing risks associated with unsustainable development and attaching a price to it in a bid to discourage laggards—and a proactive level-making direct investments in the sustainability space. The paper will focus on the rationale for banks to pay heed to sustainability issues not just from a risk mitigation angle but also from the perspective of exploring commercially viable alternative investment opportunities that in turn enhance the longevity of the institution's business itself. In doing so, the paper will explore emerging sustainability avenues in both the environmental and social arenas for banks such as clean energy, health and education services and sustainable livelihoods among others.

The paper will, therefore, showcase fourth generation sustainability within the context of financial institutions and their role in establishing crucial missing markets essential to realise the vision of an inclusively sustainable development.

INTRODUCTION

If globalisation was the buzzword for the 1990s, then sustainability is most definitely the topic *de jour* for the first decade of the 21st century. In the recent past, enormous amount of newsprint, public debate, academic effort and political will has been dedicated to understanding the concept of sustainability and its impact.

Moving through this labyrinth of intellectual hullabaloo sustainability has managed to traverse the realm of the 'alternative' to step in to the domain of reality, albeit with its fair share of sceptics. And scepticism has always been part of the sustainability debate—from being written off as a fad, a green wash or green PR to being called the altruistic vision of scientists, environmentalists and social activists. Even so, sustainable development has quietly but steadfastly seeped in to the day-to-day lexicon of global business and more importantly in to core business strategy.

And there is a simple explanation for this transition—it makes business sense! Terms like corporate social responsibility, triple bottom-line and corporate citizenship have been flying thick and furious through halloed corridors of wealthy business houses across the world, lending a somewhat lofty air to a concept that in reality harks back the 'waste not want not' and 'a penny saved is a penny earned' category of idioms that you would have learnt in school. Sifting through the jargon, you'd realise that sustainability in business quite simply boils down to being accountable for the finite resources that you use to conduct business in a manner that takes into account the environmental, social and governance issues faced by society at large.

Paradigm Shift: Drivers for Sustainability

The world we live in today is changing—and changing on every front, be it ecological, social or economic. It is therefore not unexpected that the global business environment is changing as well. And change it will, for businesses do not operate in a vacuum—they have to respond and adapt to their immediate environment in order to secure their existence and ensure their longevity. It is therefore not unusual to expect cola companies to ponder over where they will source clean drinking water for their business in the future. Or, for businesses heavily dependent on finite natural resources to worry about alternatives, i.e. the Toyotas, GMs and Fords of the world.

The days of adopting a Friedmanisque stance of 'the business of business is business' are fast fading as companies take cognisance of changing market realities and incorporate sustainability principles within their core business strategies. While there is no denying that a business needs to create wealth for those who manage it and those who have invested their capital in it, there is no escaping the fact that a business does not operate in isolation—it can only create wealth if there is a demand for its goods and services and the manner in which it delivers these.

Growing awareness that the benefits of economic development has come at the cost of significant deterioration in our ecosystem is resulting in a shift in consumer attitudes and preferences towards 'clean' products and services. According to the Natural Marketing Institute, the demographic sector known as the lifestyles of health and sustainability (LOHAS) today consists of 50 million people or one-sixth of the US population—and, these consumers spend more than USD 220 billion annually on a wide range of products and services including yoga, organic food and cosmetics, acupuncture, ecotourism and organic cotton clothing (Pernick and Wilder, 2007).

While consumer preference is driving companies to change tack to cater to growing demand for clean products and services, regulation is also playing pivotal role. This is as much true for developed economies as for developing countries—in 2000, the Brazilian state-owned oil company, Petrobas was fined USD 28 million and USD 118 million after two oil spills from its refineries, one of the highest fines ever recorded in Latin America (ECOFACT, 2002).

In the current capitalistic framework, business has emerged as a powerful institution. Today there are 60,000 multinational corporations (MNCs) accounting for 25 per cent of the world's economic output; in fact, during the 1990s, foreign direct investment (FDI) by MNCs overtook official development assistance (ODA) and by 2000, it exceeded ODA by more than a factor of five (Hart, 2005). It is only logical therefore that business should take a lead in the transition towards sustainability, albeit in a collaborative effort involving stakeholders such as the government, civil society, academia and religious entities. According to Hart (2005), "Ultimately the challenge is to develop a sustainable global economy; an economy that the planet is capable of supporting indefinitely, while simultaneously providing for the entire human community in a way that respects cultural, religious, and, ethnic diversity."

There are businesses across the world that are taking the lead in mainstreaming sustainability and according to Hart (2005) these businesses could be said to be working along the Schumpeterian notion of creative destruction wherein these companies are "turning the existing technology and business models on their heads...think(ing) as disruptors especially when conducting R&D and market research focused on unique situations and requirements..."

Sustainability in Finance

While one can understand the need for companies (especially those selling directly to consumers) to align their businesses along sustainability principles, where does the financial sector—financial institutions, private

FIGURE I

Stakeholders for Sustainability

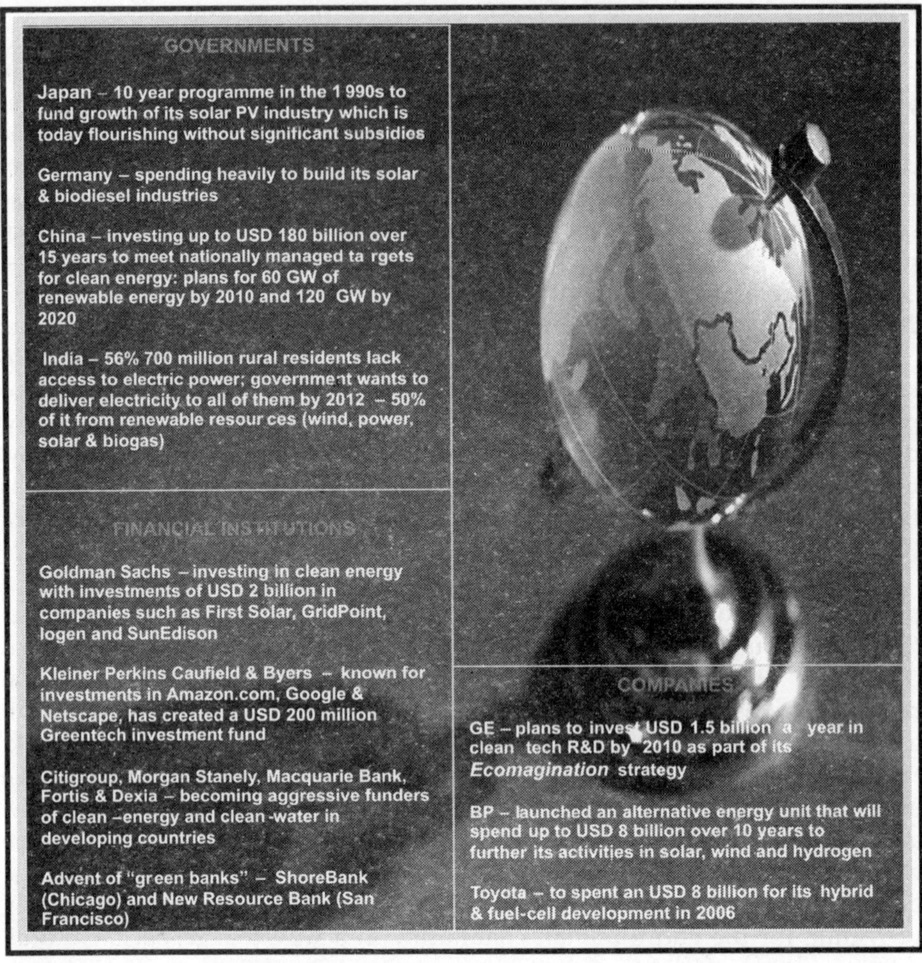

Source: Pernick, R. and Wilder, C (2007)

investors, pension funds *et al.*, fit in to all of this, especially since their products and services do not pollute?

Being a tertiary sector, the financial sector does not have a significant ecological footprint of its own but it has a multiplier impact on sustainable development through allocation of finances to various economic activities which have direct and measurable social and ecological externalities. For the financial sector, therefore, ecological and social imbalances represent both risks and opportunities.

More and more players within this sector are waking up to this reality and incorporating sustainability principles in their core business functioning. So much so that the past few decades have seen the emergence

FIGURE 2

Strategic Sustainability

DuPont transformed itself in the late 1800s from being a gunpowder and explosives manufacturer to a chemical company producing products such as Nylon, Lycra, Teflon, Corian and Kevlar. In late 1900s, it moved from being an energy-intensive petrochemical company to a renewable resource company focused on sustainable growth setting targets to reduce its greenhouse emissions by 2/3rd and increase its use of renewable resources to 10% of global energy needs.

Novio Nordisk & Empresas La Moderna are exploring "green chemistry" and finding substitutes for synthetic chemicals.

Sanyo, fourth largest solar cell manufacturer in the world, has said it will invest USD 350 million over 5 years to expand its solar operations

Monsanto, Hoechst & Rhone-Poulenc have spun off their chemical business to concentrate on life sciences, food, pharmaceuticals and biotechnology.

Suzlon Energy Ltd, an Indian company, is one of the largest pure-play wind companies in terms of market capitalisation and 4th in global sales, making its consistently profitable corporation in the sustainability space

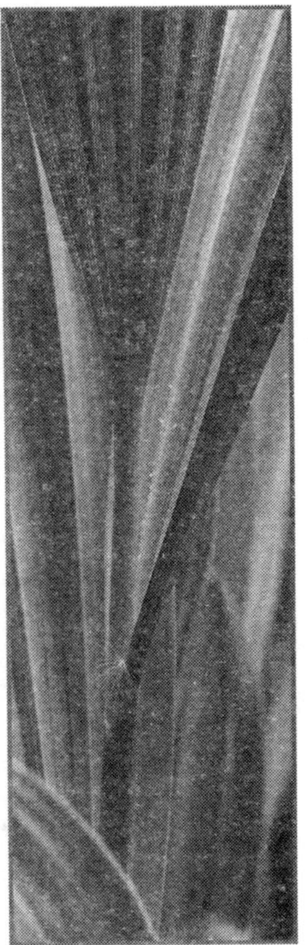

Source: Pernick, R. and Wilder, C. (2007) and Hart, S. (2005).

of a new class of investments, i.e. Socially Responsible Investments (SRI) wherein investors "invest in manner that takes in to account the impact of investments on wider society and the natural environment, both today and in the future" (WEF, 2005).

In fact, according to the World Economic Forum (2005) over USD 2 trillion under professional management in the US is linked to some kind of socially responsible investment strategy (this figure itself reflects a four-fold growth since the early 1990s). The past decade has seen the advent of a number of SRI funds such as Calvert Social Balanced Fund and the Domini Social Equity Fund as well as various indices to assess the performance of a broad universe of socially responsible stocks e.g. Citizens Index in the US, Dow Jones Sustainability Group of Index and FTSE4 Good Index for global portfolios.

Socially Responsible Investment (SRI) does not involve a Faustian choice between following one's conscience and following one's pocketbook;

FIGURE 3

Beyond Greeting

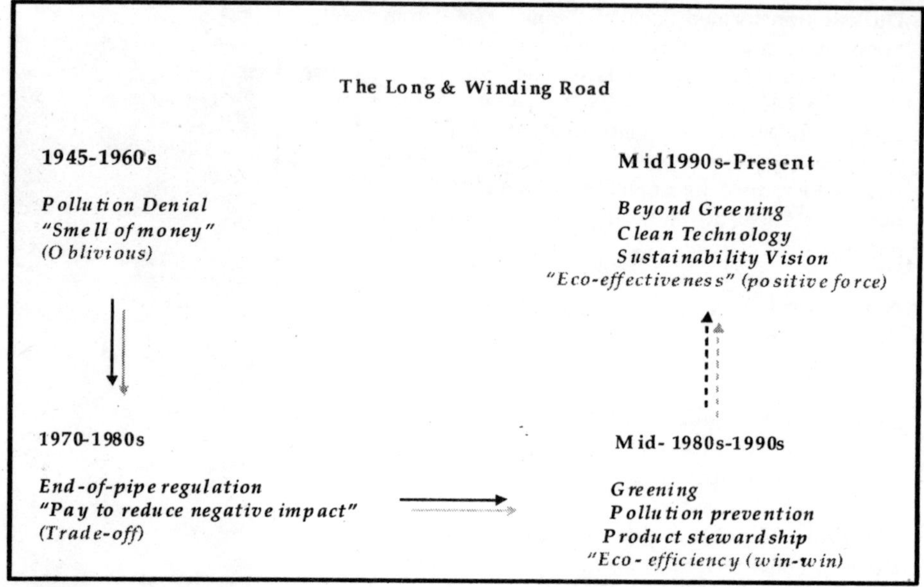

Source: Hart, S. (2005).

instead it is a legitimate investment approach that can be expected to investment performance on par with investment funds that do not formally apply SRI principles.

—*Philips, Hager and North Investment Management Ltd. (2007)*

Investors are clearly channelling more money into sustainability "...This year, 27 members of the Investor Network on Climate Risk promised to invest USD 1 billion in companies with green products (*New York Times*, 2005)." Participation is not limited to private investors alone, there are a number of investors who have a fiduciary duty to maximise financial returns such as public sector pension funds, churches and charities that are active in the SRI space. In fact, two of California's prominent pension funds—the California Public Employees Retirement System (CalPERS) and the State Teachers Retirement System (CalSTRS)—have both committed to investing USD 500 million in clean tech and environmentally responsible companies in so-called Green Wave initiatives (Pernik and Wilder, 2007).

For banks in particular, sustainability issues represent both risks and opportunities. On the credit side, for example, banks can be exposed to a risk of default in case a borrower is suffers losses on account of environmental issues due to pollution or non-compliance with environmental regulations or when properties assigned as collateral suffer depreciation risks because of pollution. A case in point is A bank transforms money in to place, term, size and risk in an economy and, as such, it affects economic development. This influence is not only quantitative but can be qualitative since banks can influence the nature of economic growth.

—*Marcel Jeucken (2001)*

the Colombian bank, Banco de Colombia, which was held responsible for cleaning up a site received from the National Federation of Cotton Growers in payment of a loan as the property was contaminated with agrochemicals (ECOFACT, 2005). Taking into account environmental and social imbalances and structuring its business along a sustainability mandate, therefore, helps a bank to mitigate risk—both credit and reputation risks.

Opportunities present themselves in the form of direct investments in sustainable development, i.e. clean energy sectors as well as developing customised products and services such as environmental funds, microfinance offerings. There are numerous examples of the financial sector making efforts to mainstream these 'niche' products and service—Deutsche Bank s Microcredit Development Fund (MDF) for financing microfinance institutions across countries; Citigroup's USD 17 million grant to 178 microfinance partners over the past five years and ABN Amro's micro-credit programmes in India and Brazil (Lafon-Vinais, 2006).

Going beyond individual operations, the financial sector as a whole, given its unique intermediary position in an economy and its vast ambit of influence over diverse stakeholders, can play a potentially catalytic role in the transition towards sustainability. It can, in fact, leverage their position of indirect control over investment and management decisions to influence the business community at large to align itself with broader sustainability goals. According to Jeucken and Bouma (1999), banks in particular are suitably equipped to weigh risks, attach prices to these risks and use price differentiation to foster sustainability. The authors have also proposed using a carrot-and-stick approach persuading banks to lend at higher rates to environmental laggards and at lower rates to environmental front-runners.

On the whole, the financial sector, given its unique intermediary position in an economy and their vast ambit of influence over diverse stakeholders, can play a potentially catalytic role in the transition towards sustainability. It can, in fact, leverage it's their position of indirect control over investment and management decisions to influence the business community at large to align itself with broader sustainability goals.

In our view, to truly achieve the desired outcomes through the adoption of Sustainability principles, companies need to incorporate the following in their business processes:

- Define what sustainability means to their business
- Align sustainability policy with core business strategy

FIGURE 4

Banks and the Economy

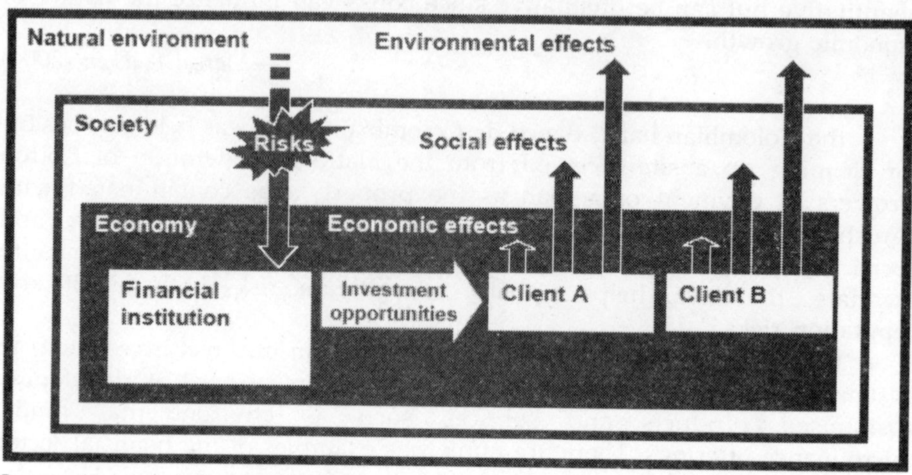

Source: Heim and Zenklusen (2005).

- Buy-in from Board, support of senior management
- Percolate sustainability principles at all levels of management
- Formulate a well defined environmental and social policy that is integrated with core business strategy
- Record, maintain and publish relevant information
- Engage with various stakeholders to ensure regular communication
- and feedback on sustainability initiatives
- Support sustainable business opportunities.
- Mainstream sustainability by bringing niche products like environmental funds or financing of sustainable livelihoods into the conventional framework
- Participate in various voluntary global initiatives on sustainability such as the UN Global Compact United Nations Environment Programme—Finance Initiative (UNEP-FI) to further enhance the adoption of sustainability practices on an international level

Global Initiatives in Sustainability: Enabling Corporate Citizenship

While companies can choose for themselves the scope of their sustainability activities, initiatives such as the UN Millennium Project, through the Millennium Development Goals, provide a useful guide as to the critical areas that need to be addressed. There are also numerous global voluntary initiatives—aimed at business in general, such as the UN Global Compact, and those focused primarily on the financial sector such as the UNEP-FI and the Equator principles—that the private sector can use as tools to translate their respective visions of sustainability into concrete and measurable actions.

FIGURE 5

Risk Matrix for Banks

Risk category	**Mechanism** Losses may result if environmental and socio-economic issues ...	**Examples**
Market risk	... influence the level or volatility of prices	Effect of weather conditions on global market prices for agricultural commodities
Liquidity risk	... cause the obligation of payments that cannot be covered by the bank	–
Credit risk	... influence a counterparty's ability to fulfil its obligations ... raise the bank's loss in the event of default	Inappropriate health and safety standards negatively affect a client's financial performance. Market value of property that serves as collateral is weakened by contamination
Operational and legal risk	... cause damage to the bank's assets	A flu epidemic or a natural disaster disrupts a bank's services
Reputational risk	... may harm the reputation of a bank if badly managed by the bank or its clients	Media campaign against a bank investing in projects which are related to child labour and large-scale environmental damage

Environmental and socio-economic risks translated into a bank's business risks. Categories adapted from the Financial Risk Manager Handbook (Jorion, 2003).

While the Equator Principles focus on managing social and environmental risks of major infrastructure projects through stricter guidelines and criteria for project financing, the UNEP-FI concentrates on developing and promoting linkages between the environment, sustainability and financial performance. The International Finance Corporation's Equator Principles currently have 41 financial institutions as signatories while the UNEP-FI is working with over 160 financial institutions across the globe.

FIGURE 6

Investment Opportunities for Clean Tech

Industrial Pollution Abatement	Water Supply & Sanitation	Renewable energy	Environmental Monitoring & Measuring
Air pollution control & monitoring equipment in thermal power plants *Water & waste treatment; material recovery & utilization of chemical; pulp & paper and steel industry* *Hazardous waste treatment facilities (landfill sites, recycling and incineration) from various industries* *Electronic waste (e-waste) treatment in IT centres: Bangalore, Pune and Nagpur*	*Efficient use, re-use & circulation of water in industrial processes, esp. in pulp & paper, steel & chemical industry* *Equipment & materials for water and sewage network leakage control* *Waste water treatment equipment, especially bottom aeration (to compensate surface aeration)* *Dewatering, thickening & digestion of primary sludge; utilisation of biogas as an energy-source, digestion of sewage sludge.*	**Biomass** - *small biomass 1–3 MW in rural areas. Larger capacities in co-generation in sugar mills (bagasse) and pulp & paper factories: advanced biomass gasification technologies, biomass combustion systems and high pressure cogeneration systems* **Small Hydro Power** *(5–25 MW) - Himalayan region: low head power generation systems, high efficiency systems and portable hydro sets* **Waste to Energy** - *municipal & industrial solid waste in major cities such as Mumbai; high rate biomethananisation systems, incineration and sanitary landfills Financing plays a very important role in Waste to Energy projects (BOT or BOOT concepts should be considered)* **Wind Energy** - *latest technologies & higher capacities needed: over 1–2 MW size wind power systems, wind machines for low wind*	*On-line water & wastewater monitoring on pH, TSS, BOD, COD, conductivity (following parameters studied & analysed case by case O_2, SS, N, P, As, Hg, Pb, Cd, Cr, Cu, Zn, Se, Ni, F, S, phenolic compounds, Mn, Fe)* *On-line air pollution monitoring SOx, NOx, RSPM/ SPM/ PM10, benzene, VOC, multi-gas analyzers*

Source: Asian Environment Outlook 2005, ADB.

FIGURE 7

Global Environmental Market (USD billions)

By Region	Actual						Forecasts	
	2000	2001	2002	2003	2004	2005	2010	2015
USA	210.5	215.2	221.4	227.5	233.7	240.2	275.1	315.0
Western Europe	157.8	160.8	165.0	169.1	173.4	177.7	201.0	227.5
Japan	93.7	93.3	92.4	92.6	92.9	93.1	94.4	95.6
Australia / NZ	8.4	8.6	8.8	9.1	9.5	9.8	11.7	14.0
Rest of Asia	24.0	25.6	28.16	31.0	34.1	37.5	66.1	116.4
Other Regions	47.6	48.5	45.4	46.6	47.8	49.1	57.0	67.6
Global	542.0	552.0	561.1	575.9	591.3	607.4	705.3	836.1

Source: Environmental Business International Inc. and ADB staff estimates

These initiatives provide an ideal cooperative platform for the financial community to move beyond compliance to initiate long-term positive changes centred around commonly agreed upon global standards.

Sustainability @ YES BANK: Walking the Talk

So why and how does India's latest greenfield private sector commercial bank incorporate sustainability within its business strategy?

SUSTAINABILITY FINANCING
(select transactions)

The Bank used complex structured trade transaction solutions to augment ***sustainable livelihoods*** *of over 2000 honey bee producers, winning the* **EUROMONEY Deal of the Year Award**

The Bank provided structured trade facility to **Paramparik Karigar**, *an NGO of Indian Craftsmen, enabling over 27 craftsmen to exhibit* ***indigenous Indian handicrafts*** *at an international platform 'Gateway of India Exhibition' to be held in New York in March 2007*

FIGURE 8

Sustainability Benchmarking

The Ten Principles

Human Rights

Principle 1 | Businesses should support and respect the protection of international human rights within their sphere of influence; and
Principle 2 | make sure they are not complicit in human rights abuses.

Labour

Principle 3 | Businesses should uphold the freedom of association and the effective recognition of the right to collective bargaining;
Principle 4 | the elimination of all forms of forced and compulsory labour;
Principle 5 | the effective abolition of child labour; and
Principle 6 | the elimination of discrimination in respect of employment and occupation.

Environment

Principle 7 | Businesses should support a precautionary approach to environmental challenges;
Principle 8 | undertake initiatives to promote greater environmental responsibility; and
Principle 9 | encourage the development and diffusion of environmentally friendly technologies.

Anti-Corruption

Principle 10 | Businesses should work against corruption in all its forms, including extortion and bribery.

http://www.unglobalcompact.org/

The why—at this early stage in our evolution, we have adopted sustainability as one of the cornerstones of our business strategy, not because we want to be a Don Quixote tilting at imaginary wind-mills, but because we believe that this focus gives us a truly winning competitive edge. YES BANK's vision is to create a commercially viable financial institution that incorporates sustainability within its core business focus. We have evolved an innovative business model entailing a conscious move away from philanthropy to sustainability as a critical business driver.

The how—embodied in organisation's 'Responsible Banking' philosophy, and driven by the Bank's founder and managing director himself, our sustainability approach is a well-defined, comprehensive strategy that is embedded across all businesses/departments. In fact, YES BANK has become the first Indian Bank to be a signatory to the United Nations Environment Programme—Finance Initiative (UNEP-FI) with the aim of percolating sustainability principles across the local banking industry.

Overarching Directional Strategy

Encapsulated in our Responsible Banking approach, sustainability for YES BANK is a strategic tool lending a sustained competitive advantage to our core business practices. Being part of the tertiary sector, the Bank does not have a significant ecological footprint of its own but it does have a multiplier impact on sustainable development through allocation of finances to various economic activities which have direct and measurable social and ecological impacts.

As a Public Trust Institution, YES BANK is cognizant of its responsibility to augment the sustainable development of an 'Emerging India' hence our commitment to percolating sustainability principles within the organisation and in the broader context of the Indian financial community.

Sustainable Business Model

The Bank is aware that not only does it need to make direct investments in sustainable development; it also needs to use is its position of indirect influence over investment decisions to help steer the Indian business community along the sustainability path. Therefore, while building strong relations with civil society and non-governmental organisations is a key component of our approach, equally important is the conscious decision to support several sectors within the sustainable development space that can be profitable on a stand-alone basis.

There is a strong business case for projects that deal with Blue (air and water), Green (land) and Brown (waste) issues. We realise that project opportunities in areas such as energy (renewables), urban and rural regeneration, sustainable water management, solid waste management and carbon sequestration can be remunerative and can add substantial value to society. YES BANK strives to operate in what we call the 'Sustainability Zone', where wider economic, environmental and social objectives are met by supporting Businesses of the Future such as Information Technology (IT), Life Sciences and Biotechnology, Renewable Energy, Food and Agribusiness, Sustainable Livelihoods and Social Infrastructure, i.e. Healthcare and Education among others.

This translates in to a two-pronged implementation strategy which operates under the broad heads of 'SUSTAINABILITY IN THOUGHT' and 'SUSTAINABILITY IN ACTION'.

Mainstreaming Sustainability: The Bank's efforts are focused on embedding the 'triple bottom-line' ethos across the organisation thereby creating thought leadership, enduring value and competitive advantage. In our external engagements, we work towards mainstreaming sustainability within the Indian banking community by adopting a multi-stakeholder approach to dialogue with peers, governmental and non-governmental bodies, industry and academia.

SUSTAINABILITY IN THOUGHT—YES BANK establishes linkages with likeminded players of repute both locally and internationally allowing

YES BANK—Bank of Choice for Businesses of the Future

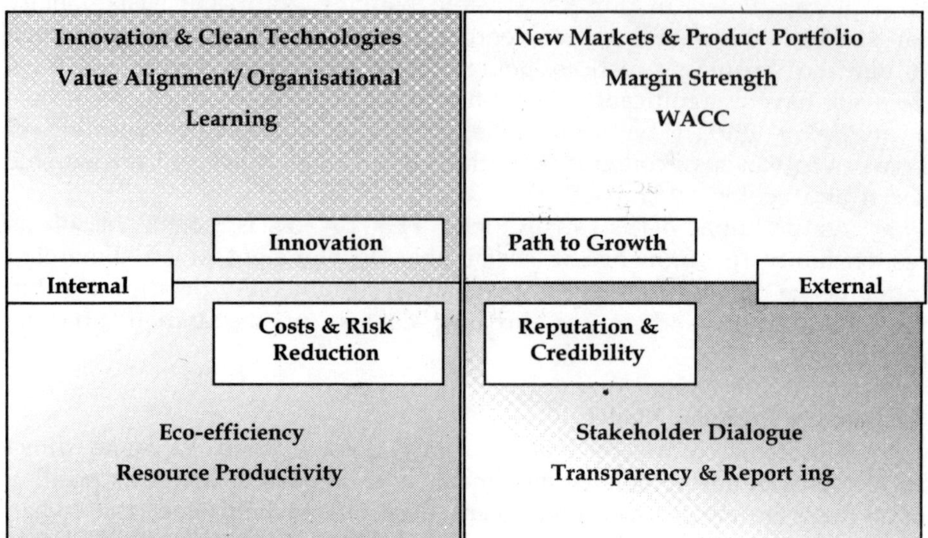

Adapted from Stuart Hart.

access to a potentially new set of investors, i.e. the Socially Responsible Investor community, academia as well as community development organisations:

- § Carbon Disclosure Product (CDP)—the BANK is the first Indian signatory to the CDP and supports the Project's endeavours in addressing issues related to climate change, in particular its initiative to formulate a single international carbon reporting standard
- § Clinton Global Initiative—as a member of the CGI, the Bank has made strategic commitments to work in area of sustainability including global health, education and poverty alleviation.
- § Triple Bottomline Investing (TBLI) Group
- § Bill and Melinda Gates Foundation
- § Clinton HIV/AIDS Initiatives (CHAI)
- § Academia—the Bank is in active dialogue with leading academic institutions including Harvard Business School and the Fletcher School (Tufts University) with aim to lend strong support to various global knowledge exchange initiatives.

SUSTAINABILITY IN ACTION—harnessing risks in to opportunities, the Bank uses its sustainability strategy to identify new markets and develop 'sustainable products'.

§ Serving New Market Segments

- Microfinance Institutions Group (MIG)—in 2005, YES BANK established credit partnerships with leading Indian microfinance institutions (MFIs) with more than 15 partner MFIs providing services to over 500,000 clients in 1000+ villages. The division's current portfolio stands at about USD 60 million and is projected to grow to USD 125 million by next fiscal. Over the year, we have expanded our product suite under MIG to include term loan, syndication advisory, securitization of receivables, PE advisory and mergers/acquisitions.
- YES SAMPANN (Direct Intervention)—in 2006 the Bank set-up a specialised division, YES SAMPANN in technical collaboration with ACCION International, to provide holistic financial solutions including savings, credit, insurance and transfer services to the bottom of the pyramid (BoP) helping the poor manage risks, build assets, develop micro enterprises, enhance income and enjoy an improved quality of life. YES SAMPANN currently focuses on urban markets operating out of three branches in Mumbai with plans to gradually expand to other cities/metros and eventually to rural markets. Starting commercial operations in July 2007 with a working capital loan product for individual micro-entrepreneurs, YES SAMPANN has over 1500 active clients now. We have recently launched a credit product for salaried individuals primarily targeting people employed in the unorganised sector who would typically not fall within the ambit of formal finance; a group loan is on the anvil while a basic savings and recurring deposit facilities were launched in Dec 2008.
- Social Investment Bank—the bank has set-up the Social Investment Bank to address the need for investment in social ventures, i.e. businesses which have significant impact on low income populations and the environment. These include renewable energy, clean technology, sanitation/sewage management, education, health care, and transportation. The Social Investment Bank offers a wide range of services, including consulting/advisory, fund raising, acting as an arranger, aggregating and trading carbon credits, and carbon financing.

§ Partnerships in Sustainability Finance

- The Bank has partnered with the Small Industries Development Bank of India (SIDBI) to offer financial products and services to small and medium enterprises. We have also signed a USD 20 million loan guarantee agreement with United States Agency for

International Development (USAID) to promote lending to clean energy enterprises, energy efficiency and water projects.

- Yes Bank is the house banker to Suzlon Energy Limited, the fourth largest wind turbine manufacturer in the world competing with industry leaders Vestas Wind Systems of Denmark, General Electric and Spain's Gamesa Corporacion Tecnologica. Suzlon's astounding success is powerful reflection of YES BANK's commitment to mainstreaming sustainability and our confidence in our ability and expertise to replicate such transactions across the sustainability spectrum
- The Bank has recently been appointed as the Country Advisor to the Global Environment Fund's (GEF) Emerging Markets Fund with a focus on identifying and evaluating investments in businesses, products, services and technologies which help to reduce carbon footprint. We are also partnering GEF for USD 200 million South Asian Clean Energy Fund that will invest across India, Sri Lanka, Bangladesh and Nepal.

§ Creating Sustainable Human Capital

The Bank's sustainability approach ties-in with its Human Resource (HR) practice on two broad levels—it helps us to attract and retain best in class professionals through regular induction and training programmes as well as to tap in to various academic institutions to augment knowledge exchange within the sustainability space. The Bank has initiated various HR practices aimed at creating sustainable human capital:

- YES—Professional Entrepreneurship Programme working towards Talent Development; aims to ensure presence of an experienced, dynamic, energetic and driven team of professionals in Junior/Middle/Upper Management to implement various strategic initiatives of the Bank.
- YES ENTREPRENEUR in ACTION—In 2006 the Bank initiated an employee programme allowing a YES BANKER to take time off to pursue his/her goals for a year during which time they will focus on a sustainability project of their choice.

§ Managing Accountability and Performance

The Bank's Environmental and Social Policy (ESP) enables us to recognise, evaluate, and monitor, the environmental and social facets of its own operations and those of its customers. The ESP reflects the "walk the talk" link between the bank's sustainability vision and its policy and processes to substantiate this.

Business as Usual—For YES BANK sustainability is a mainstream strategy and not a stand alone operation; it ensures the longevity of our business and that of our clients, helping us to not only mitigate risk but also to identify new markets and future business winners.

YES BANK has charted a novel model of banking with the Indian context, building home-grown expertise, tapping tacit local knowledge of sustainability issues and dovetailing this with international best practice such as the UNEP-FI. Benchmarking itself against the best in business globally, the Bank is using sustainability as an effective business tool with the aim to raise competitiveness of the Indian banking sector, impact regional effectiveness and global paradigms through a "glocal" approach. So even as naysayers continue to hum the scepticism tune, for us at YES BANK, like many of our global counterparts who are taking leadership positions in the area of sustainability, it is business as usual!

Awards & Recognition

- YES BANK ranked **India's No. 1 Bank by Business Today– KPMG** in BT – KPMG Best Banks Survey 2008 (balance sheet size <= INR 240 billion)
- **FT – IFC 'Emerging Markets Sustainable Bank of the Year Asia'** award 2008
- **Only Indian Private Sector Bank** to receive the **Euromoney Trade Finance 'Deal of the Year'** award 2007 for a **Structured and Innovative Rural Financing Solution**
- **Bombay Stock Exchange – NASSCOM Best CSR practice award** 2007
- **USAID Environment Leadership Award 2005**

References

Asian Development Bank (2005), Asian Environment Outlook, 2005, ADB.

Davis, I. (2005), "The Biggest Contract", *The Economist*, Business and Society, May 26, 2005.

Deutsch, C. (2005), "Saving the Environment, One Quarterly Earnings Report at a Time", *New York Times*, November 22, 2005.

ECOFACT (2002), 'Towards Green Banking Practices in the South'.

Economist (2002), "Lots of it About", *The Economist*, Corporate Social Responsibility, Dec 12, 2002.

Economist (2005), "The Good Company", *The Economist*, Survey: Corporate Social Responsibility, Jan. 20, 2005.

Friedman, M. (1970), "The Social Responsibility of Business is to Increase its Profits", *The New York Times Magazine*.

Hart, S. (2005), 'Capitalism at the Crossroads', Pearson Education inc. Wharton School Publishing.

Heim, G. and Zenklusen, O. (2005), Sustainable Finance: Strategy Options for Development Financing Institutions, Sept. 2005.

Jeucken, M. and Bouma. J. (1999), "The Changing Environment of Banks," Sustainable Banking: The Greening of Finance, Greener Management International, Issue 27, pp. 21-35

Lafon-Vinais, V. (2006), "Taking Stock: Adding Sustainability Variables to Asian Sectoral Analysis—Banking," Association for Sustainable and Responsible Investment in Asia (ASRIA).

Pernick, R. and Wilder, C. (2007), 'The Clean Tech Revolution', Harper Collins, New York.

Peters, T. and Waterman, R. (1982), In Search of Excellence, Harper and Row Publishers, New York.

Philips, Hager and North Investment Management Ltd. (2007), Does Socially Responsible Investing Hurt Investment Returns?, Canada.

Sachs, J.D. (2005), "The Business Community and the Millennium Development Goals", Speech at the international Policy Forum, Berlin, Germany, February 10, 2005.

World Bank (1997), World Development Report, 1997.

World Economic Forum (WEF) (2005), "Partnering for Success: Business Perspectives on Multistakeholder Partnerships" in collaboration with The Prince of Wales International Business Leader's Forum (IBLF) the Kennedy School of Government, Harvard University.

World Economic Forum (WEF) (2005), 'Mainstreaming Responsible Investment', World Economic Forum, January 2005, Geneva.

Zenklusen, O and Heim, G. (2005), "Just a Fad?", EcoFact AG, Zurich.

CHAPTER

13

ROAD TO COPENHAGEN ON CLIMATE CHANGE

P.K. Vasudeva

ABSTRACT

The United Nations Climate Change Conference will take place at the Bella Center in Copenhagen, Denmark, between December 7 and December 18, 2009. The conference includes the 15th Conference of the Parties (COP 15) to the United Nations Framework Convention on Climate Change and the 5th Meeting of the Parties (COP/MOP 5) to the Kyoto Protocol. According to the Bali roadmap, a framework for climate change mitigation beyond 2012 is to be agreed there. The conference is preceded by the Climate Change: Global Risks, Challenges and Decisions scientific conference, which took place in March 2009 and was also held at the Bella Center. In total 8000 people are expected to Copenhagen in the days of the climate meeting.

The host of the meeting in Copenhagen is the government of Denmark represented by Connie Hedegaard, the Danish minister of Climate and Energy and Prime Minister Lars Lokke Rasmussen.

The world's largest emitter will draw up new laws and regulations to provide a legal basis for combating climate change.

· Earlierk, China's top climate-change negotiator met with Indian Environment Minister Jairam Ramesh. Both parties insisted that they are pushing for an agreement at this year's climate change conference in Copenhagen.

In 2012 the Kyoto Protocol to prevent climate changes and global warming runs out. To keep the process on the line there is an urgent need for a new climate protocol. At the conference in Copenhagen 2009 the parties of the UNFCCC meet for the last time on government level before the climate agreement need to be renewed.

Therefore the Climate Conference in Copenhagen is essential for the worlds climate and the Danish government and UNFCCC is putting hard effort in making the meeting in Copenhagen a success ending up with a Copenhagen Protocol to prevent global warming and climate changes.

The industrialised nations—other than the U.S.—responsible for most greenhouse gas emissions causing climate change, proposed reduction by 16 to 24 per cent by 2020 relative to 1990 levels.

According to the Intergovernmental Panel on Climate Change (IPCC), if carbon dioxide emissions continue at the same or increasing rates, average temperatures may rise by as much as four degrees Celsius by 2090 globally—and the Earth will experience catastrophic impacts.

Protecting the world's forests can contribute to the achievement of global goals for emissions reductions while easing the transition to a global low-carbon economy for both the developed and the developing world.

INTRODUCTION

The United Nations Climate Change Conference will take place at the Bella Center in Copenhagen, Denmark, between December 7 and December 18, 2009. The conference includes the 15th Conference of the Parties (COP 15) to the United Nations Framework Convention on Climate Change and the 5th Meeting of the Parties (COP/MOP 5) to the Kyoto Protocol. According to the Bali roadmap, a framework for climate change mitigation beyond 2012 is to be agreed there.

Governmental representatives from 170 countries are expected to be in Copenhagen in the days of the conference accompanied by other governmental representatives, NGOs, journalists and others. In total 8000 people are expected to Copenhagen in the days of the climate meeting.

The host of the meeting in Copenhagen is the government of Denmark represented by Connie Hedegaard, the Danish minister of Climate and Energy and Prime Minister Lars Lokke Rasmussen. The official sekretariat is placed in connection to The Prime Minister's Office in Copenhagen. Originally the hosting of the climate conference was initiated by the former Prime Minister Anders Fogh Rasmussen.

The Danish government has decided that not only the subject of the conference should be focused on the climate but also the conference itself. Among other initiatives the organizers work on mounting of windmill near the Bella Center to produce climate-friendly electricity for the conference.

An important part of the scientific background for the political decisions taken on the conferences is made by the Inter-governmental Panel on Climate Change IPCC, based in Geneva, Switzerland. The IPCC is Established to provide the decision-makers and others interested in climate change with an objective source of information about climate change. IPCC is a scientific inter-governmental body set-up by the World Meteorological Organization (WMO) and by the United Nations Environment Programme (UNEP). In 2007 the IPCC received the Nobel Peace Price.

THE COUNTDOWN TO COPENHAGEN

In December 2009, 15,000 officials from 200 countries will gather in the Danish capital with 1 goal: to find a solution to global warming. Michael McCarthy, Environment Editor, presents the first in a series of dispatches on the crucial summit

The UN Climate Conference will try to work out a way for the world to act together to preserve the thin envelope of atmosphere, soil and sea which surrounds our planet and enables us to live, in the face of rising temperatures which threaten to destroy its habitability

On 7 December, the UN Climate Conference will open in Copenhagen and the world community will try to agree a solution to the gravest threat it has ever faced: global warming.

Between 10,000 and 15,000 officials, advisers, diplomats, campaigners and media personnel from nearly 200 countries, almost certainly joined by limousine-loads of heads of state and government from America's President Barack Obama down are expected to meet in the Danish capital in one of the most significant gatherings in history.

If that sounds like exaggeration, we need only glance at some historical comparisons. The Copenhagen meeting will have a far broader reach and potential impact on the world than the Congress of Vienna, say, the 1814-15 assembly which attempted to reorder Europe after the Napoleonic wars, or the Paris peace conference of 1919, which tried to construct a new global order after the First World War, or the 1945 meetings at Yalta and Potsdam which tried to do the same after the Second World War. For they were all dealing with national boundaries, politics and political structures, phenomena which of course are vital in human terms, but ephemeral and changeable. Copenhagen will be dealing with something fundamental to life on earth: the stability of the biosphere.

Known officially in UN-speak as COP 15—the 15th meeting of the parties of the UN's Framework Convention on Climate Change—the meeting in Denmark will try to work out a way for the world to act together to preserve the thin envelope of atmosphere, soil and sea which surrounds our planet and enables us to live, in the face of rising temperatures which threaten to destroy its habitability.

All the world's major governments, including the once-sceptical administration of the US President George Bush, now formally accept that temperature rises have already begun, are likely if unchecked to prove disastrous for human civilisation, and are being caused by emissions of greenhouse gases such as carbon dioxide from our power plants, factories and motor vehicles.

But if all the major governments now accept it, getting them to agree on how to tackle it still seems a very long way off indeed. The essential problem, to use the jargon, is burden-sharing. We know the world has to cut its CO_2 emissions drastically, and soon. But which countries are to cut them, by how much?

The Chinese, for example, with their scarcely believable economy growing at 10 per cent a year, have now overtaken the Americans as the biggest carbon emitters; but historically, America has emitted far more; and on a per capita basis, US emissions still dwarf those of China. So the Chinese have felt (so far) that they have a moral right for their economy to grow unchecked, and their carbon emissions to grow with it; but many Americans have felt (so far) that they see no reason to act unilaterally to cut their own CO_2 if the Chinese are not willing to do the same.

Differences like those stubbornly percolate the whole negotiating process and make achieving a universal agreement mind-bogglingly hard. "This is the most complicated deal the world has ever tried to put together," says Tom Burke, visiting professor at Imperial College and an adviser on climate change to the Foreign Office. "In effect, you're asking nearly 200 countries to align their energy policies—to create a common world energy policy. If you look at how hard it has been for the member states of the European Union to align their energy policies, you get an idea of the difficulty of attempting it with the whole world."

Yet it has to be done, and the penalty for failure could not be higher. It is just 20 years since the world woke up to the danger of rising carbon emissions destabilising the atmosphere. Two decades ago it seemed a fairly distant threat, prefigured principally in supercomputer climate prediction programmes; something that was likely to happen a comfortably long distance away, such as at the end of the 21st century.

Three things have altered since then. First, the changing climate is now visible, not just in computer predictions, but all around us: spring in southern Britain, for example, is arriving about three weeks earlier than it did 40 years ago. At this time last year a red admiral butterfly, an archetypal creature of the summer, was photographed perching on a snowdrop, a flower of the winter—a previously unheard-of occurrence.

Second, it has become clear in the past five years that the earth is responding to the increasing CO_2 loading of the atmosphere much more rapidly than scientists initially thought. There are numerous examples but to instance just one, the summer sea ice of the Arctic Ocean is melting far more quickly than anyone imagined.

Third, it has become apparent, even more recently, that global emissions of CO_2 are shooting up at a rate that far exceeds anything the UN's Inter-governmental Panel on Climate Change (IPCC) thought possible when it sketched out future emissions scenarios in a special report in 2000. Even though we have had 20 years to think about emissions cuts, and 11 years of the Kyoto protocol, the treaty which actually prescribed the first cuts for the industrialised countries, emissions are soaring as never before.

Some leading climate scientists are now openly voicing concerns that this makes it increasingly unlikely we can meet the aim of keeping global temperature rise to about 2C above the pre-industrial level, which is generally regarded as the most that may be endured by human society without mortal danger. (We are now at about 0.75 degrees C above pre-industrial, and another 0.6 of a degree is thought to be inevitable because of the CO_2 which has already been emitted).

Certainly, if we are to have any chance at all at holding the increase to two degrees, there is wide agreement that global emissions have to peak very soon—probably by 2015 or 2016—and then rapidly decrease, to 80 per cent below present levels by 2050. The later the peak, the greater (and therefore more difficult) the subsequent decrease would have to be.

That's the pathway the world has to follow. Copenhagen offers the chance to set out along it. But even if the deal in December is not as ambitious as scientists and environmentalists insist is necessary—and at the moment, that seems pretty likely—it is vital that there is actually an accord. Disagreement would be a catastrophe.

Three conditions, according to Britain's Energy and Climate Change Secretary, Ed Miliband, have to be fulfilled for Copenhagen to be regarded as a success. First, the wealthy industrialised countries have to agree tough new targets for cutting their CO_2. Second, the developing countries led by China, even if they do not take on the same sort of numerical targets, have to move away from "business as usual". And third, the rich nations have to agree a way of financing the developing countries, especially the poorer ones, in the measures they take to adapt to the climate change that is coming anyway. Otherwise they won't sign up to anything.

Securing such a deal will be a matter of political will: a global political consensus will have to be hammered out. It is becoming clear that, over the next 11 months, the world could well do with a high-level political fixer, jetting unceasingly from capital to capital, to pull such a consensus together, in the manner in which the Argentine diplomat, Raul Estrada, managed to pull the original Kyoto agreement together in the Japanese city in December 1997. It could be Britain's Ed Miliband, according to Tom Burke. "There has to be someone who can put the time in, and go round various capitals and talk to the key people at a very high level, and not just environment ministers," he says. "Ed Miliband could play that role. He's known to be close to Gordon Brown, and Britain is reasonably respected for its record on climate change. It doesn't have to be him. But there probably needs to be someone."

However, Mr Miliband, and the British Government, may face a problem of reduced credibility in climate change terms as a result of two policy decisions likely to be taken in the next few weeks. One, which Mr Miliband will take personally, is whether or not to agree to a new coal-fired power station at Kingsnorth in Kent. If he gives it the go-ahead, without strict controls over its emissions, environmentalists will accuse him of sanctioning a new generation of power plants run on the most carbon-intensive fuel. The other is whether or not to allow Heathrow airport to build a third runway, and thus expand British aviation, whose CO_2 emissions are growing faster than those of any other sector.

If both these projects go ahead—as seems perfectly possible—there is no doubt that the UK's position as a potential Copenhagen broker will be weakened. "If countries like Britain, who, for better or worse, are the global leaders, go to Copenhagen with new coal-fired power stations and expanding airports at home, it's very difficult to see how we will be taken seriously by other countries which have even more serious energy security problems and concerns about economic growth," said Robin Oakley, the head of climate change at Greenpeace UK. "That leadership can't just be shown by grandstanding at the meeting. It has to be shown by what we do in our domestic policy."

In the absence of Mr Miliband or any other leading politician emerging as the Copenhagen fixer, the key player in the process is likely to be Barack Obama. The President-elect has already opened a chasm, in terms of climate change policy, between himself and the outgoing George Bush, who, in 2001, withdrew the US from Kyoto and began years of climate policy obstructionism.

Mr Bush wanted no truck with emissions cuts of any sort; Mr Obama has pledged he will get US emissions down to 80 per cent of 1990 levels by 2050 (a target identical with Britain's) and "engage vigorously" with the international negotiating process over the next few months. Hints have been dropped that he may convene meetings of key world leaders to speed the negotiations along. It seems highly likely that he will go to Copenhagen himself—which means every other world leader will want to be present.

Whether or not they can do the deal the world needs is another matter. Yet there is no doubt the world needs it. It may seem reasonable to think, in the coldest winter for years, that global warming has gone away, yet nothing could be further from the truth.

In December, thousands of government leaders, policy-makers, scientists, and civil society representatives will gather in Copenhagen under the United Nations Framework Convention on Climate Change (UNFCCC). There, it is hoped national governments will agree upon an ambitious and effective international response to the global threat of climate change.

The conference is preceded by the Climate Change: Global Risks, Challenges and Decisions scientific conference, which took place in March 2009 and was also held at the Bella Center.

On January 28, 2009, the European Commission released a position paper, "Towards a comprehensive climate agreement in Copenhagen". The position paper "addresses three key challenges: targets and actions; financing of "low-carbon development and adaptation"; and building an effective global carbon market".

Bonn—Second Negotiating Meeting

Delegates from 183 countries met in Bonn from 1 to 12 June 2009. The purpose was to discuss key negotiating texts. These will serve as the basis for the international climate change agreement at Copenhagen. At the conclusion the AWG-KP negotiating group was still far away from the emission reduction range that has been set out by science to avoid the worst ravages of climate change: a minus 25 per cent to minus 40 per cent reduction below 1990 levels by 2020. The AWG-KP still needs to decide on the aggregate emission reduction target for industrialised countries, along with individual targets for each country. Progress was made in gaining clarification of the issues of concern to parties and including these concerns in the updated draft of the negotiating text.

The world's largest emitter will draw up new laws and regulations to provide a legal basis for combating climate change. A Chinese draft resolution on climate change, which has been submitted to the Standing Committee of the National People's Congress (NPC), proposes to include emissions control by law.

According to China, the draft law states that China "should make carbon reduction a new source of economic growth, and change the economic development model to maximize efficiency, lower energy consumption and minimize carbon discharges."

"China already has a bunch of laws and regulations related to climate change and environmental protection, but the climate legislation will give the forces fighting global warming more legal power," Zhang Jianyu, China Programme Head of the US-based Environmental Defense Fund, says.

Earlier, China's top climate-change negotiator met with Indian Environment Minister Jairam Ramesh. Both parties insisted that they are pushing for an agreement at this year's climate change conference in Copenhagen.

"Both of us were of the view that we should be part of the solution...We want an agreement in Copenhagen", Ramesh said, according to Bloomberg.

In 2012 the Kyoto Protocol to prevent climate changes and global warming runs out. To keep the process on the line there is an urgent need for a new climate protocol. At the conference in Copenhagen 2009 the parties of the UNFCCC meet for the last time on government level before the climate agreement need to be renewed.

Therefore the Climate Conference in Copenhagen is essential for the world's climate and the Danish government and UNFCCC is putting hard effort in making the meeting in Copenhagen a success ending up with a Copenhagen Protocol to prevent global warming and climate changes.

CLIMATE CHANGE: '15 DAYS TO COPENHAGEN'

The disappointing results of negotiations in Bonn are indication that industrialised countries are unwilling to make substantial contributions to reducing their greenhouse gas emissions.

They failed once again to meet the expectations formulated in 2007 by the IPCC. In a report in February 2007, the IPCC called for reductions of up to 40 per cent up to 2020. Without substantial reductions, it warned, the average earth temperature would rise by more than two degrees Celsius by 2050.

Two degrees is considered the most that earth can tolerate if it is to maintain its ecological equilibrium. A temperature rise beyond this point, the IPCC said, would lead to environmental catastrophes from severe droughts to further melting of glaciers and rise in sea level, and stronger and more frequent cyclones and hurricanes.

The industrialised nations—other than the U.S.—responsible for most greenhouse gas emissions causing climate change, proposed reduction by 16 to 24 per cent by 2020 relative to 1990 levels.

The U.S., the largest polluting country per capita by far, did not commit itself even to this. The total reductions offered by industrialised nations add up to far less if U.S. emissions are taken into account.

"If we count the U.S. emissions, then the reductions proposed in Bonn by industrialised nations fall to 10 to 15 per cent," Martin Kaiser, climate change expert with the environmental organisation Greenpeace told IPS.

"If we continue at this rate we're not going to make it," Yvo de Boer, head of the United Nations Framework Convention on Climate Change (UNFCCC), which hosted the meeting in Bonn, told a news conference after the closing of the negotiations. Some 2,000 delegates from 192 nations took part in the Bonn talks.

The conference in Copenhagen is expected to produce a binding global agreement on reducing emissions, to take over from the Kyoto protocol on climate change which expires in 2012.

De Boer said there are now only 15 days of negotiations left until the Copenhagen meeting. "A climate deal in Copenhagen this year is an unequivocal requirement to stop climate change from slipping out of control," he said.

Eighty least developed countries, including several small island states, collectively called for reductions of at least 45 per cent below 1990 levels by 2020, in order to keep the global temperature rise below 1.5 degrees.

There is little sign of any such pledge. "Industrialised countries are playing poker with climate change," Stephen Byers, chair of the Global Legislators Organisation for a Balanced Environment (GLOBE), told IPS.

Byers said industrialised countries are waiting until the very end of the negotiations for reduction commitments by emerging economies, and only then reveal their hand. "This is a gambler's behaviour, and it's as wrong." Byers urged the industrialised countries to "take a strategic approach to the climate change negotiations and commit to medium-term emissions reductions in line with the IPCC's analysis and an overall goal of limiting global temperature rise to two degrees Celsius."

Byers also demanded that the industrialised countries "recognise the scale of the required financial support from developed to developing economies to ensure effective implementation of the diverse outcomes of the Copenhagen conference."

GLOBE estimates that some 90 to 140 billion dollars a year might be needed to pay for climate change mitigation technologies and adaptation. GLOBE says predictable and sustained finance must be raised "according to the principle of common but differentiated responsibility, for example a levy on bunker fuels or aviation."

Delegates from the emerging new economies such as India and China accused industrialised countries of trying to shift the burden of reductions on to poorer countries.

"We still have the same problems that have been holding back an agreement," China's climate ambassador Yu Qingtai said at a press conference in Bonn.

Yvo de Boer had said at the last round of talks in June in Bonn that there remained "tough nuts to crack." Those nuts still remain, and remain just as hard.

U.S. Media Ignores Warning of Climate Scientists

In the last two years, our scientific understanding of business-as-usual projections for global warming has changed dramatically (see "M.I.T. doubles its projection of global warming by 2100 to 5.1°C" and "Hadley Center projects 5-7°C warming by 2100"). Yet, much of the U.S. public—especially conservatives—remain in the dark about just how dire the situation is (see "Gallup poll shows catastrophic failure of media, conservatives still easily duped by deniers").

The U.S. media is largely ignoring the story. Where was the coverage of the Copenhagen Climate Science Congress, attended by 2000 scientists, which concluded with this Key Message:

> Recent observations confirm that, given high rates of observed emissions, the worst-case IPCC scenario trajectories (or even worse) are being realized. For many key parameters, the climate system is already moving beyond the patterns of natural variability within which our society and economy have developed and thrived. These

parameters include global mean surface temperature, sea-level rise, ocean and ice sheet dynamics, ocean acidification, and extreme climatic events. There is a significant risk that many of the trends will accelerate, leading to an increasing risk of abrupt or irreversible climatic shifts.

What is the worst-case IPCC scenario trajectory? That would be A1F1 (the red dotted line in the Figure below from Figure SPM-3 of the 2001 *Intergovernmental Panel on Climate Change, Synthesis Report*):

(f) CO_2 concentration (ppm)

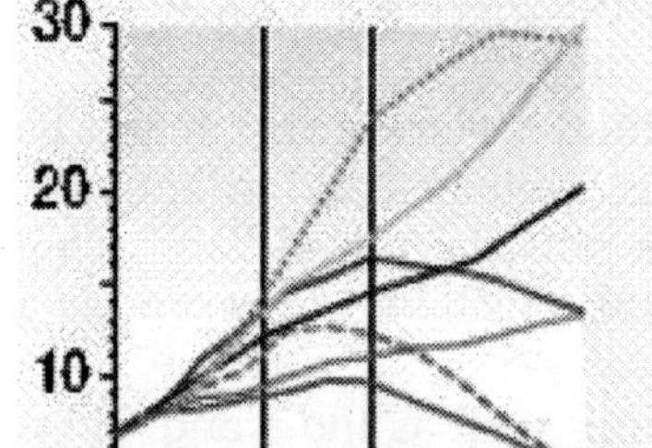

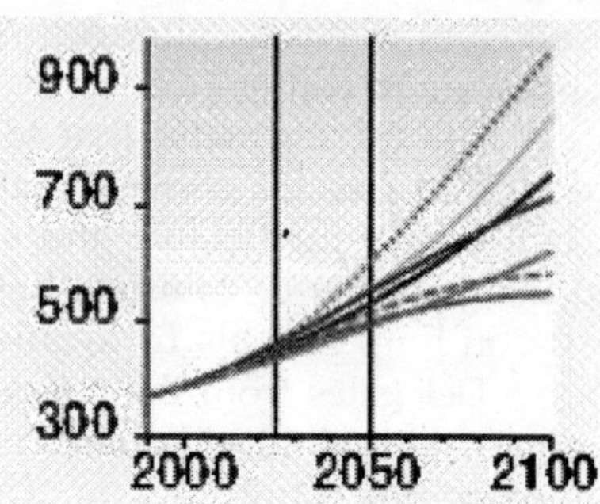

The A1F1 scenario takes us to atmospheric concentrations of carbon dioxide of 1000 ppm in 2100—otherwise known as the end of human civilization as we have known it. Actually it's worse than that. The 2001 IPCC report largely failed to model amplifying carbon cycle feedbacks. The 2007 IPCC report, which began to consider such feedbacks, warns that even averaging 11 GtC (billion metric tons of carbon) a year this century could take us to 1000 ppm (see "Nature publishes my climate analysis and solution"). The A1F1 scenario averages well above 15 GtC a year through 2100 as you can see from the figure on the left.

The United Nations and Climate Change

The UNFCCC aims to stabilize greenhouse gas (GHG) concentrations at a level that would prevent dangerous human impacts on climate systems. At the December meeting in Copenhagen, the 192 national governments that are party to the UNFCCC will seek to agree upon a global path forward. Conservation International (CI) and others are working to support governments in their efforts to reach consensus within the UNFCCC, and to promote an agreement wherein Parties participating in the UNFCCC:

- commit to a global climate agreement that will prevent dangerous levels of greenhouse gas emissions and the resulting impacts,

- incentivize the role avoided deforestation and forest degradation can play in achieving climate mitigation goals,
- include necessary measures to help developing countries and vulnerable communities adapt,
- incorporate the impacts to and contributions of nature in amplified adaptation efforts, and
- ensure that indigenous peoples and local communities are represented in international negotiations and their rights are respected.

Negotiations in preparation for the Copenhagen meeting are ongoing, and CI is working hard to develop tools and work with national governments to support and inform these discussions.

The Plan

To achieve these goals, CI has committed to a major initiative designed to: advance the science of climate change solutions; identify options and possible incentives for reducing emissions and coping with climate impacts; support governments and communities in developing climate change policies and solutions; and promote international agreement to mitigate and adapt to climate change while incorporating the role of healthy ecosystems in the global solution.

The Science

According to the Inter-governmental Panel on Climate Change (IPCC), if carbon dioxide emissions continue at the same or increasing rates, average temperatures may rise by as much as four degrees Celsius by 2090 globally—and the Earth will experience catastrophic impacts.

Already we have witnessed sea level rise, ocean warming, coastal flooding, more intense storms, shrinking glaciers, drier soils and even infectious disease scares over the last decade. All have been linked to noticeable changes in our climate.

FEATURE: Galapagos and Climate Change

These and other impacts of climate change threaten food and water security in some of the world's poorest regions. As these incidents escalate, they will tax global humanitarian efforts, as well as threaten global security and diplomatic relations. Additionally, climate change is expected to become the main driver of species extinction by 2050.

Forests can Contribute to Mitigation

Protecting the world's forests can contribute to the achievement of global goals for emissions reductions while easing the transition to a global low-carbon economy for both the developed and the developing world. Research shows that we cannot prevent dangerous impacts from climate change if we don't reduce emissions from deforestation and forest degradation, no matter how aggressively mitigation measures are taken in other sectors.

Adapting to Climate Change

Healthy natural ecosystems allow people to adapt to a changing climate by providing food, clean water and income. These ecosystems—including forests, oceans, coastal zones and freshwater areas—provide a natural infrastructure which enables communities to more easily adapt to some of the worst impacts of a changing climate by performing vital tasks like buffering communities from storms, providing water sources during times of drought, and supplying alternative food sources and livelihoods when agricultural crops fail.

Engaging Communities

People who live and work in natural areas are likely to be more affected by the direct impacts of climate change and also by actions implemented to address the problem. These groups—including indigenous peoples and other local communities—need to be actively involved at the earliest stage possible in the decision-making process of any plans that may affect them.

CI is working within the UNFCCC process towards an international climate agreement that incorporates the incentives necessary to ensure that forests and other ecosystems can continue to remove and store carbon in order to contribute to climate mitigation, and help all communities—human and otherwise—adapt to a changing climate.

India has the Will to Fight Climate Change

Climate change secretary praise India's renewable targets and 'big ambitions', cementing cordial relations between the countries Ed Miliband, Britain's climate change secretary, hailed India as a potential "deal maker" in the forthcoming talks in Copenhagen for an international treaty to tackle global warming, stating that the country would not face targets to cut its emissions in the near future because it "took climate change seriously". The UK's "softly-softly" approach has won plaudits in India, and contrasts with that of US secretary of state, Hilary Clinton, whose visit in July resulted in a spat with Indian environment minister Jairam Ramesh. India has categorically ruled out greenhouse gas cuts, arguing that rich nations caused the problem and must not deny Indians the opportunity to grow out of poverty. In an interview with the *Guardian*, Miliband and development secretary Douglas Alexander said India would not have to reduce emissions by 2020—the year when the European Union has offered to cut by a third its greenhouse gas output—given that Delhi was "not doing things on a 'business as usual basis'".

"India has very stretching targets on solar energy, on renewable energy ... it has big ambitions on energy efficiency ... I think India wants to be a deal maker not a deal breaker in Copenhagen," said Miliband. India already generates 8% of its power from renewables—more than the UK. It says it aims to have 20,000 mW of solar energy in place by 2020 and make fuel efficiency standards mandatory for cars from 2011 as part of a package to reduce the nation's carbon footprint. After Clinton's visit, Delhi accused the United States of applying pressure on India to curb its greenhouse gas emissions. The United States wants big developing countries such as India and China, whose emissions are quickly rising as their economies grow, to agree to rein them in before Washington commits to any global deal.

CONCLUSION

In conclusion, the outcome of Copenhagen could be similar to the outcome of the Kyoto Conference. There will be some targets and a formula "allowing for" cap and trade, but no binding obligation for a global cap and trade system. So the outcome might be not enough and not sustainable—a more progressive approach would be needed. China and India, in particular, should agree that from 2020 onwards, they will behave like developed countries. However, it all depends if both countries have achieved its status of developed nations which is likely the way their economic growth is progressing globally.

References

Alamy forum (2009), Briefing on Climate Change, 9 January.

Alex MacLennan (2009), The Road to Copenhagen: Climates Big Picture, June 9.

http://climateprogress.org/2009/03/17/media-copenhagen-global-warming-impacts-worst-case-ipcc/

Julio Godoy' (2009), Analysis on Climate Change, WIKIO, March.

Michael McCarthy (2009), "The Countdown to Copenhegen", Environment Editor

Rie Jerichow (2009), Green rooftops create a better climate in Mexico City by planting flowers and vegetable gardens on rooftops, the temperature on roofs may fall by half. 27 August.

Yvo de Boer (2009), Press briefing by UNFCCC Executive Secretary, 17 March, BonnerwirtschaftBlog.

Index